four precepts for guiding the comparative analysis of phenomena:

1. focus upon environmental influences emanating from societal structure and processes.

2. a multi-disciplinary perspective, so as to incorporate economic, political and socio-cultural factors.

3. emphasis upon explanatory variables rather than descriptive categories.

4. the importance of utilising a historical as well as contemporary dimension.

pp 8 - 10

Industrial Relations: Origins and Patterns of National Diversity

The author

Michael Poole is Reader in Industrial Relations in the Cardiff Business School at the University of Wales Institute of Science and Technology. He has also lectured at the University of Sheffield, and in 1983 he was Research Associate of the Institute of Industrial Relations at the University of California at Berkeley. He has published widely in the fields of industrial relations, management and industrial sociology, and his previous books include *Workers' Participation in Industry* (revised edition, 1978), *Theories of Trade Unionism* (revised edition, 1984), with Brown, Rubery, Sisson, Tarling and Wilkinson, *Industrial Relations in the Future* (1984) and *Towards a New Industrial Democracy* (1986) all published by Routledge & Kegan Paul.

Industrial Relations: Origins and Patterns of National Diversity

Michael Poole

Routledge & Kegan Paul
London and New York

First published in 1986 by
Routledge & Kegan Paul Ltd
11 New Fetter Lane, London EC4P 4EE
Reprinted in 1987

Published in the USA by
Routledge & Kegan Paul Inc.
in association with Methuen Inc.
29 West 35th Street, New York, NY 10001

Printed in Great Britain
by Billing & Sons Ltd., Worcester

ISBN 0−7102−1415−4

For
Anne
and
Adam, Thomas, Alice and Edmund

Contents

Figures

Tables

Foreword

Despite a considerable literature, comparative industrial relations is a field struggling to be born. There are numerous collections of individual country studies, but this book is among the few to attempt a comparison of industrial relations systems in various countries in a systematic, theory-oriented way.

Like other new academic fields, comparative industrial relations must face two sets of questions. Firstly, why study the field? And secondly, on what issues should the field be focused?

Why study comparative industrial relations? Isn't it hard enough to understand one's own? Except for managers of international firms, why should Britons concern themselves with Italian or American labour relations?

One reason might be that, like other foreign curiosities (Arabian harems, New Guinea sing-sings, or moonlit Venetian canals), industrial relations elsewhere are quaint, even charming. (Americans think of British labour relations in terms of *I'm All Right, Jack;* similarly, for many Britons, US labour relations mean *On the Waterfront.*) But voyeurism is hardly enough to justify a field of study.

Other people study foreign industrial relations practices with the hope of adopting them back home. But transplants are seldom easy. In 1971 Britain made the great mistake of trying to graft American industrial relations institutions on to an alien British host without giving sufficient consideration to the context in which these institutions were imbedded in their home environment. A more thorough analysis of comparative industrial relations – or perhaps a better developed comparative industrial relations theory – might have saved Britain much agony.

Comparative industrial relations may help scholars in any one country better understand (and criticize) their own industrial relations system. Excessive concentration on one's own system makes one provincial and smug.

Here is an example. The founders of American academic

industrial relations, during the 1920s and 1930s, were reformers, if not radicals. They advocated fundamental changes in the nature of employee-employer relationships. By the 1940s and 1950s, however, they became more interested in facilitating union-management co-operation, and in the process became technicians and defenders of the status quo. In so doing they convinced themselves that American industrial relations was the best in the world. Criticism from either the left or the right was almost completely stilled. Indeed, many leading American scholars transformed themselves into hucksters, selling their system's advantages throughout the world. Only recently, after the system has gone through much turmoil, have its basic premises been questioned. More awareness of developments in other countries might have stimulated greater humility.

Some people argue that if industrial relations is to become a science or even a respectable discipline, it needs a theoretical base of its own. Others believe that industrial relations, like engineering or medicine, is merely an applied field; and like engineering and medicine it must draw its theories from the basic disciplines, which in the case of industrial relations, include economics, sociology, political science and psychology.

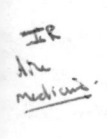

If the first position is correct, comparative industrial relations has a very important and difficult task. It must construct (or at least test) the theories on which the field can rest. After all, a theory can't be much if it explains behaviour in merely a single country.

The second approach still casts comparative industrial relations in an important role: it must specify the key variables necessary to understand how (and why) industrial relations differ from one country to another.

This brings us to our second initial question. What are these key variables?

On what should the field focus? Many sociologists view contemporary industrial relations as a reaction to industrialization. Back in 1960, a landmark work by Kerr, Dunlop, Harbison and Myers predicted (as did Marx, a century earlier) that the forces of industrialism would inevitably lead toward *convergence*, that is that industrial relations systems would become increasingly alike. During the twenty-five years since this seminal work appeared technology throughout the world has indeed become more alike; however, as Kerr, himself, concedes, we have seen little convergence in such social processes as industrial relations.

Technology has not become the great homogenizer. Each country has adapted to industrialization in its own fashion. (Nevertheless, technology helps explain differences in industrial relations among industries. For example, strike rates among coal miners are high throughout the world.)

Economic factors help explain changes over time. Both strike rates and extent of unionism are affected by the business cycle. But economic factors tell us little about differences among countries.

Historical, cultural, political and ideological variables are clearly relevant, but even these provide no simple answers. Superficially, the United States and Australia are much alike. We are both countries of wide open spaces; we are at about roughly the same stage of industrialization; we share a common motherland, a common legal system, and a common written (though not spoken) language. The orientation of unions in both countries is 'instrumental' rather than 'radical' (to use Poole's terminology). And yet our industrial relations systems are very different. American industrial relations are based on fairly decentralized collective bargaining for example, while those in Australia are based on centralized arbitration decisions. The US is noted for its relatively few, but long strikes, Australia for its frequent short ones.

Even where the two countries share the same institutions they operate quite differently. Twenty-six American states require compulsory interest arbitration for certain public sector activities. Where interest arbitration exists, strikes are almost unknown, and arbitration awards are accepted automatically by the parties, though sometimes grudgingly. In Australia, by contrast, the Arbitration Court is really an interested party; its awards are always subject to further bargaining and are frequently accompanied by strikes.

Differences such as these can be understood only in terms of history (and perhaps accidents). So far we have developed few simple hypotheses as to why they occur. Indeed, comparative industrial relations is a laggard among the social sciences in developing testable hypotheses. One reason for this is that there are few sets of meaningful comparative data. We do have an international set of strike data, for example, but aside from inaccuracies in the data themselves, strikes serve such different functions in different countries that analyses based on such data may yield only superficial, even misleading findings.

Thus, in writing this book, Michael Poole has set himself an awesomely challenging task. But he asks the right questions. He keeps the essential variables up front. He stresses that industrial relations is a system of interrelated parts, and he makes an important contribution by insisting that there are at least three interconnected sets of industrial relations, those occurring at the national, organizational and shop levels. In short, this is an important beginning of a difficult quest.

George Strauss
Institute of Industrial Relations,
University of California,
Berkeley

Preface and acknowledgments

My aim in this study is to analyse comparatively a wide range of industrial relations phenomena with a view to uncovering some of the origins of national diversity. In many respects the book is best regarded as a sequel both to *Theories of Trade Unionism,* in which I first formulated the outlines of a comprehensive explanatory framework, and also to *Workers' Participation in Industry,* which had kindled an early interest in the experiences of countries with different political and economic systems and at various levels of development. More specifically, its essence is the fruit of a six-months' sabbatical period as a Research Associate on the Visiting Scholar Programme of the Institute of Industrial Relations at the University of California at Berkeley.

All comparative studies should ideally be embarked upon in a country other than one's own, but the additional advantage of undertaking such a project at Berkeley were immense. The library facilities were of a quality which made it a joy as well as a privilege to work at the University while, in the Institute, specialist advice could be obtained and a strong American element incorporated. In my entire academic career, no one has ever been as helpful or as encouraging to me as Professor George Strauss, who read through part of the book and made very many detailed and valuable suggestions. Other members of the Institute also contributed in specific areas (notably Professors Joseph Garbarino, Raymond Miles, Michael Reich, Karlene Roberts, Lloyd Ulman and Harold Wilensky together with Mr Tom Janoski). Further assistance was given by fellow visiting scholars (and especially Professors David Brody, Nelson Lichtenstein and Eliezer Rosenstein), while Joan Lewis (Senior Administrative Assistant) and Barbara Porter (Managing Editor of *Industrial Relations*) were both supportive. Nanette Sand and Joan Nakano of the Institute's library helped me greatly with references, and Marjorie Morrissette typed roughly two-thirds of the Berkeley draft of the book with remarkable patience and resilience.

In the UK, Colin Crouch of the London School of Economics and Political Science read through and offered valuable thoughts on the chapter on the state, while John Donaldson of the Imperial College of Science and Technology supplied a number of references on the distribution of economic rewards. My exchanges on comparative issues with Professor Malcolm Warner of the Management College, Henley and Brunel University have been both enjoyable and instructive. To embark on the project, I was granted paid leave of absence by the University of Wales Institute of Science and Technology, while a number of my colleagues (notably Catherine Bailey and Paul Blyton) in the Department of Business Administration and Accountancy provided information on specific works. Moreover Jane Sparks of the UWIST library gave substantial assistance with references and compiling the bibliography. Margaret Pritchard (Mrs 'P') will always be remembered for her valiant efforts with typing and re-typing and there was also vital assistance from Sally Jarratt, Kath Hollister, Stevie Burges and Carol Andrewartha. It is worth mentioning, too, that at Routledge & Kegan Paul, for a number of years, I have had a valuable working relationship with both Peter Hopkins and David Stonestreet. David Luke helped me greatly with the compilation of the tables in Chapter 6. My wife Anne was her usual tower of strength, her own professional expertise contributing at many points to both the style and structure of the manuscript. The children very much enjoyed the trip to America but, while the book was being compiled on both sides of the Atlantic, suffered from a degree of paternal neglect. However, I hope all in their different ways consider the project to be worthwhile though, of course, responsibility for the contents is entirely my own.

A prefatory note is also invaluable for recording acknowledgments to produce figures and tables from copyright work. Indeed, without such goodwill, the processes of scholarship would be substantially restricted. The following copyright holders are thus gratefully cited for granting permission to reproduce the material listed below: (1) Basil Blackwell: G. S. Bain and R. Price (1980), *Profiles of Union Growth*, Oxford, Blackwell, p. 170; also from the *British Journal of Industrial Relations*; R. O. Clarke (1980), 'Labour-management disputes – a perspective', 18, pp. 16, 18; and A. Sorge (1976), 'The evolution of industrial democracy in the countries of the European Community', 14, pp. 284 and 286–7; (2) Cambridge University Press: P. C. Schmitter (1981), 'Interest intermediation and regime governability in contemporary Western Europe and North America', in S. Berger, A. Hirschman and C. Maier (eds), *Organizing Interests in Western Europe*, Cambridge, Cambridge University Press, p. 294; (3) The Controller of Her Majesty's Stationery Office: D. Marsden (1981), 'Vive la différence: pay differentials in Britain, West Germany, France and Italy', *Employment Gazette*, 89, p. 310; (4) Elsevier Science Publishers BV: P. Wiles (1974), *Distribution of Income in East and West*, Amsterdam, North Holland Publishing Company, p. 48; (5) Harvard University Press: C. Kerr (1983), *The Future of Industrial Societies*, Cambridge, Mass., Harvard University Press, p. 143; (6) Houghton Mifflin: P. R. Gregory and R. C. Stuart (1980), *Comparative Economic Systems*, Boston, Houghton Mifflin, p. 21; (7) International Institute for Labour Studies: E. C. Iwuji (1980), *Labour and Society* (Geneva, International Institute for Labour Studies), 5, p. 154, Table 2; (8) International Labour Office (1969), *Bulletin of Labour Statistics*, ILO Geneva, 2nd quarter: Results of the ILO October Inquiry on Wages, Hours of Work and Retail Prices for October, 1968; published in Part 1, 'Average hourly wages of adult workers in selected occupations', October 1968, of the section entitled 'Results of the ILO October 1968 Inquiry'; (9) J A I Press: J. Child (1981), 'Culture, contingency and capitalism in the cross-national study of organizations', in B. M. Staw and L. L. Cummings (eds), *Research in Organizational Behaviour*, vol. 3, Greenwich, Conn: J A I Press, p. 326; (1) D. Lane (1970) and Weidenfeld & Nicolson: *Politics and Society in the USSR*, London, Weidenfeld & Nicolson, p. 306 (see also D. Lane (1985), *Soviet Economy and Society*, Oxford, Blackwell, p. 30); (11) D. Lane (1971) and Penguin Books; *The End of Inequality?*, Harmondsworth, Penguin, pp. 64–5; (12) Macmillan, London and Basingstoke: J. Wilczynski (1983), *Comparative Industrial Relations*, London, Macmillan, p. 188; for North American rights: St. Martin's Press, New York; (13) Pergamon Press: J. G. Chapman (1979), 'Recent trends in the Soviet industrial wage structure', in A. Kahan and B. Ruble (eds), *Industrial Labor in the USSR*, New York, Pergamon, p. 173; A. Pravda (1979), 'Spontaneous workers' activities in the Soviet Union', in A. Kahan and B. A. Ruble (eds), *Industrial Labor in the USSR*, New York, Pergamon; and W. Bornschier (1983), 'World

Part 1

The comparative approach

Chapter 1 Introduction

Diversity rather than uniformity characterizes the industrial relations experiences of nations. The search to resolve or to accommodate conflicts which arise in the conduct of work and in the distribution of the fruits of labour is universal. But varied strategic choices set within heterogeneous cultures and ideologies, political and economic conditions, industrial relations institutions and power distributions have occasioned a rich array of global outcomes.

In this study, some of these multiform patterns are charted, interpreted and explained. The aim is to contribute to the analysis of comparative industrial relations, partly by drawing together certain of the main strands of current knowledge, but more especially by establishing a series of explanatory theories and frameworks. These incorporate historical as well as contemporary insights and provide the basis for the formulation of a focused account of differences amongst countries in the strategies of the main industrial relations 'actors' (employers and managers, labour and trade unions and the state and various of its agencies) and in industrial conflict, industrial democracy and the distribution of economic rewards.

The book itself should be timely given that, in recent years, there have been signs of an appreciable revival of interest in comparative issues. In several texts and readers the main characteristics of the industrial relations systems of different countries have been charted (e.g. Kennedy, 1979; Torrington (ed.), 1978; Martin and Kassalow (eds), 1980; Blum (ed.), 1981; Doeringer (ed.), 1981; IDE, 1981a; Wilczynski, 1983). Pathbreaking cross-national collaborative surveys (e.g. Crouch and Pizzorno (eds), 1978a, 1978b) and penetrative studies with a focused theoretical and empirical compass have been conducted (e.g. Clegg, 1976). Further symptoms have been the series of impressive investigations of matched enterprises in country pairs (e.g. Dore, 1973; Gallie, 1978, 1983; Sorge *et al.*, 1983) and, latterly, the spectacular improvements in the quality of collaborative cross-national empirical research in industrial democracy (IDE, 1981b) and incomes policy (Flanagan, Soskice and Ulman, 1983). Hence, while it is premature to predict a new dawn for comparative industrial relations, not least because, in the past, a number of 'waves' or 'cycles' of commitment followed by periods of dormancy can be identified (Scoville, 1982), the prospects for substantial further progress in the late 1980s and the 1990s are excellent.

Definitions

At the outset, however, a word is in order about the position adopted here on the definition, scope and principles of comparative industrial relations. The view is advanced that industrial relations is a discipline concerned with the systematic study of all aspects of the *employment relationship*. It is assumed that, in every industrial and industrializing country, there are three main industrial relations 'actors' or parties with partly common and partly divergent interests: employers and managers, labour (and usually trade unions), and the state. A degree of conflict between these groups is regarded as inevitable, but there are generally mechanisms to ensure that it is channelled or accommodated, notably: (1) *individual resolution* supported by freedom of contract and by the lack of any substantial restrictions to the operation of the labour market; (2) *unilateral determination* by employers, managers, the state, trade unions or workers; and (3) *plural modes of regulation* (typically under collective bargaining) in which differences are 'expressed, articulated and defended' through independent associations of employers and working people and in which joint determination and responsibility for the terms and conditions of employment have been instituted.

For comparative purposes, too, it is considered elemental that interests may be shared or conflicting in both so-called *production* and *distribution* spheres (the first encompasses the actual work process, the second economic rewards which accrue from employment). On the one hand, then, a series of 'creative' or 'productive' activities are defined by the *functions* of all organizations. But while their performance may be free of conflict (for example, when managerial decision making is legitimated), equally there are often fundamental struggles along the so-called 'frontier of control', between working people who seek 'freedom on the job' (Perlman, 1928: 9), and managers and supervisors who endeavour to plan the overall organization and conduct of work. On the other hand, the allocation of rewards from work may also occasion consensus or conflict. The former depends on 'fairness' or justice governing the principles of distribution. However, in its absence, antagonism is likely and is reflected in familiar disputes over pay and income.

These definitional criteria for the study of comparative industrial relations have support amongst comparative scholars but they diverge in a number of important respects from earlier approaches. In Britain, the dominant focus has been on different patterns of job regulation associated with variations in the institutions of collective bargaining (cf. Flanders, 1970; Clegg, 1976, 1979). This perspective has the advantage of incorporating conflicting interests and it applies to the production as well as to the distribution spheres. But its anchorage in collective bargaining makes it too specific to cover experiences in eastern Europe, in the Third World and in western societies in which collective bargaining plays only a circumscribed role in regulating employment relationships. By contrast, the alternative radical conception in which the subject of industrial relations is defined in terms of 'processes of control over work relations' (Hyman, 1975: 12) is in principle applicable to all types of employment relationship. However, this fails to satisfy the rigorous requirements of comparative analysis, partly because it underestimates the extent of common interests, but above all as a consequence of an inadequate treatment of issues of distribution and of the *creative* properties of work roles that underlie the fundamental demands for, say, job autonomy or industrial democracy in the first place.

On the face of it, the basic constituents of an adequate definition of comparative industrial relations are more readily apparent in American literature. After all, for scholars in the United States, the field of industrial relations has always been broad ranging and inclusive of a substantial number of issues involved in the employment relationship. Indeed, until the 1930s the two main topics in American industrial relations were social security, and protective legislation and trade unionism, with the first often receiving the most attention. Only as collective bargaining became better established did industrial relations become primarily (but never exclusively) a study of labour-management relationships. Moreover, with the progressive weakening of trade unions, industrial relations scholars in the

USA have once again returned to their traditionally broad conceptions of this field of study. Kochan (1980) thus views collective bargaining in union-management relations as only one subject area, and industrial relations, in its broadest sense, as comprising an 'interdisciplinary field that encompasses the study of all aspects of people at work', including 'the study of individuals, groups of workers who may or may not organize into a union or an association, the behaviour of employer or union organizations, the public policy or legal framework governing employment conditions, the economics of employment problems, and even the comparative analysis of industrial relations systems in different countries over different time periods' (Kochan, 1980: 1).

But if British approaches are too narrow in compass, American conceptions do not obviously differentiate the boundaries of industrial relations from a range of related 'behavioural sciences'. By contrast, to focus *on conflict and the accommodation and reconciliation of partly common and partly divergent interests of the three main parties to all industrial relations systems (employers and managers, labour and trade unions, and the state and its agencies) in both production and distribution spheres* is both sufficiently general for comparative purposes and also focused enough to provide a *raison d'être* for a distinctive discipline of industrial relations.

The scope of comparative analysis

Furthermore, comparative studies of industrial relations are ultimately concerned with *analytical* and not *substantive* relationships. The central thrust of the approach is to assess the impact of a number of environmental conditions on divergencies in industrial relations phenomena amongst countries. The effects of intervening forces have also to be incorporated and the possibility of a complex interrelationship between different analytical levels must be acknowledged. But comparative studies 'refer to a method for the examination of general analytical problems in which environmental variables are controlled, so as better to perceive the relation between independent environmental variables and the hypothetically dependent phenomena examined.' As such, they contrast with *international studies* which comprise the 'substantive description and case analysis of supranational phenomena', and with *foreign studies* which encompass the 'case examination of phenomena in a foreign environment and, for theoretical purposes, do not differ qualitatively from like case studies of the home environment' (Meyers, 1967: 27–8).

There are several important implications here. To begin with, international phenomena (e.g. trade unions transcending national frontiers) are not in themselves necessarily relevant topics for comparative study. Secondly, *country by country descriptive modes of enquiry have to be rejected*. Indeed, such theoretically limited approaches cannot in the long run be expected to survive the advance of the conceptually sophisticated explanatory comparative investigations that are likely to become dominant during the next decade. Thirdly, the comparative approach is concerned chiefly with factors which reveal: (1) relatively strong differences amongst countries; and (2) considerable homogeneity within any given nation. As a consequence, the problem of how to deal with elements which do not systematically differ amongst countries is vital. However, this may be resolved partly by extending the range of countries studied (for example, including the Third World and eastern Europe ensures that political economy is a variable and not a constant), partly by including several levels of analysis (in particular, the institutional) and partly by accepting that inter- or intra-industry explanatory variables have to be discarded for this type of investigation.

More generally, too, the approach adopted here focuses largely on *national uniqueness* and *cross-national contrasts* rather than on similarities and comparabilities (see Elder, 1976). To be sure, this presents problems in the selection of adequate supporting data which necessarily rest on secondary sources. But, depending on availability, the solution is to choose in *descending order* from the following types of material:

(1) Cross-national systematic research data from studies designed to test specific propositions and based on large samples (e.g. IDE, 1981b).

(2) Secondary data having problems of validity and reliability but with a very broad coverage of countries (e.g. material on strikes in the *Yearbook of Labour Statistics*: ILO, 1973–82).

(3) Detailed research material gathered in a small number of nations often with purposes other than those of the analyst (e.g. Dore, 1973; Edelstein and Warner, 1975; Gallie, 1978; 1983; Maitland, 1983; Sorge *et al.*, 1983).

(4) Data from a wide range of countries on a specific issue typically arranged by nation and hence having to be re-

worked (e.g. Flanagan, Soskice and Ulman, 1983; Windmuller and Gladstone (eds), 1984).

(5) Primarily illustrative data from detailed single country studies (e.g. Windmuller, 1969; Clegg, 1979; Valente, 1979) or on specific themes within one nation (e.g. Dubin and Aharoni, 1981; Fishbein, 1984).

Principles of comparative analysis

But what are the guidelines of comparative analysis? Four central principles may be identified here: (1) a focus on broad societal structures and processes; (2) a multidisciplinary perspective; (3) an explanatory core; and (4) an historical as well as a contemporary dimension.

Firstly, then, explanations for divergent types of industrial relations phenomena have at least *originally* to be sought in the environmental context, in broad societal structures and processes, and not in the framework of regulatory institutions in the employment relationship itself. This is implied to some extent by the definition of comparative studies, but it also follows from the conception of organizational phenomena and the structure of collective bargaining (and other institutional relationships) as logically *intervening* and not *independent* in analytical sequence. In this respect the position adopted here does not substantially depart from that of Schregle (1981: 28–9):

> A comparative study of industrial relations shows that industrial relations phenomena are a very faithful expression of the society in which they operate, of its characteristic features and of the power relationships between different interest groups. . . . In the final analysis, industrial relations can be understood and explained only as an offshoot of all the characteristic features of a given society – economic and legal, political and cultural, rational and irrational . . . the pattern of industrial relations is but an expression, a reflection of the power structure of a society, its decision-making processes and habits, its economy, history and traditions, the attitudes and behaviour of its people, its past experience, its aspirations and values.

Secondly, a satisfactory comparative approach to industrial relations must be built on multidisciplinary foundations. After all, however valuable the insights of a single discipline may be, there can be no prospect of developing a satisfactory comprehensive account on that basis alone. This is not to suggest that the contribution of each main discipline is of equal significance, but it is to argue that an adequate comparative analysis must include the explanatory dimensions of a variety of mainstream social sciences (sociology, political science, economics, social psychology, law and history), of fields which straddle traditional boundaries (e.g. organizational behaviour) and of institutional industrial relations scholarship itself.

The third principle of comparative analysis is that explanatory conditions should be the centrepiece of the overall framework and that descriptive categories and methods should be eschewed. This is again built into the definition of comparative studies since to encompass a broad group of environmental influences and to examine the effects of each, leads to explanatory modes of enquiry. Put technically, there is a preference in the long run for *nomothetic* (or 'law' posing) rather than *idiographic* (i.e. describing the particular) investigations. However, it should be stressed that the two approaches are complementary rather than mutually exclusive and it is doubtful whether the search for law-like causal relations in the social sciences is a valid exercise. The differences analysed may be both *genotypical* and *phenotypical* (i.e. they include broad divergencies of type as well as peculiarities in any given form). Variations, too, may be of degree, trait, relationship or type (see Lammers and Hickson, 1979b), but in each case, it is the aim of the comparative scholar to explain rather than merely to describe the observed disparities.

Fourthly, comparative analysis should consider historical or temporal *as well as* spatial insights. Essentially, industrial relations phenomena may be examined comparatively either by keeping locations constant and conducting the enquiry over different periods in time or by holding time constant but varying the settings (or, preferably, by a combination of both approaches). The first entails a so-called *longitudinal* or *diachronic* design, and the second, the *cross-sectional* or *synchronic* method (see Lammers and Hickson, 1979b). Both are vital, but the special significance of the temporal approach is linked with: (1) the importance of understanding the origins of institutions; (2) the distinction between correlation and causation (see Shalev, 1980); (3) the ways in which strategic decisions take time to become effective; and (4) the relationships which can be established with broader processes of social change and general forces shaping long-run patterns of divergence and evolution within industrial societies as a whole.

The investigation

So far, then, we have examined the main problems of definition and analysis of comparative industrial relations and have highlighted four central principles which have guided our own approach. These considerations also structure the design of the overall project. The focus on broad environmental as well as intervening conditions, the multidisciplinary and explanatory objectives of the study, and the significance of an historical dimension shape the arguments in the following chapter. The resulting analytical frameworks are then deployed, in Section 2, to generate more specific theories to interpret divergent patterns in the strategies of three main 'actors'. And they also form the basis, in Section 3, for highlighting differences in conflict and in the accommodation of interests in both production and distribution spheres in which industrial conflict, industrial democracy and the distribution of economic rewards are the main concerns.

The upshot should be the elucidation of some highly interesting issues in countries with varying politico-economic systems, diverse cultural and historical backgrounds and disparate levels of development. At the current stage in our knowledge, it is admittedly only possible to attach some very general weights to the most salient environmental and other conditions of relevance to comparative analysis. Indeed, rigorous empirical investigations in this area of enquiry are still in their infancy. But the integration of conceptual and empirical themes should be conducive to a valuable analysis of issues central to some of the uppermost problems of mankind.

Chapter 2 Comparative frameworks

The thrust of the theoretical position advocated here is that variations in industrial relations institutions and practices have their roots in the strategic choices of the parties to the employment relationship. That is to say, employers and managers, workers and their representatives, and officials of the state and various of its agencies are essentially social 'actors' who shape the institutional arrangements in which they operate. Of course, this in no way is to posit a one-sidedly 'voluntarist' thesis. On the contrary, choices are influenced by broad meanings and patterned and constrained in their formulation, implementation and formation by economic, political and social structures, by organizational and institutional forces and by the distribution of power. But to adopt the concept of social action as the primary point of departure in theoretical modelling ensures that the comparative approach is not weakly formulated in opposition to untenable unidimensional and unilinear interpretations of long-term social evolution. After all, to presuppose that societies with diverse political economies and at varying stages of development are becoming increasingly convergent in *industrial relations structure and process* is to strain credibility. *Ceteris paribus*, it is the obverse case which is persuasive. That is to say, unless it can be clearly demonstrated to the contrary, it is to be expected that, as more countries become industrialized and as already complex modes of accommodation of interests amongst the parties are shaped by a progressively diverse range of socio-cultural forms, a rich, heterogeneous and variegated pattern of industrial relations institutions will unfold in future years.

The central theoretical approach

Although specific focused theories have to be elaborated within given substantive areas, the contribution to analysis here is founded first on the notions of strategy and strategic choice and their connections with the orientations of social 'actors' (and, above all, with *instrumental* and *value* rationality). These are then combined with broad 'subjective' *meanings* which are multiform and diverge amongst nations (being inclusive of culture and ideology as well as public and legal policies).

But in no sense is a one-sidedly 'voluntarist' thesis propounded, for a series of social, economic, political, technological and demographic *structural* constraints in the wider environment of industrial relations are also isolated for comparative purposes. Moreover, further checks on the choices of 'actors' stem from *organizational* and *institutional* factors (the first encompassing cognitive-attitudinal and technological-structural conditions, and the second the impress of collective bargaining structure and other systems of industrial relations) and the *distribution of power*. Finally, an historical or temporal as well as spatial or cross-sectional mode of analysis is deployed in which emphasis is placed on long-run movements which induce divergence and greater diversity, 'late development' effects and heterogeneous trajectories of economic and industrial growth.

Strategy, strategic choice and social action

The approach to theoretical modelling thus begins with the notions of strategy and strategic choice anchored in the categories of social action. Strategy has been recently located at the core of industrial relations theorizing (Poole, 1980; Thurley and Wood, 1983; Kochan, McKersie and Cappelli, 1984), but for comparative purposes it must be combined with the orientations of the 'actors' or parties to the employment relationship and with the broader cultural values and ideologies of given societies (see Poole, 1984).

But what, first of all, are strategies? For Miles and Snow (1978) they are 'consistent *patterns* in streams of decisions or actions' and include the stages of formulation (intention), implementation (re-working the design of an institution or organization) and formation (in which unintended byproducts of decisions affect action) (see Meyer, Snow and Miles, 1982). They are intertemporal, describing 'a set of choices taken over a period of time for a given objective', the industrial relations variants referring to 'long run policies which are developed . . . in order to preserve or change the procedures, practice and results of industrial relations', usually over several years (Thurley and

Wood, 1983: 197–8). *Strategic choices* imply *discretion* over decision making (i.e. no environmental *determinism*), while *strategic decisions* should be capable of *altering* a party's role or its relationship with other 'actors' (see Kochan, McKersie and Cappelli, 1984). Finally, the concept of strategy can apply at several levels of analysis including the macro or global level of key institutions, the industrial relations system and the workplace itself (Kochan, McKersie and Cappelli, 1984).

At root, the notion of strategy encapsulates the idea of an overall design within social action, and *rationality* and calculus in the patterning of decisions (see Poole, 1980). As such, it is associated with the general categories of social action (i.e. with *instrumental-rational* and *value-rational* orientations); the one referring to the means to utilitarian ends (reflecting material interests and the 'will to power') and the other to ethical, aesthetic, religious, political or other *ideals* (involving identification and commitment) (see Table 2.1). Affectual or emotional conduct is not strategic but enhances value-rational commitments; while traditional behaviour ('ingrained by habituation') encompasses *institutionalized*, utilitarian or idealistic, strategic decisions. Strategy and action are also integral to the analysis of industrial relations systems – Dunlop (1958: 8) using 'actor' in the sense of 'doer or reagent' – and, for comparative purposes, include three main parties: employers and managers, labour and trade unions and the state and various of its agencies (see Chapter 1).

Strategic choices of the 'actors' and the overall framework for analysis

But the strategic choices of the 'actors' are in practice set within a multiplicity of environmental, organizational and institutional, and processual conditions. The overall framework is presented in Figure 2.1 and it should be stressed that, despite reciprocal influences in the overall pattern of relationships, the broader rather than specific elements have the greatest analytical consequence.

Taking first the *environmental* conditions, these are classified into two groups: (1) 'subjective' meanings and policies at a 'macro' level; and (2) 'structural' forces (or broad phenomena which constrain the choices of the human 'actors' concerned). Given the importance of environmental factors in the definition

TABLE 2.1 *Strategies and the general categories of social action (orientations)*

General categories of social action (orientations)	Strategies
(1) *Instrumental-rational* (Zweckrational) that is, determined by expectations as to the behaviour of objects in the environment and of other human beings; these expectations are used as 'conditions' or 'means' for the attainment of the actor's own rationally pursued and calculated ends	Utilitarian, based on material interests and a 'will to power'
(2) *Value rational* (Wertrational) that is, determined by a conscious belief in the value for its own sake of some ethical, aesthetic, religious, political or other form of behaviour, independently of its prospects of success	Idealistic, based on identification and commitment
(3) *Affectual* (especially emotional) that is, determined by the actor's specific affects and feeling states	Not strategic but sentiments and emotions can enhance value-rational commitments
(4) *Traditional* that is, determined by ingrained habituation	The institutionalization of previous strategic decisions of an utilitarian or idealistic character

Note: For a further elaboration see Mueller (1979); Poole (1980, 1984).

of comparative studies, organizational structures and processes and *industrial relations* institutions are assumed to be *intervening* and not independent in analytical sequence. The former cover formal and informal aspects of organizations and include the corporate strategies of managerial personnel. The latter comprise the patterned relationships between employers' associations and management, trade unions and other workers' associations and various governmental and 'third party' agencies in the industrial relations system. Again, while reciprocal relationships are

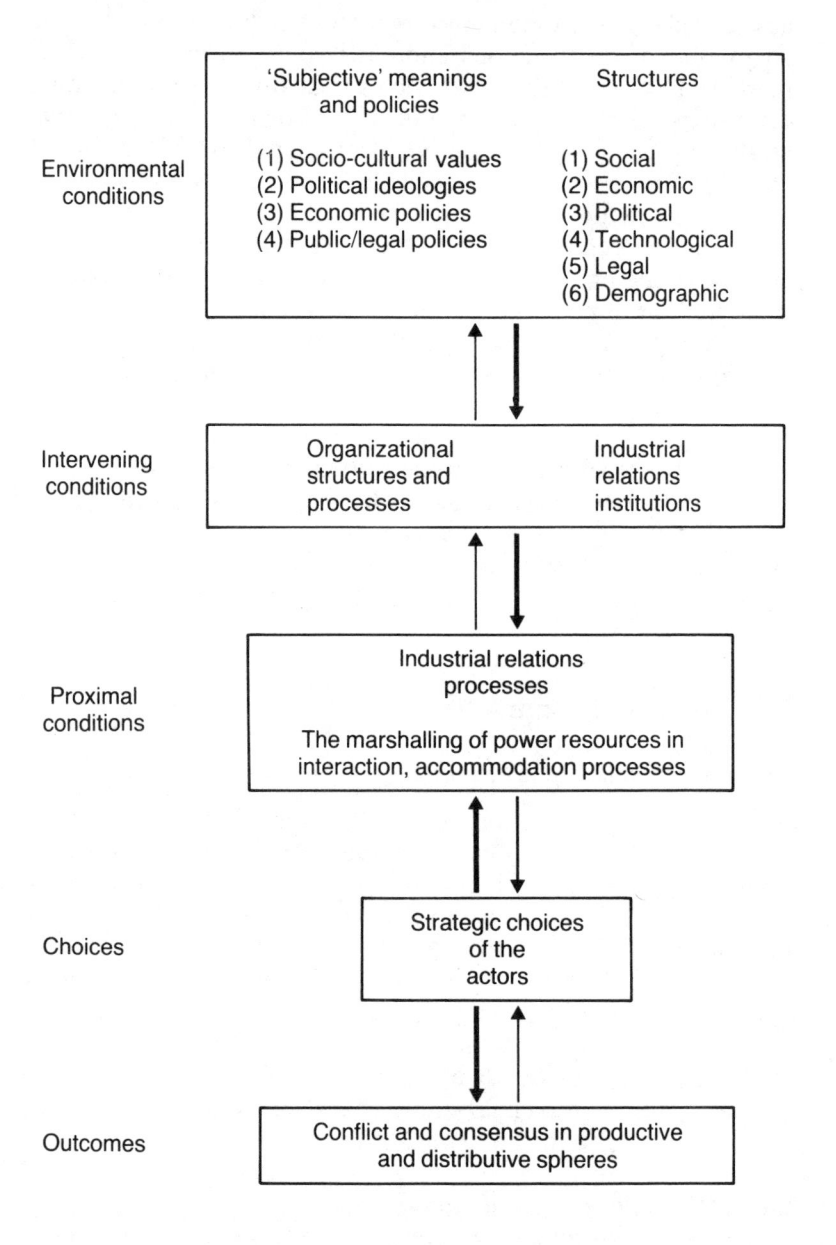

FIGURE 2.1 *The overall framework of analysis*

acknowledged, the dominant direction of influence involves the adaptation of organizations and institutions to wider environmental influences rather than vice versa. But these intervening conditions in turn take analytical precedence over industrial relations processes which are *proximal* to choices and outcomes. Here, power resources are marshalled and there are procedures for accommodation and reconciliation of interests.

Finally, outcomes in the production and distribution spheres are wide-ranging and inclusive of strikes and other forms of industrial unrest, participation in decisions, agreements and rules, wage and salary scales and differentials between groups, the consequences of incomes policy, management of human relations or human resourcing practices, the effects of laws governing the employment relationship and so on. But these are *not* strictly dependent, because although in most cases even strikes and other forms of conflict have only a limited reciprocal effect (most disputes do not occasion major changes even in established industrial relations processes), in isolated instances their impact can extend to the reshaping of the entire political, economic and social fabric.

Environmental conditions

Subjective meanings and policies

At the heart of the action approach is the assumption that an analysis at the *level of meaning* must be deployed alongside structural-type explanations. Hence we begin by identifying a series of macro-level subjective meanings and policies, for not only are these elements inseparable from the notion of strategic choice but they also comprise the foundations of an adequate approach to understanding national diversity. The principal 'subjective' elements in the wider environment of industrial relations are isolated, then, under the following heads: (1) cultural values and civilization; (2) ideologies; (3) economic policies; and (4) public and legal policies.

Cultural values and civilization
In countries with roughly equivalent politico-economic structures, there are pronounced differences in trade union density, structure and policy, managerial employee relations 'styles', the extent of legal regulation of the employment relationship, the

degree of integration and conflict, and so on. To explain these variations the meanings of 'actors' enshrined in cultural values are crucial. However, analytically, there are problems in demonstrating the influence of culture because of imprecise definitions, diverse usage of the term and its specification in a *post hoc*, even residual fashion.

The central properties of culture encapsulate the distinctive achievements of human groups, historically-related and transmitted values and the 'creative' properties of human action. As Kroeber and Kluckhohn (1952: 181) have observed, culture

> consists of patterns, explicit and implicit, of and for behaviour acquired and transmitted by symbols, constituting the distinctive achievement of human groups, including their embodiments in artifacts; the essential core of culture consists of traditional (i.e. historically derived and selected) ideas and especially their attached values; culture systems may, on the one hand, be considered as products of action, on the other hand as conditioning elements of further action.

Critically, too, values are founded on 'principles of orientation to a commonly felt good' and embrace morality, aesthetics and truth, characteristics which, in turn, 'show different degrees of prominence' in each culture (Giner, 1972: 91). Civilizations are created on the basis of an upsurge of 'higher values,' which, as Kroeber (1969: 763) has noted, tend to be transient:

> the patterns which we adjudge of higher quality are selective from among a number of potentialities. They cannot remain undifferentiated and attain quality. As they begin to select, early in their formation, they commit themselves to certain specializations, and exclude others. If this arouses conflict with other parts of the culture in which the pattern is forming, the selection and exclusion may be abandoned . . . and nothing of much cultural value eventuate. If, however, this does not happen, but the other patterns of culture reinforce the growing one, or at least do not conflict with it, the pattern in question tends to develop cumulatively, in the direction in which it first differentiated, by a sort of momentum.

But even if the concepts of culture, values and civilization can be defined in a focused way, their deployment in actual research investigations is problematical, partly because of a tendency to avoid a clear specification of cultural meanings and also from the indiscriminate use of the term to explain phenomena which cannot be accounted for by varying political economies or contingencies. Yet, as Child (1981: 305) has argued in the context of organizational behaviour, 'a test of national differences which are culturally intrinsic would require an examination of whether organizational characteristics continue to differ across nations when contingencies and economic systems are similar or controlled, *and* a demonstration that remaining differences are explicable in terms of an adequate theory of national cultures.' And this stricture applies with no less force in industrial relations where variations in patterns of employment relationships amongst countries are greater than those of organizational characteristics.

As we shall see in Chapter 3, there are solutions here, and notably to identify a number of cultural-value orientations (which encompass actors' meanings) along which societies may be shown to differ. These include views on human nature, the relationship of man to nature, time orientation, orientation towards activity and types of relations between people (Kluckholn and Strodtbeck, 1961). More specifically, too, cultural values may be expressed in moral codes (especially in employment relations), commitments to legalism or voluntarism, regionalism, religious values and in the extent to which social integration and accommodation are widely accepted social goals. (See Table 2.2)

Ideologies

Cultures, then, encapsulate the creative properties of societies, inform strategic choices in the industrial relations sphere, and, above all, vary widely from one country to the next. They also contrast sharply with ideologies which enshrine the goals of political systems and are inexorably bound up with the exercise of power.

An ideology is a 'conception of the social world explicitly and coercively maintained by a collectivity, which derives from it a general plan of action and an identification of the sources of legitimate authority, and attempts the control of its social environment in a way consistent with this conception' (Giner, 1972: 218). For use in comparative explanatory analysis, the term is subject to many of the same problems as that of culture. It is necessarily at a high level of generality. It is hard to operationalize or to show its distinctive effects as against those of contingencies, economic systems or culture. And it is by no

TABLE 2.2 *The meanings of social actors*

---

(1) Cultural values
    a. Moral codes (especially in employment relations)
    b. Legalism or voluntarism
    c. Regionalism
    d. Religious values
    e. Social integration and accommodation

(2) Ideologies (political strategies)
    a. Capitalism
    b. Centralised communism
    c. Corporatism
    d. Decentralised communism and democratic socialism
    e. Liberal pluralism and social democracy
    f. Syndicalism, anarchism and guild socialism

(3) Economic policies
    a. Fiscal
    b. Monetary
    c. Incomes

(4) Public and legal policies

---

means easy to demonstrate close interconnections with more specific strategies for control over work-place relationships.

Nevertheless, ideology remains an indispensable concept for the comparative analysis of industrial relations phenomena (see Poole, 1974; Crouch, 1977; Wood, 1979; Hartley, 1983). Moreover, the spectrum of ideas which gives meaning to action here is very extensive, being inclusive of free-enterprise capitalism, corporatism, liberal pluralism and social democracy, democratic socialism, centralized forms of socialism and communism and syndicalism, anarchism and guild socialism. (See Table 2.2.)

Economic policies
The meanings of social 'actors' are also expressed in diverse economic policies which, in socialist societies, fluctuate according to the extent to which market forces are promoted as a supplement or alternative to state planning; whereas, in western nations, diversities typically reflect the specific forms of fiscal, monetary and incomes policies.

Taking the west for illustrative purposes, fiscal policies refer to national government programmes on taxation, spending and borrowing, although, since the 1930s, their area of application has been largely confined to the 'purposeful manipulation of public expenditures and taxes – to modify the aggregate demand for goods and services of society upon which the levels of output and employment depend' (Estey, 1950: 394–5). These are applied variously amongst nations, but from the 1940s to the late 1970s, monetary policies were generally combined with fiscal policies to affect levels of employment. Moreover, while not sufficient, the conditions of full employment that resulted were necessary supports for the rise in trade union influence and activity in much of western Europe, stimulating major changes in bargaining relationships, with shop stewards and other plant-based officials assuming an increasingly prominent role. But practice has varied in the 1980s and nations where the tight monetary policies of the 'post-Keynesian' era have been ascendant have experienced particularly high levels of unemployment and consequently sharp declines in union membership (Price and Bain, 1983) and more 'directive' managerial 'styles' (Storey, 1983).

Incomes policies have usually been advocated as a means for allowing a community to enjoy full-employment and price stability *at the expense* of 'free' collective bargaining (cf. Ulman, 1982: 113–14). In the post-war period they have been widely but non-uniformly used throughout the western world, being applied with differing degrees of severity (statutory freezes and norms, voluntary guidelines and guideposts and so on). Effective incomes policies impact in large measure upon bargaining relationships and restrict the scope for manoeuvre of plant-based management and union representatives. They encourage centralization of collective bargaining machinery (and, arguably, are most likely to be successful when this is present). They also significantly enhance the role of the state in the industrial relations system and the formation of centrally organized bodies of employers as well as trade unions (see Flanagan, Soskice and Ulman, 1983).

Public and legal policies

In recent years, particularly in the USA, there has been much interest in public and legal policies, even though these broad subjective meanings are as difficult to define and to operationalize as culture and ideology and are far weaker concepts. The term public policy is notoriously vague and applies variously to interventionist strategies by governments in the employment relationship and the opinions of the broad majority of people which are channeled into focused approaches to industrial relations issues. But there is consensus that changes in public policy relate to legal policies and to various legislative enactments, the resort either to 'common law', 'business law', 'labour law' or broader 'economic and social policy' stemming from diverse public opinion pressures (Kochan, 1980).

Structural conditions

Yet a broad endorsement of the social action perspective is not to reject the *constraints* of structure in the wider environment of industrial relations. On the contrary, strategic choices are clearly patterned by external forces over which the 'actors' themselves frequently have very little impact, if any at all. To be sure, the Althusserian position of *determination by structure* is dismissed (after all, most such conditions are ultimately the product of purposive action and are in principle alterable by human agency) (see Poole, 1984), but the constraints of structure merit examination under the following six heads: (1) social; (2) economic; (3) political; (4) technological; (5) legal; and (6) demographic (see Table 2.3).

Social

A social structural explanation of comparative industrial relations is founded on an examination of the effects of inequality in the distribution of power, class and status in the 'larger' society. Its origins can be traced to Weber (1968) and Marx (1974), both of whom detailed social inequality in *production* and *distribution* relationships. Weber's approach, stressing that power is decisive in social stratification (the allied but derivative variables being 'class', 'status' and 'party'), has been echoed in industrial relations analysis (Dunlop, 1958; Bain, Coates and Ellis, 1973) and in organizational behaviour theory (focusing on structures of domination and control in the enterprise and in its environment; see Dahrendorf, 1959). Moreover, the utility of the Marxian perspective here was enhanced in the 1970s and 1980s, when attention shifted from distribution issues (e.g. inequalities in wealth and income) to control of the forces of production in actual enterprises (cf. Balibar, 1970; Bettelheim, 1976; Carchedi,

TABLE 2.3 *The structural environmental conditions*

(1) Social
    Class, status and power differences in the larger society

(2) Economic
    a. Types of economic systems
    b. Rates of inflation, unemployment and economic growth; industrial concentration

(3) Political
    a. Type of political system
    b. Pluralism, corporatism and socialism
    c. Political parties

(4) Technological

(5) Legal
    a. Provisions in the private and public sectors
    b. Legalism, voluntarism and the role of written constitutions

(6) Demographic
    a. Age
    b. Percentage of women economically active
    c. Ethnic structure

1975a, 1975b; Poulantzas, 1975; Crompton and Gubbay, 1977; Burawoy, 1979; Clegg and Dunkerley, 1980). Giddens (1973), too, has identified *mediate* and *proximate* types of 'structuration', the first being based on market capacity and including ownership of the means of production, possession of educational and technical qualifications and manual labour power, and the second being located within productive enterprises, in the division of labour, in authority relations and in various internal 'distributive groupings'. Moreover, to encompass forces of this type avoids excessive 'subjectivism' and supplements an analysis at the level of meaning by so-called 'casual adequacy' (Weber, 1968).

Economic
The wider structure of the economy also impacts upon industrial relations, being bound up with distinctive political systems (see the section which follows). Gregory and Stuart (1980) noted four dimensions on which economic systems differ: organization of

decision-making arrangements (centralism or decentralism affected by the distribution of authority and the utilization of information); mechanisms for the provision of information and co-ordination (planning or markets, reflecting planners' preference or consumer sovereignty); property rights (disposition, utilization and the right to use products and/or services – private, public, and collective); and incentives (material or moral) (see Table 2.4). Under capitalism, decentralized control runs counter to state regulation of income and incentives. But because the owners of capital or their representatives (i.e. management in private enterprises) have at least formal 'powers' of domination over the workforce, struggles along the 'frontier of control', as well as over pay and salary levels, may feature prominently. Market socialist systems in principle reduce the extent of conflict over control of decision making in the firm but, because of the extensive use of market mechanisms, they frequently produce major regional and other variations in income. Moreover, under planned socialism, the capacity of management and the workforce to determine substantive and procedural rules is highly circumscribed. The state becomes the dominant 'actor' in the industrial relations system and, although the centralized regulation of income and pay differentials reduces problems over comparability, a degree of frustration and tension arises because decision-making power is located away from workplace organizations.

TABLE 2.4 *The classification of economic systems*

	Capitalism	Market Socialism	Socialism
Decision-making structure	Primarily decentralized	Primarily decentralized	Primarily centralized
Mechanisms for information and co-ordination	Primarily market	Primarily market	Primarily plan
Property rights	Primarily private ownership	State and/or collective ownership	Primarily state ownership
Incentives	Primarily material	Material and moral	Material and moral

Source: Gregory and Stuart, 1980: 21.

Especially in 'western' countries, rates of inflation, unemployment and economic growth and the degree of industrial concentration also impact on industrial relations. Inflation is in turn, of course, affected by political and monetary policies, but a high rate is conducive to trade union growth and militancy. It also undermines established 'status' hierarchies (reflected in traditional differentials over pay and conditions), while being associated with so-called 'threat' and 'credit' effects on trade union density. That is to say, threats to living standards stemming from a high rate of inflation encourage large numbers of employees to seek protection through collectivism, while the extent to which the union is able to maintain or to improve material rewards in these circumstances ensures a corresponding 'credit' for the leadership (cf. Price and Bain, 1976). High levels of unemployment tend to reduce union power and enhance managerial attempts to regain control over shop-floor decisions, whereas economic growth is conducive to relatively buoyant product and labour markets and augments the relative position of employees against employers in production and distribution relationships. And finally, industrial concentration (which can vary greatly amongst societies with otherwise broadly similar political systems) can influence density of unionization, the degree of 'formalization' of procedures for handling disputes, the extent of organized and unorganized conflict and many other facets of industrial relations (cf. Ingham, 1974; Brown (ed.), 1981; Wilensky, 1981).

Political

The economic structures of particular societies are intimately related to their political forms and dominant ideologies. But it is valuable to identify separately a number of contrasting characteristics of political systems and, here, the most appropriate classification for comparative industrial relations is by Blondel (1969: 37–42) who highlighted three main comparative variables: (1) participation in decision making; (2) the means of achieving decisions; and (3) general policy ends. At a structural level, the last is irrelevant, but the others comprise two main axes: *populist-oligarchic* (the degree to which the mass of citizens participate in decision making); and *liberal-democratic-totalitarian* (the degree to which voluntary actions by autonomous groups are allowed and engoured). In combination, as Wilensky (1975: 21) has observed, these two dimensions yield four types of political system: 'liberal-democratic', 'authoritarian-populist', 'authoritarian-oligarchic', and 'totalitarian.'

With respect to industrial relations, in liberal-democratic societies, there are likely to be independently organized trade unions and extensive voluntarism in the employment relationship. Under authoritarian-populism, independent organizations of labour are not encouraged but 'mass' forms of involvement through referenda and limited types of employee participation frequently emerge. Authoritarian-oligarchic regimes may be conducive to the emergence of labour organizations but typically in the form of 'centralized peak' structures or 'popular bossdoms', which have little rank-and-file participation. Finally, under totalitarianism, the organs of labour (so far as they surface at all) usually become part of the machinery of state administration.

But no analysis of political structures in industrial relations could afford to ignore the consequences of pluralism for shaping diverse industrial relations practices. Pluralism is based on concession and compromise, a body of rules (laws and customs) which guarantee freedom of operation for the main industrial relations groups, a moral imperative in the duty to compromise, varying distributions of power, an adequate material base to ensure all parties can achieve some of their interests, and certain restrictions on the power of the state (Clegg, 1975, 1979). Of course, there are many versions of pluralism, including Fox's radical conception, in which a restructuring of relationships outside the factory is viewed as an indispensable basis for achieving justice rather than merely a number of procedural rituals (Fox, 1974; cf. also Hyman, 1978). But, as a political type, pluralism differs from free market capitalism (the effects of which are checked through intermediary institutions), corporatism and socialism, and above all is associated with strong trade unions and securely founded machinery for collective bargaining.

The characteristics of the main political parties in any given nation are, of course, closely connected with dominant ideologies. But in structural terms, the presence of a distinctive party of labour (comprising the political rather than industrial wing of a given labour movement) may have a profound impact on indigenous patterns of industrial relations. After all, this affiliation will tend to extend the role of the welfare state, reduce social inequality and encourage the adoption of the 'social wage' (cf. Wilensky, 1976, 1979, 1981). It is also conducive to the application of effective incomes policies and, by ensuring a sharp separation of political and industrial issues, it sustains 'positive sum' attitudes on the part of labour in the actual process of production.

Technological

Arguably, few phenomena have shaped industrial relations as much as technology but, ironically, few concepts are of less utility for comparative purposes. Its impress is manifest in trade union structure and policy, in the composition of the labour force and in employer strategies in the 'contested terrain' between management and worker at the point of production. But the obstacles to handling it comparatively arise partly because of its reference to materials and knowledge as well as to operations (Kmetz, 1977/78; Gerwin, 1979; Fry, 1982), but above all because it produces convergence or even uniformity in industrial relations amongst countries (its value is thus largely confined to comparisons between societies at different levels of development or to institutional forms which still reflect the state of technology at their inception).

Legal

However, the principal types of legal provision and the extent to which the existence of a written constitution favours legalism as against voluntarism are vital for comparative purposes. In countries with written constitutions, the highest forms of law rest on documents and specific industrial relations legislation has to be concordant with their premises. Statutory law refers to the enactment of laws and statutes (in the USA by such groups as Congress, state legislatures and other representative bodies). Common law is based on the action of the courts and the customs of the people in which issues of precedence are paramount. Finally, administrative law refers to the application of particular statutes and the regulations of administrative agencies by specified governmental bodies (see e.g. Mills, 1982).

Moreover, the degree of legalism or voluntarism varies amongst countries. Above all, the existence of written constitutions helps to explain the greater degree of legal intervention in industrial relations in countries such as the United States compared with Britain. Flanders (1970) attributed the early British commitment to voluntarism to the cultural commitment to freedom, but, however important this may be, it cannot account for the greater prevalence of legalism in, say, the United

States, where the endorsement of such values is if anything greater than anywhere in western Europe. The constitution of the United States (a written document and the highest form of law), which has no parallel in Britain, may however provide the crucial underpinning for extensive legal regulations, not least because these wider legal provisions are endorsed by all the main parties to industrial relations.

Demographic

The demographic characteristics of populations underlie distinctive labour markets and patterns of segmentation. For instance, a rise in the birth rate presents difficulties in the absorption of a substantial new labour force, while in a declining population, problems of ageing and of a high 'dependency ratio' may be met by the use of older workers in secondary forms of employment (see for reviews of the effects of age on employment patterns, Federal Civilian Workforce Statistics, 1974; Meier, 1976). In most industrial countries, the percentage of 'economically active' women in the labour force has risen substantially, but diversities remain in overall rates of female participation and in the extent of equal pay and equal opportunities (Fogarty, Rapoport and Rapoport, 1971; ILO, 1976b; Lewenhak, 1977). Moreover, the ethnic structure of the population is intertwined with segmentation and partly explains variations in the degree of trade union solidarity amongst countries as well as specific types of industrial militancy (Laslett and Lipset (eds), 1974; Crouch and Pizzorno (eds), 1978a, 1978b).

Intervening conditions

Organizational structures and processes

But although environmental forces are of elemental explanatory significance for comparative industrial relations, intermediary conditions embedded in distinctive organizations and institutions are also integral to the overall framework. In principle, organizational structures and processes embrace two specific sets of influences: cognitive-attitudinal (management *organizational* strategies, employee and employee representatives' orientations and democratic versus efficiency norms in organizations); and technological-structural (types of technology, dimensions of organizational structure, organizational size and formal democratic procedures in labour organizations) (see Table 2.5).

TABLE 2.5 *Organizational structures and processes*

(1) Cognitive-attitudinal

    a. Management *organizational* strategies
    b. Employee and employee representatives' orientations, traditional proletarian, traditional deferential, instrumental-privatized, class solidarity and economism
    c. Democratic versus efficiency norms in labour organizations

(2) Technological/structural

    a. Types of technology: mechanized manual production, mechanized production, integrated mechanized production, automated production, integrated automated production
    b. Dimensions of organizational structure: specialization, standardization, formalization, centralization, configuration and traditionalism
    c. Organizational size
    d. Formal democratic procedures in labour organizations

Managerial *organizational* strategies encompass disparate approaches to administration, the balancing of interests and the organization of legitimacy (cf. Mansfield, 1980; Heller and Wilpert, 1981). The first includes activities such as planning, organizing, staffing, directing and controlling (e.g. Koontz and O'Donnell, 1955), all of which may potentially emerge in multiform ways cross-culturally (see Roberts and Boyacilliger, 1983). The second relates to the functional separation of ownership and control (Nichols, 1969) and the managerial requirement (which varies cross-nationally depending on the power structure of the wider society) to take account of the interests of divergent 'stake-holders' in the enterprise. And the third applies to the distinctive use of moral and material rewards as a basis for authority.

In the case of employees and their representatives, patterns of conflict and accommodation in industry are enmeshed with the dominant orientations of the workforce and the extent to which these are consistent with solidary forms of action and opposition to the employer (see e.g. Brown, Curran and Cousins, 1983). For instance, in the British literature, the distinction between 'traditional proletarian', 'traditional deferential' and 'privatized' has been used to interpret different types of trade union activity (cf. Lockwood, 1966; Brannen, 1983). In comparative terms, the extent to which 'class solidarity' or 'economism' is pervasive amongst the rank and file also has implications for the character of labour movements, while within the labour organization, a varying commitment of the membership and leadership to democratic or efficiency norms helps explain variations in union democracy amongst nations (see e.g. Edelstein and Warner, 1975).

Technological-structural conditions, are of course set in the wider environment of industrial relations as well as within productive organizations. A classification of the latter types of technology includes mechanized manual production, mechanized production, integrated mechanized production, automated production and integrated automated production (ILO, 1966), the problem again remaining that these distinctions are better for explaining inter-organizational variations in industrial relations rather than the differences amongst countries.

However, the potential effects of organizational structure on the locus of decision-making power on labour issues and the degree of formality in the procedures for handling disputes are considerable. The usual dimensions of organizational structure are formulated on the Aston studies, while in recent cross-national research, further scales have been constructed for dependence, automaticity, functional specialization, formalization and centralization (Hickson and McMillan (eds), 1981). Comparatively, too, as Roberts and Boyacilliger (1983: 39) have pointed out, the better cross-national studies using this technique 'couple the Aston measures with a sufficiently well-versed interpretation of the cultural, economic and socio-political milieu of the country.'

Finally, for studies of union government, formal democratic potential is a vital concept, being connected with the so-called formal organizational approach to union government and with the extent to which representative as well as administrative structures have been established within labour organizations (Child, Loveridge and Warner, 1973). Anderson (1979), too, has noted here that the criteria for union democracy include legal and behavioural variables as well as 'responsiveness and control', the behavioural group representing such issues as institutionalized opposition, close elections and high participation, with responsiveness and control covering the ability of officers to respond to and reflect members' interests and to allow a substantial amount of control to reside in the membership.

The institutional framework of industrial relations

The institutional analysis of comparative industrial relations has two main aspects: (1) the patterns and structures which obtain under collective bargaining; and (2) the modes of regulation of employment relationships where collective bargaining is either non-existent or of limited consequence. The main components of collective bargaining have been outlined by Clegg (1976) and Kochan (1980) and, for systematic purposes, the former's approach is set out in Table 2.6, the main dimensions of collective bargaining structure including the extent, level and depth of bargaining, union size and union security, the degree of control and scope of collective agreements and union structure (morphology).

TABLE 2.6 *The institutional system of industrial relations*

---

(1) Dimensions of collective bargaining structure

    a. Extent, depth and level of bargaining
    b. Union depth and union security
    c. Degree of control and scope of collective agreements
    d. Union structure (morphology)

(2) Institutional systems of industrial relations without extensive collective bargaining

    Extent of centralization and decentralization of decision making in production and distribution relations

---

For the study of institutional conditions in industrial relations systems without collective bargaining machinery, analysis is still in its infancy. However, the degree of centralization of decision making in the establishment of procedural and substantive rules is basic and depends greatly on the degree of state intervention, the autonomy of management and the relative power of the various industrial relations 'actors' in any national industrial relations system.

Industrial relations processes

At the proximal level, the processes of interaction between the main parties are the focal concerns, although again these issues have been better handled under collective bargaining systems than where other types of machinery for the accommodation of conflicting and common interests prevail. Industrial relations processes refer to the *exercise of power* and the *marshalling of power resources* in negotiational and other labour-management encounters. Here, for the isolation of specific elements, Walton and McKersie (1965) have developed the best classification of dimensions of collective bargaining processes, there being strong grounds for supposing that the focus on conflict resolution and the attempt to discover complementary interests vary amongst societies.

Indeed, in explanatory terms, processes relate to the exercise of power in interaction, being commonly measured by the relationship between *revealed preferences* and *outcomes* (Abell, 1975, 1977). Power *exercise* in turn depends on power *resources* that differ under integrative or disjunctive conditions respectively. In the first case, certain power bases and values predispose *harmonious outcomes* (e.g. when knowledge and expertise are the criteria for decision-making power and when dominant attitudes encourage conceptions of consensus). In the second, *conflictual outcomes* are typical and the respective power bases and values include 'organizational mobilization' within distinctive opposition groups and 'militancy' (see Table 2.7). But however power is conceived, it is integral to the processes of interaction and not solely a 'defocalized' constraint in the wider environment. This is not to disavow structural inequalities in power in the larger society, but it is to stress that power is also basic to endogenous interactions within the industrial relations system itself. Furthermore, the exercise of power also encompasses processes of accommodation (as is shown in Table 2.7, these can include negotiation, arbitration, conciliation and mediation, grievance procedures, day-to-day interpersonal relations and wider enquiry and other commissions). And again, substantial divergencies are to be expected amongst countries in these processes as well as in environmental and intermediary sets of constraints.

TABLE 2.7 *Industrial relations processes*

Conflict and consensus in production and distribution relations

(1) Marshalling of power resources in interaction

    a. Integrative: exclusiveness and essentiality; knowledge and expertise

    b. disjunctive: numbers, organization, resources (e.g. educational skills, material resources)

(2) Accommodation processes

    a. negotiation

    b. arbitration, conciliation, mediation

    c. grievance procedures

    d. day-to-day interpersonal relations

    e. enquiry commissions

Historical or temporal forces and movements

So far, we have proposed that the comparative approach to industrial relations may be most appropriately conducted in terms of an 'action' perspective in which diverse meanings which link motive and behaviour are examined alongside structural and processual modes of explanation. Nevertheless, much of the account developed up to this point is better suited to cross-sectional than to historical analysis of variations in the employment relationship amongst nations. Hence, long-run trends and movements in industrial and industrializing societies are now highlighted and, here, the explanatory significance of major episodes in institutional construction are uppermost. An overall framework of analysis is specified prior to an appraisal of the notions of 'divergence' 'convergence' and 'late-development'.

A temporal explanatory framework

In Figure 2.2, the underlying relationships between the sets of variables in an historical or temporal framework of industrial relations are presented. The broad group of environmental conditions is identical to that of the previous analysis and comprises both 'subjective' meanings and 'structural' conditions. Similarly, organizational structures and processes and the institutional framework of industrial relations can be seen to

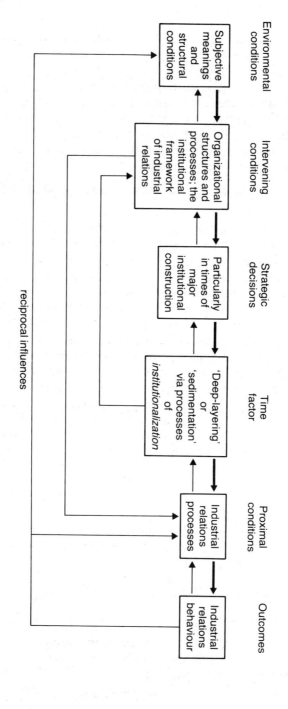

FIGURE 2.2 *A temporal framework of industrial relations*

have long-term as well as short-term effects on patterns of action and behaviour. Again, the proximal forces of process are essentially common to both approaches and, in each case, reflect the exercise of power in interactive encounters.

However, temporal analysis is different in its concentration on the way in which *strategic choices become 'deeply layered' or 'sedimented' through processes of institutionalization* (see Giddens, 1979). On such assumptions, then, at crucial historical junctures, fundamental *decisions* on appropriate industrial relations forms are taken that gradually become embedded in particular societies and transmitted from one generation to the next through institutions. The examination of strategic decisions frequently requires detailed historical accounts of periods of 'diachronic' change and the variety of choices and constraints which informed particular outcomes. At these points in time, too, the distribution of power and the patterns of conflict and 'strategic alliances' amongst the three main parties to industrial relations (and among wider social classes and groups) are vital.

Above all, by means of historical or temporal analysis, an explanatory usage of the concept of institutionalization can be advanced. Indeed, institutions established at critical periods of transition and change assume a degree of 'functional autonomy' from wider environmental and organizational exigencies. Moreover, through processes of internal socialization, there is a gradual 'layering' of traditional practices and the entrenchment of particular methods of handling industrial relations issues. Further, once these processes of so-called 'sedimentation' have been completed, the institutions attract personnel into administrative and other leadership roles who have a vested interest in the survival of established procedures and practices themselves.

Forces for divergence and convergence in industrial relations

No account of long-term movements in comparative industrial relations could of course afford to ignore wider issues of divergence and convergence which are associated with long-standing exchanges on the forces for change in industrial societies as a whole. In a sense, the comparative scholar inevitably adopts a polemical position since the compass of his or her analysis centres largely on the variations and not the similarities of pattern in the employment relationship. But the further argument advanced here is that although technology and associated processes of rationalization are potent sources for similarity and convergence, in the long run, *increasing diversity* can be expected to stem from varied institutional responses to conflict in production and distribution relationships in the developing countries, accompanying the rapid spread of industrialism.

Given the focus and emphasis of comparative analysis, it is certainly not our aim to revisit the convergence thesis or to begin with its assumptions (for a review see Form, 1979). But Clark Kerr's (1983) *The Future of Industrial Societies* provides a recent valuable springboard for our distinctive position emphasizing: (1) continuing substantial dissimilarity, and in many cases mounting diversity in industrial relations; (2) the vital effects of power amongst the 'actors' in fashioning the outcomes of conflict and accommodation; (3) the 'functional autonomy' of values; and (4) above all, a widening global variety stemming from the presence of a progressively *larger* number of industrialized societies.

For Kerr (1983), then, the non-determinist conception of the future proposed originally in *Industrialism and Industrial Man* should now be reaffirmed in which the 'threads of diversity' and 'source of uniformity' are in continual conflict. Broadly speaking, it is possible to identify areas of current comparability, increasing similarity and continuing substantial dissimilarity. In respect of industrial relations, comparability is evident in the creation of a 'web of rules' governing the workplace, hours of work per week, wage differentials for skill, prestige scores of occupations and welfare expenditures as a percentage of Gross National Product; increasing similarity in the percentage of adult women in the labour force and in service and white-collar occupations, in the ability of managers to dismiss workers, the content of work rules and the distribution of income; and continuing substantial dissimilarity in the comparative rate of pay for white-collar workers, the use of plans and markets and the autonomy of workers' organizations. More generally, too, the trend to similarity is most apparent in those parts of societies that bear the imprint of industrialism: the extent of knowledge, mobilization of the resources of production, organization of productive processes, patterns of working life, patterns of daily living, and patterns of distribution of economic rewards. Bipolar arrangements tend to occur in economic and political structures. And heterogeneity remains in the area of beliefs with the 'most impenetrable barriers to convergence' being 'the power and tenacity of the elites that lead the process, the invariable eternal conflict over the highest economic and political goals, and the ingrained beliefs of the people' (Kerr, 1983: 85).

For my part, however, there is convincing evidence for increasing dissimilarity (the fourth logical possibility) in a number of industrial relations patterns. At many points in the chapters which follow empirical data are presented that reveal that current institutional forms and practices are more polymorphous than was once the case, there being no obvious reason to suppose that this will not continue in the years ahead. The distribution of power is also basic to understanding disparate outcomes to continuing struggles over those ideals which move the 'actors' the most forcefully. Moreover, while diversity in the sphere of ideologies and culture is underscored, both value and instrumental rationalities are viewed as potent sources of national differences. Finally, experimentation in advanced industrial societies and the ambitious programmes of industrialization in the Third World are seen to encourage increasing diversity not least in socialist countries.

Late development

The experiences of the developing nations also lead to a further interesting temporal theoretical approach to the study of industrial relations, associated with the concept of late-development (Dore, 1973). Essentially, on this view, the later a society comes to industrialization, the more likely it is that a number of central characteristics in the industrial relations system and in its wider environment will be present or absent (Dore, 1973: 415–16): (1) the laissez-faire philosophy will be less pronounced and the state will play a particularly major role; (2) there is less chance of a slow evolution of putting-out into factory systems; (3) educational development will precede the growth of a substantial manufacturing section; (4) the 'technological leap' will be more substantial; (5) the 'organizational leap' will be greater with industries commencing with a bureaucratized and rational form of organization; (6) the impact of human relations (and, by extension, participative) philosophies of management will be pervasive; (7) the larger organizations will be more secure; and (8) the differences between large and small organizations and sectors will be greater.

In developing societies, then, the role of the state in industrial relations is pronounced, the chances of, say, craft unions emerging are limited (because of the large technological leap), the prospects for advanced personnel and human resourcing techniques are enhanced, and dual labour markets have far-reaching consequences for the distribution of rewards accruing from work, resulting in sectoral variations in income and security. To be sure, such relationships have to be carefully demonstrated in concrete cases and they underestimate the range of choice available to developing societies (cf. Poole 1975, 1982a) and the pervasiveness of the ideologies of industrial elites (Loveridge, 1983: 56). But the existence of *qualitatively* distinct temporal periods is highlighted and, above all, the improbability that modern industrializing societies will follow step by step the processes of economic transformation of the major countries in the 'capitalist' and 'state socialist' worlds is underscored. And finally, the thesis of late development involves focusing on a source of diversity in global industrial relations stemming from different trajectories of development at distinctive time periods.

Summary and developments

During the first part of this investigation, the aim has been to establish a number of core principles of comparative analysis and to absorb a wide range of multidisciplinary concepts within inclusive spatial and temporal analytical frameworks. More specifically, the case for an 'action' approach, centred on the notion of strategic choice, and acknowledging the significance of a series of environmental, organizational and institutional constraints and the distribution and mobilization of power in interaction, has been formulated. But of course to begin to *explain* variations in industrial relations phenomena systematically amongst countries requires the development of more focused theories in particular substantive areas. Analytical frameworks are invaluable as a source of relevant concepts but they are merely a prelude for the establishment of incisive propositions to account for observed differences and not ends in themselves. It is now appropriate, therefore, to attempt to generate a series of more confined theories covering differences amongst countries in the strategies of the 'actors' (employers and managers, labour and trade unions and the state and various of its agencies) and in central comparative themes (industrial conflict, industrial democracy and the distribution of economic rewards).

Part 2

The 'actors' in the industrial relations system

Chapter 3 Managers and employers' associations

The development of industrialism is one of an ever-increasing capacity amongst human populations to fashion a multiplicity of employment relationships. Earlier, the exigencies of the physical environment largely determined task-based behaviour and, to a substantial degree, the social organization of work as well. By contrast, in advanced industrial societies, there is widespread variation in managerial strategies and 'styles', in trade union density, structure and policy, in the extent of legal or voluntary regulation of the terms and conditions under which work takes place and in the effectiveness of employers' associations and governmental agencies. Thus, the parties to the employment relationship may be seen as creative 'actors' who, within acknowledged limitations of economic, political and social forces *and* the distribution of power, have a progressively rich and varied range of options available to them in the construction of distinctive national institutions. The more substantive parts of this study thus appropriately begin by a comparative assessment of the 'actors' in the industrial relations system, focusing first on diverse managerial strategies and 'styles' and the varied impact of employers' associations.

A theory of managerial strategies and 'styles' in industrial relations

Managers are an ubiquitous and expanding group in all industrial relations systems. To explain the principal contrasts in their strategies and 'styles' amongst nations, attention centres on choices, patterned in terms of the general categories of action and wider cultural values and ideologies (see Figure 3.1). But the formulation and outcomes of particular choices are modified by powerful constraints that include economic forces (particularly diverse product and labour markets), politico-economic systems (notably the overall extent of central regulation by the state) and,

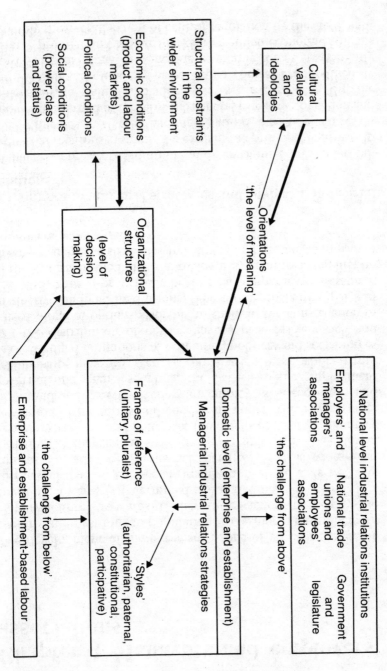

FIGURE 3.1 *Managerial strategies and 'styles' in industrial relations: the overall pattern*

to a lesser extent, social structures (including power, class and status in the 'larger' society). The structures of organizations are also consequential (especially the levels at which strategic choices are formulated and 'the challenge from below' from plant-based organizations of labour), as is the institutional structure of industrial relations (for instance, when agreements amongst employers' associations, trade unions and government are framed at a national level, this circumscribes the domestic autonomy of management). In addition to 'the challenge from above', the main changes over time reveal a very broad movement away from authoritarian managerial 'styles', but overall a complex pattern of increasingly 'hybrid' types.

Managerial strategies and 'styles'

The notion of strategy is basic to the analysis of managerial roles in industrial relations. Formulated to take account of the interests and roles of labour and government, it includes a recognizable content and distinctive outcomes (Kochan, McKersie and Cappelli, 1984). Moreover, an industrial relations 'style' embodies a coherent approach to the problem of motivating and controlling employees, of handling grievances and conducting relationships with organized labour (see e.g. Brown and Sisson, 1984: 21–3), while a 'frame of reference' refers to managerial conceptions of the authority structure of the firm (see Fox, 1974).

The connections between these primary analytical building blocks of the industrial relations of managers are set out in Figure 3.2 where strategic decisions are seen to be taken at the macro level in the higher level interchanges between employers, government and organized labour, at the level of the industrial relations system where the characteristics of the employment relationship are ultimately determined, and at workplace level amongst individuals and groups (Kochan, McKersie and Cappelli, 1984). The distinctive 'styles' of management include directive (authoritarian), directive but welfare-oriented (paternalist), negotiational and based on reaching agreements with organized labour and government (constitutional), and the involvement of employees in decisions (participative) (see Kerr *et al.*, 1960). The first two 'styles' reflect a unitary frame of reference where the enterprise has a unified authority structure with common objectives and values. The second pair are more likely to be associated with a

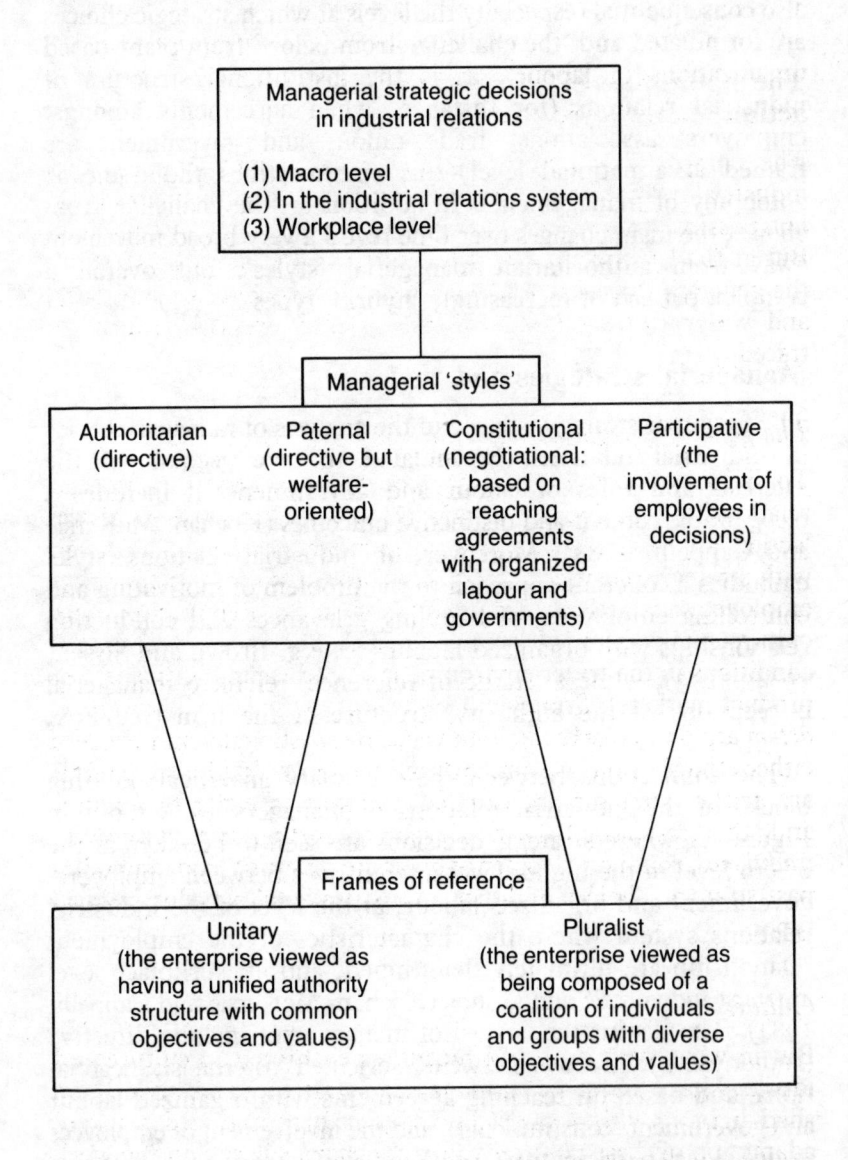

FIGURE 3.2 *Strategy, 'style' and frame of reference: the industrial relations of managers*

pluralist conception of the firm as comprising a coalition of individuals and groups with diverse objectives and values.

The patterning of choices: general categories of social action, culture and ideology

The comparative analysis of managerial strategic choices in industrial relations would present an insuperable problem were it not possible to discover patterns which vary amongst nations. But at the level of meaning, links between strategy and 'style', the general categories of social action (focusing on orientations), and wider cultural and ideological conditions can readily be traced.

The general categories of social action

To begin with, then, the choices of managers in industrial relations can be located within the primary categories of the 'action' approach (see Table 3.1). *Instrumental action* is associated with strategies designed to enhance productivity and efficiency, employee satisfaction, adaptability and so on. Relating partly to culture, it is also connected with economic and technical conditions in the wider environment (e.g. the competitiveness of product markets). Strategic decisions grounded in *value rational action* are particularly likely to vary cross-nationally and concern either ethical or moral standards or ideologies. *'Affectual'* choices are neither strategic nor rational, unlikely to differ by country and, therefore, need not be developed further here. However, *traditional* conduct is potentially more relevant and embodies past strategic choices of either an instrumental or value-rational type.

Culture

But in what ways do broad meanings enshrined in culture and ideology have a bearing on managerial strategies and 'styles'? To shed light on this issue, Child (1981) has produced a useful adaptation of these cultural-value dimensions based on the work of Kluckholn and Strodtbeck (1961), to relate to management action. Adapted here to cover the industrial relations of managers in diverse national contexts, it will be seen in Table 3.2

TABLE 3.1 *The location of managerial strategic choices in industrial relations in terms of the categroies of social action*

General categories of social action (orientations)	Managerial strategies in industrial relations
(1) Instrumental-rational	(1) The development of industrial relations strategies as a means to such ends as increased productivity and efficiency, employee satisfaction and adaptability (especially during conditions of rapid economic and technical change)
(2) Value-rational	(2) Strategic choices based on: (i) values reflecting a primacy of ethical and moral considerations. (ii) ideologies associated with certain dominant political creeds (e.g. capitalism, corporatism, managerialism)
(3) Affectual	(3) Lack of an overarching strategy: non-rational, affectual conduct divorced from instrumental-rational action (e.g. productivity and efficiency), or value-rational action (e.g. notions of 'fairness'). Includes 'favouritism' in the distribution of rewards or the application of sanctions
(4) Traditional	(4) Managerial-type 'custom and practice' based on unreflective, habituated modes of behaviour. The embodiment of past strategic choices

that, at least in principle, a positive assessment of 'subordinate' groups should encourage decentralization of powers to work groups and job enrichment; emphasis on human mastery is associated with non-fatalistic views and a stress on choice in the selection of industrial relations 'styles'; a future orientation is connected with long-term strategic policies in industrial relations rather than with short-term so-called, 'fire fighting' policies; an orientation towards activity favours human relations and employee-centred practices; and finally the de-emphasis of hierarchical distinctions tends to facilitate a reduction in status and power 'distances' within the organization.

Given the dearth of cross-national research on managerial industrial relations strategies and 'styles' and the lack of any real attempt to relate these to the value-orientations identified above, an examination of the substantive effects of culture is inevitably illustrative. Examined in turn, the three distinctive national cultures of Japan, the USA and Nigeria are shown to have informed diverse managerial approaches to labour issues.

Culture is not solely responsible for 'benevolent paternalism' in the Japanese system of industrial relations, but the modified Confucian world-view which prevailed in the late nineteenth century is a vital factor. Assuming original virtue rather than original sin (Dore, 1973; Ichiro, 1975), it encouraged employers to evoke moral appeals to authority and to stress the efficiency of benevolence. And it also helped to shape personal objectives (the desire of private industrialists and managers to appear to be good moral citizens) and economic goals (such as public reputation *as well as* greater profits and efficiency and faster expansion) (Dore, 1973: 401–2). Indeed, the patterns of institutionalization which emerged in industrial Japan reflected a creative synthesis of new elements which conformed to cultural predispositions, the direct borrowing from abroad in certain instances and, in other respects again, the institutional continuation of pre-industrial practices (Dore, 1973: 375–6).

In the USA, the effects of value systems (and ideologies) are most obviously manifest in union avoidance practices, a pronounced 'unitary' perspective and the deployment of sophisticated human relations and human resourcing 'techniques'. Managerial preferences have fluctuated over time, but against the general trend towards a tacit acceptance of trade unions, a substantial number of US employers publicly espouse a 'union-free' policy. And the origins of this approach can be traced in part to 'individualism' in the wider culture, coupled with prevalent private enterprise commitments (Rothenberg and Silverman, 1973; Myers, 1976; Foulkes, 1980a; Kochan, McKersie and Cappelli, 1984). Indeed, in recently established enterprises, care is commonly taken in the size of operating units to prevent excessive concentrations of employees in a single site and in the 'screening' of potential applicants prior to selection. In addition, non-union grievance procedures have been introduced, together with 'rational' wage and salary administration, advanced systems of communication and information sharing and foremen and supervisors trained in human relations and human resourcing

TABLE 3.2 *Examples of relationships postulated between cultural value orientations and organizational and industrial relations characteristics*

Value orientation ($>$ = stronger than, or preferred)	General organizational characteristics	Examples of specific practices	Adaptations for industrial relations
(1) Human nature: good $>$ evil	Emphasis on subordinate autonomy and intrinsic motivation	Subordinate goal setting: job enrichment	Subordinate goal setting: job enrichment
(2) Man to nature: mastery $>$ subjugation	Policies of innovation, and of developing individual expertise	Support for venture management; positive exercise of strategic choices including active negotiation of boundary conditions with external groups	Emphasis on choice in selection of different industrial relations 'styles'

(3) Time orientation: future > past	Strategic emphasis and long-term planning; formal schemes for thorough organizational socialization and career planning	MBO approach rather than budgetary control: use of manpower planning and assessment centres	Preference for long-term industrial relations strategies over fire fighting
(4) Orientation towards activity: being > doing	Human relations philosophy: emphasis on interpersonal sensitivity; interest in social as well as economic and technological criteria in work organization	Management style high on consideration relative to initiating structures; organizational morale and climate included in performance monitoring	Human relations and employee-centred management style rather than focus on productivity
(5) Relationships: individual > hierarchical	Minimization of hierarchy; emphasis on delegation and participation; control through assessment of achievement rather than through insistence on conformity to rules	Amenities and fringe benefits not differentiated between status; employees deal directly with members of the public (where relevant) without referral upwards	Amenities and fringe benefits not differentiated by status; power distances minimal

Note: Adapted from Child (1981: 326).

techniques (see Foulkes, 1980b: 17–44; Kochan, 1980: 185).

Nigeria is not entirely typical of the Third World, but its managerial industrial relations strategies are instructive, being based on culture, and reflected in an authoritarian but people-centred African 'arbitrary paternalistic style' (Damachi, 1978: 113–21). This leads to an informal and frequently perfunctory treatment of trade union demands so that 'it appears to be rare to find that the eventual settlement is arrived at wholly through collective bargaining' (Diejomaoh, 1979: 193). Further, it encourages (and partly emanates from) a corresponding willing-ness amongst trade unions 'to strike over situations which are merely misunderstandings' rather than over issues in which substantial and sharply focused grievances are manifest (Damachi, 1978: 192–4). It also occasions a lack of proper institutionalized grievance channels and persistent 'high-handedness' in the treatment of the workforce and it ensures that, to some extent contrary to the logical expectations of the late-development effect, the influence and prestige of human relations and personnel departments in the entrerprise are no higher than in comparable western concerns (cf. Akinmayowa, 1980, 1981).

Ideologies

Managerial ideologies are designed to facilitate control over 'labour resources' and vary significantly amongst nations. Early 'entrepreneurial' ideologies were elaborated in an effort to promote industry in a relatively hostile environment against a politically dominant aristocracy and a newly recruited industrial workforce. 'Managerial' ideologies, however, arose originally from the problems of exerting *control* over labour and varied according to the size and complexity of industry and the degree of 'trust' or 'good faith' in management-employee relations. Critically, too, as Bendix (1956) has shown, diverse managerial ideologies emerged in Britain, the USA, Russia and East Germany, which were partly independent developments reflecting particular historical conditions, but also derived from the degree of autonomy of the entrepreneurial 'class' and the role of the state in the development of industry itself.

But the link between managerial ideologies, strategies and 'styles' is exemplified most of all by the French case. Based on individualism, paternalism and legalism (cf. Gallie, 1978), management 'style' here reflects the vitality of ideology in the context of an intense struggle for control incessantly waged between employers and unions at both national and enterprise levels. Indeed, the strategy of French management is 'to maintain the maximum degree of managerial discretion while seeking to tie workers directly to the firm' (Gallie, 1978: 183; 1983). Moreover, such a policy is related to the high levels of political consciousness of organized labour and to the determination of the key unions to eradicate the system of private ownership of the means of production in the long term, a situation which rules out any prospect of an evolution towards constitutional management.

Structural constraints

Cultural values and ideologies are thus basic to understanding the strategic choices and 'styles' of management in industrial relations in particular countries. But structural constraints make intelligible some of the variation as well and encompass broad economic, political and social conditions in the wider environment, the structure of organizations and the institutional characteristics of the industrial relations system.

Environmental conditions

The growth of distinctive managerial strategies in industrial relations can thus be attributed in part to economic conditions and especially to the nature of product markets (see Purcell, 1983; Kochan, McKersie and Cappelli, 1984). Above all, a mature market and the will to compete across all segments can lead to a 'shift in emphasis in industrial relations away from maintaining labour peace in order to maximise production to one of controlling labour costs, streamlining work rules, and increasing productivity in order to meet growing price competition' (Kochan, McKersie and Cappelli, 1984 – see also Slichter, 1941; Livernash, 1962; McKersie and Hunter, 1973; Kochan and Katz, 1983). In short, a highly competitive product market leads to directive managerial 'styles', the abandonment of constitutionalism and the focus on individual employees at the expense of trade union representatives.

Labour market conditions also modify managerial 'styles', for high levels of unemployment affect power relationships and further encourage 'directive' forms of decision making. But these show little uniformity amongst nations with the result that in the recent recession, the Scandinavian countries (with more favourable employment conditions than, say, the UK) have found their labour relations institutions to be correspondingly more robust and less liable to fundamental transformation by unilateral managerial action.

The effects of political economy on 'styles' of management is best illustrated in countries with wholesale state regulation and planning. In the socialist countries of eastern Europe, then, 'the exercise of authority is interpreted in a much more complete way' than in the west, 'because it is seen ultimately to represent the supreme authority of the state' (Bendix, 1956: 10). More particularly, in the USSR, the predominant managerial 'style' is 'constitutional', a situation which reflects the numerous checks on managerial autonomy by the state and the Party and, to some extent, by the trade unions as well. Hence, in the Soviet Union, ownership and control of enterprises are vested in government ministries. The minister (responsible to the council of ministries) appoints directors who are in charge of 'enterprises' or production units (cf. Lane, 1970: 299–300), with the result that it is 'the state bureaucrats who have the power and organization to run the state' and that 'the industrial manager is a subordinate'. (Lane, 1970: 300; see also, Berliner, 1957; Granick, 1960, 1972; Lane, 1976). This 'structural propensity' is reinforced by the direct control by the trade unions of various human relations functions, for Soviet Union labour organizations are liable for the administration of various schemes for 'social insurance' (e.g. sickness, maternity, industrial injury and factory 'allowances').

However, the effects of class, status and power in the 'larger' society on managerial strategies and 'styles' are probably weak. It is feasible to point to distinctive 'class constellations' which serve as background conditions for the early development of particular managerial strategies (cf. Bendix, 1956), but the extent that these currently persist depends almost entirely on their reinforcement through a series of *institutional* processes. As for status, a comparison between the USA and France is instructive since, despite high employer aspirations for control in both countries, the American managerial 'style' is obviously more personal. This, in turn, could result from the greater flexibility of the system of social ranking in the USA that tends to counter a high degree of 'social distance'. But such differences may have little bearing on the actual content, target and outcomes of strategic decisions.

Organizational and industrial relations structures – the locus of strategic decision making

The choice of particular bargaining relationships and the chance of developing, say, union-free enterprises also hinge on whether strategic policies on labour issues are formulated at corporate or plant level (see Purcell, 1983: 7–9; Kochan, McKersie and Cappelli, 1984). The growth of conglomerate multinational enterprises presents clear opportunities for management to shape policies at corporate level where they are relatively unrestricted by intervention by government or by plant-level agreements with labour. This is contingent on the distribution and locus of power amongst the 'actors' in the industrial relations system, for, broadly speaking, the decision-making control of managers is subject to two main challenges (Flanders, 1970). The first (the so-called 'challenge from above') refers to the intervention of governments and the impact of centrally organized trade unions. By contrast, the second ('the challenge from below') applies to the penetration of factory-level representatives of labour into managerial decision making and to the existence of either unilaterally regulated zones for labour or, perhaps more typically, a degree of power sharing via locally based substantive and procedural rules (see e.g. Poole, 1974; Batstone, Boraston and Frenkel, 1977).

Taking the UK as an example, the power of the various 'actors' in the industrial relations system is closely entwined with the shifts in emphasis in managerial 'styles' over time. Until recently, a 'semi-constitutional style' of management predominated, accompanying a progressive evolution from 'unitary' to 'pluralist' conceptions of the appropriate structure of enterprise authority (cf. Fox, 1966, 1974; Gallie, 1978). However, latest researches reveal a pronounced *preference* for a 'unitary' frame of reference (Poole *et al.*, 1981, 1982) and suggest that *the more that managers are able to formulate strategic policy at corporate and to some extent domestic levels, the more will strategies aimed to reduce the role of trade unions prevail.* By contrast, 'constitutional' rule making emerges when governments, central federations of trade unions and, to a lesser degree, shop stewards and other domestically based representatives of labour are able to enforce such an outcome. Certainly this proposition is strongly supported in the USA where the *'ability* of a firm to pursue nonunion options' is seen to be 'negatively related to its current level of unionization and positively related to the extent to which collective bargaining is decentralized in the firm' (Kochan, McKersie and Cappelli, 1984: 26).

Temporal diversity

Examining variations in managerial strategies and 'styles' in industrial relations on a long-term scale points not to a pronounced evolutionary or convergent pattern but rather to a progressively rich array of 'hybrid' forms accompanying the proliferation in number of industrialized countries and fluctuating movements in 'mature' industrial societies.

The evolutionary approach elaborated by Kerr *et al.* (1960) suggests that, if management is completely free to construct its own rules in the industrial workplace, it will adopt either dictatorial (authoritarian) or pragmatic 'styles'. A commonplace in the early phases of industrialism, these types of management decision-making procedure have proved to be unstable over time through a failure to enhance loyalty and productivity. Sometimes they have been superseded by the philosophy of paternalist management which 'carries forward the traditions of responsibility and subordination of the master-servant relationship' and generally is most stable: (1) when the 'pre-existing culture and social structure are congenial' to this type of relationship; (2) when strong labour unions do not challenge management's decision-making authority at work; and (3) when the community does not provide extensive welfare facilities (Kerr *et al.*, 1960: 126–7). But in the modern era, constitutional management and, less typically, democratic or participative 'styles' predominate.

Yet, while a near-universal concern for human resources is recognized here, rather than any particular managerial 'style' prevailing, an interesting array of types seem to exist. While authoritarian or directive forms of management were dominant in the nineteenth century, they are still widespread in many countries. Hybrid types, such as the African arbitrary-paternal style and the tendency of US managers to exact control and to eschew constitutional modes of decision making but to experiment with shop-floor participation, have proliferated. Even the distinctive Japanese style of welfare corporatism has become more consultative in character. So-called 'sophisticated paternal' patterns have also emerged in which trade unions are recognized but, consistent with 'unitary' objectives, are enmeshed in company procedures and even encouraged to enter into 'no strike agreements'. (Purcell and Sisson, 1983). Hence, while research into these developments has scarcely begun and it is simply not feasible to develop a valid comparative explanation for changes over time, the propensity to *divergence* and to the parallel development of ever more complex 'styles' of management in the industrial relations sphere is stressed.

Employers' associations

Unlike administrative or managerial personnel, associations of employers are not universal throughout all industrial and industrializing societies. To be sure, they 'hold a key position in the industrial relations system' in almost every western nation and Japan (Windmuller and Gladstone (eds), 1984: v). But they have a limited role in the USA and Canada, are patchy in development in much of the Third World and entirely absent from the state socialist countries of eastern Europe. Furthermore, although they have sufficient ubiquity to merit separate treatment here, our analysis is hampered by fragmented knowledge of their origins, activities and strategies, a dearth of rigorously formulated explanatory propositions which have been tested in research designs, and the tendency for genuinely comparative accounts to be inhibited by the treatment of cases by country.

In the exposition which follows, a comparative theory of the evolution and influence of employers' associations is first presented. Following a brief classification of the diverse experiences of nations, there is then an attempt to isolate a series of contributory forces derived from the overall analytical frameworks elaborated earlier.

A theory of employers' associations

Coupled with the strategic choices of employers themselves, substantial explanatory weight must be attached to the constraints of political economy since, in certain cases (and particularly in state socialist countries), these in practice imply that collective bodies of employers cannot emerge at all. Vital also are variations in the power of the actors in the industrial relations system. The presence of strong, centralized and independent trade unions is thus a spur to countervailing employer activity. Similarly, a powerful state with an interventionist role in industrial relations encourages employers to establish centralized 'peak' organizations to influence government policy at source. By contrast, autonomous professional management in large corporations prefer to handle labour policy internally and, other than for information and advice, will eschew employers' associations for collective bargaining purposes.

A number of supplementary influences on employers' associations also merit attention, above all, material 'infrastructure', culture and ideology, the structure of industrial relations institutions and the timing and pace of industrialism. Medium-sized companies in competitive markets are particularly likely to require the services of employers' associations. Cultural conservatism and an attachment to tradition also favour their persistence as do industry-wide and national systems of collective bargaining. And finally, the timing and pace of industrialism relate to the experience of Third World countries, where a dominant role by the state in economic planning and an established network of trade unions reinforce employers' associations. However, obverse pressures originate in the influence of professional managers in the advanced sectors of the economy, the 'infrastructural' consequences of a dualism between the largest enterprises and the very small concerns and, in terms of power in the 'larger' society, the absence of a strong indigenous entrepreneurial class to provide a firm basis for a forcefully articulated employers' viewpoint.

Variations in the incidence and impact of employers' associations

Given the current limitations to our knowledge of employers' associations, it is unrealistic to embark upon a comprehensive analysis of variations in their strategy and structure. The treatment here is thus, advisedly, focused on their varied incidence and impact, in terms of which countries are classified under three heads covering those: (1) with strong or influential employers' associations; (2) with weak or uninfluential bodies; and (3) with no independent organizations of employers at all.

The cradle of powerful employers' associations is continental Europe, for the bulk of countries here (e.g. Austria, Belgium,

Denmark, France, Italy, the Netherlands, Norway, Sweden, Switzerland and West Germany) have influential organizations which engage in collective bargaining and attempt to ensure that governments are regularly appraised of employers' viewpoints. Moreover, in many of these countries, the relevant employers' associations are formally implicated in national policy through extensive tripartite machinery. Elsewhere, Australia and Japan also have groupings of employers which have a notable impact on the industrial relations system, while in a number of Third World countries (e.g. India and Kenya), these associations are again well entrenched. By contrast, in North America and to some extent the UK, employers' bodies are fragmented and do not have the same cohesive and significant role at the centre. But at least employers' associations are present, while this is not true of the advanced state socialist industrial societies of eastern Europe and the USSR, Yugoslavia and other decentralized self-managed systems and the fully socialized political economies of the Third World (e.g. China, Cuba, South Yemen).

Explanations

Strategy and political economy

Employers' associations are not the product of ineluctable economic forces over which the members themselves have no control, but are better understood as the outgrowth of consciously formulated strategies which are designed to promote employer interests in given environmental, institutional and organizational circumstances. Indeed, Windmuller's (1984: 1) observation here is apposite, that

> Organizations for employers generally owe their establishment to attempts, initiated mostly by employers themselves and only rarely by outsiders, to achieve one or several aims in pursuit of their collective interests: to regulate matters of trade and competition by mutual agreement; to seek statutory protection in matters of trade, particularly with regard to imported goods; to erect a united front in dealing with trade unions; to provide services in labour relations and personnel administration; and to contest the passage of social and labour legislation.

Moreover, guiding the tactics of employers' associations are three central strategies or 'models of organization': defensive, procedural-political and market or economic (Jackson and Sisson, 1975; Armstrong, 1984). The first encapsulates employer hostility to the aims of trade unions and embraces coherent policies to arrest the influence of labour over the employment relationship. By contrast, the second involves the recognition of trade unions and collective bargaining in return for employee acceptance of the employers' 'right to manage' and the orderly handling of disputes. And the third is designed to prevent excessive competition for labour and to avoid pirating and the 'bidding up' or 'undercutting' of the price of labour. Indeed, political-economy only has a determining effect upon outcomes in countries without employers' associations, where private ownership of the means of production has been eradicated by one or other of the leading forms of socialism.

The power of the 'actors' in the industrial relations system

But if employers' associations are interpreted as the product of conscious strategy and a necessary condition for their existence is a substantial private sector, other contingent factors underlie their origins and varied impact. The power of the other 'actors' in the industrial relations system is all-important: namely, organized labour, the state, and professional managements in the large corporations. In countries with strong employers' associations, then, the emergence of influential trade union movements was originally met with a determined collective counter-offensive by industrialists. For instance, in the case of Sweden, the Swedish Employers' Confederation (Svenska Arbetsgivar Foreningen: SAF) was founded as a direct concerted response to the three-day general strike of 1902 to check the rising industrial and political power of labour organized in the Landsorganisationen (LO). In the official constitution of the SAF, the primary purpose is explicitly to promote interests common to all employers including assistance 'in negotiations with organised labour' and compensation 'for damages caused by labour conflicts' (Swedish Employers' Confederation, 1950: 3; see also Skogh, 1984). In Australia, the rise of trade unions was indisputably the overriding factor behind the proliferation of employers' associations (Walker, 1970: 71–84; Dabscheck and Niland, 1981: 171–85). As Dufty (1984: 117) has cogently observed:

Generally speaking, early employers' associations [in Australia] were formed as a result of a learning process; they learned that unless they stood together they were picked off one at a time by the increasingly powerful unions. For example, in the early 1870s the unions made successful claims on individual employers for an eight-hour day. The New South Wales (NSW) employers responded by forming the Iron Trades Employers' Association and when the union tried to retain the customary two breaks in the working day the employers, acting together, refused on the grounds that with the shorter day one was enough.

It is clear, too, that Australian employers' associations sometimes became defunct when the threat from labour was no longer exigent, only to re-form again when pressure was renewed. Italian history also 'confirms the thesis that both the structure and initiatives of employers' associations tend to parallel those of trade unions' (Treu and Martinelli, 1984: 264). The function of early German employers' associations was closely related to the rise of trade unions (Bunn, 1984). And, in Israel, the challenges posed by the labour movement (the Histadrut) 'more than any other reason prompted employers to establish associations' (Shirom, 1984: 295).

But the state also has a powerful impact on the strength and vigour of employers' associations. Corporatist-type structures and institutions support employers' bodies as centralized 'peak' organizations for dealing with governmental agencies. And more generally, a pronounced state presence with widespread economic controls, coupled with an extensive role for the legislature in industrial relations, stimulates concerted employer pressure for a voice in national policy and the provision of a representative channel for members.

Italy provides a valuable example of this link between corporatism and centrally organized and influential employers' bodies, for here, despite the weakening of nationally based systems of negotiation since the late 1960s (IDE, 1981a: 200–18), Confindustria maintains 'great power both politically and economically', a situation which 'derives in good part from the Fascist period'. At that point, employer federations actually had wide government powers, and changes affecting employment conditions of groups of workers could only be made through their agency (Stagner, 1957: 5). Indeed, as Treu and Martinelli (1984: 265) have observed:

With the rise of Fascism to power in 1922, the relationship between organized business and the state became consolidated. Confindustria backed the Fascist party and ideology, thus reflecting a position widely held among industrialists who, with some notable exceptions, tended to see in Fascism a means of containing organized labour and for restoring order in a society beset by severe social conflicts.

Confindustria's domination over state policy in the Fascist period included rejecting the attempt to build global integrated unionism (*sindacalismo integrale*), maintaining organizational autonomy and ensuring that Socialist and Catholic unions were replaced by the Federation of Fascist Guilds (*Confederazione delle corporazioni fasciste*).

But, on the whole, a strong state role in industrial relations is an advantage for employers' associations. For example, although in the case of the Netherlands, the ascendency of labour was once more the catalyst for the formation of employers' bodies, their continued vitality owes much to a highly interventionist state. Thus the preponderance of economic controls and of centralized decision making instituted after the Second World War encouraged the engagement of employers in 'pressure group' participation and a high level of demand for technical services was fuelled by a large volume of labour legislation (Windmuller, 1967: 49–50). This also contributed to the predisposition for strong (if internally divided) employers' associations in the Netherlands and for the industrial relations system to be 'characterized, by and large, by centralization, strong government influence, and rather tight discipline in the ranks of unions as well as employers' associations' (Voorden, 1984: 202).

Moreover, in countries with typically weaker, decentralized and more fragmented employers' federations, the impact of the strategies of professional managements in the large corporations has been crucial. The most obvious example of this is the USA, which exemplifies a number of conditions in an advanced, predominantly private enterprise economy that undermine the growth of strong employers' associations. Three of these are particularly salient: (1) the independent power of professional managers in large multinational corporations; (2) the comparative weakness of trade unions; and (3) the local levels at which collective agreements are typically concluded. Above all, then, although American employers have established several small and overlapping associations, which, in some states (notably California)

are of consequence, generally, the industrial relations responsibilities of these bodies are circumscribed (Mills, 1982: 163;
Derber, 1984). The largest national groupings are the United
States Chamber of Commerce and the National Association of
Manufacturers although the three main attempts (in 1900, 1920
and 1934–5) to create an effective body of American employers
all ended in failure. This followed the rise of professional
managers in the large corporations who were deploying advanced
'human relations' and 'human resourcing' techniques and had no
real need for wider employer associations since they could handle
employee grievances and disputes internally and, where necessary,
call up other services (e.g. for legal advice) from within their own
departments or from elsewhere within the company.

Supplementary influences

It has been argued above that strategy and political economy and
the power of the 'actors' in the industrial relations system are
critical in explaining the origins and varied impact of employers'
federations amongst nations. But these factors do not exhaust all
the relevant conditions and it is worth examining now, if only
rather briefly, the further effects of material 'infrastructure',
culture and ideology, the structure of the institutions of
industrial relations and the timing and pace of industrialism.

Material 'infrastructure'

The case for material 'infrastructure' is superficially persuasive,
but on close examination appears to be of limited relevance.
Essentially, the argument reflects the proposition that industrial
concentration and technical and organizational complexity favour
the growth of employers' federations, whereas their development
is impeded by a fragmented industrial structure comprised of a
large number of small and medium-sized companies (Ingham,
1974). The reasons for this are complex, but are associated with
the tendency for concentrated industries to have close links with
governmental agencies and with the greater ease of combining
employer interests when the numbers involved are relatively few.
Moreover, the thesis has certainly been applied to Sweden and
has some applicability in the case of countries such as Australia
where the difficulties posed by free trade for Australian
manufacturers and for the orderly marketing of products in the
world economy were important in the early formation of

employers' associations (Dabscheck and Niland, 1981: 173).

But the argument would seem to be unsatisfactory on at least four counts. To begin with, as we have observed, in the largest enterprises there is a preference for independently formulated corporate strategies. Secondly, on a global scale, it would seem to be the middle-sized companies in competitive markets that typically require the services of employers' associations (cf. Jackson and Sisson, 1976). After all, these firms are more likely than the smaller concerns to attract recruitment drives by trade unions and also to seek regulation of competition to facilitate financial planning, while being unable to provide a full range of detailed specialist services from their own resources. Third, in critical cases such as Sweden, the timing of the development of employers' federations does not really fit the 'infrastructure' thesis (rather, as we have seen, the emergence of the SAF closely paralleled the rise of trade unions and industrial conflict). And finally, countries such as the UK, with relatively weak employers' associations, actually have high levels of industrial concentration and comparatively few small-scale concerns.

Culture and ideology

At a more 'subjective' level, it is probable that strategic decisions by employers to establish collective organizations and their subsequent effectiveness are informed by distinctive national cultures, religious values and political ideologies. Certainly ethico-political values have engendered structural divisions within notable national federations. The Dutch case illustrates the effects of religion for here, at the centre of the network of employers' associations, four main bodies have been traditionally pre-eminent, the Non-Confessional Federation of Netherlands Industries, the Central Social Confederation of Employers, the Confessional Catholic Employers' Federation and Federation of Protestant Employers (Windmuller, 1967; IDE, 1981a; Voorden, 1984).

The culture thesis has been posited by Windmuller (1967: 49) who noted that conservatism and attachment to tradition give rise to securely founded employers' associations. For instance, continental European countries and Japan (in which there has been a pronounced commitment to establishing cohesive national industrial relations institutions) have cultural proclivities which foster centralized associations, including those for employers. But the links are, to say the least, tenuous, while the effects of ideology are also difficult to demonstrate. Indeed, employers' associations in the same country do not automatically share a common political or ideological position, as Windmuller (1984: 5) has forcefully argued:

> To refer to the views generally held by employers' associations as constituting an ideology would probably be an exaggeration. Unlike a substantial number of trade unions in Western countries and Japan, employers' associations do not generally subscribe to an encompassing *Weltanschauung*, an integrated explanation of history and society, nor do they offer a prospectus of the ideal shape of social organizations in some indefinite future. After all, for most of them the present is generally quite satisfactory. In any case, they are not a political or social movement, nor do they constitute a part of such a movement in the sense in which trade unions, fraternal socialist or social-democratic parties, and sometimes cooperative societies constitute together a comprehensive national labour-oriented movement.

The structure of industrial relations institutions

Without a doubt, industry-wide, regional and national systems of collective bargaining enhance the role of employers' associations, whereas decentralized bargaining within companies tends to have the reverse effect. For example, centralized bargaining systems in Scandinavia and regional agreements in France and West Germany have encouraged a united employer response through collective associations. Moreover, the decentralized collective bargaining agreements of the USA, Canada and the UK are related to less cohesive and influential employers' bodies.

But the relationships here are somewhat fortuitous, since centralized bargaining systems are ultimately a product of the power and organization of national trade unions and of a dominant state role in the industrial relations system, while decentralized bargaining in given companies stems from managerial strategies and policies. In the one case, then, employers are constrained to form associations and to reach agreements at the centre, while in the other, their role is undermined by professional managements. The structure of the industrial relations system is thus to be regarded as a supplementary influence on the impact of employers' associations depending largely on the power and organization of the 'actors'.

The timing and pace of industrialism

Nevertheless, to understand the varied patterns in Third World countries a somewhat more complex explanation than the one formulated so far is appropriate which recognizes that, although the power of the 'actors' is critical, the timing and pace of industrialism are also relevant. There are thus two main late-development effects which encourage the growth of employers' bodies: an extensive participation by the state in economic planning, and the fairly advanced network of trade unions (underpinned by legislative action to secure certain basic 'employee rights' that is manifest in certain countries). However, three significant forces appear to run counter to the growth of effective employers' associations in many Third World nations: (1) the rise of the professional manager in the advanced sectors of the economy; (2) the 'infrastructural' consequences of a dualism between the largest enterprises and the very small concerns (the first having no real need for employers' associations and the second being too weak to establish them) coupled with the multinational links of many companies; and (3) in terms of power in the larger society, the lack of a strong indigenous entrepreneurial class to provide a secure basis for a forcefully articulated employers' viewpoint.

Turning, then, to examine the cases of India and Kenya as examples of Third World countries with well-organized and influential employers' associations, the main Indian associations (the Employers' Federation of India, the All-India Manufacturers' Association and the All-India Organization of Industrial Employers) originally grew in size and strength following the emergence of a politically conscious and increasingly militant labour movement (Ross, 1966; Mathur, 1968: 77–98; Myers and Kannappan, 1970; Venkatachalam and Singh, 1982). Undoubtedly, too, the central planning controls exercised by the state have ensured a centralized and effective presence of these bodies since their prime function is to persuade governments to follow policies consistent with employers' interests and to articulate an ideology emphasizing the scope for private enterprise in a mixed economy (Mathur, 1968: 77–98). The Federation of Kenya Employers has also been described as 'a compact and formidable force in the industrial scene' (Amsden, 1971: 95). Moreover, its effectiveness has been ascribed to the ascendance of Kenya's labour movement and to the existence of a larger number and broader range of enterprises including several in the crucial 'middle range'. This can be defined as an 'infrastructural' effect reflecting uneven paths of industrialization (Amsden, 1971: 94).

However, in most Third World countries with a prominent private sector, employers' associations do not appear to be as well entrenched as in, say, continental western and northern Europe. In much of Africa, this situation is attributable to the virtual absence of an intermediary group of enterprises between the very large concerns (which frequently have multinational links and whose professional managements typically eschew the constraints of a national federation) and the small family firms which are difficult to link under the aegis of an overall association. There are also the limitations imposed by the so-called 'politics of industrial relations' in developing societies which operate against the formation of cohesive bodies of employers (Amsden, 1971: 94). This contributes to the situation, in much of the English-speaking Caribbean, where, despite having the same legal basis as the trade unions, employers' associations are by no means as influential in the industrial relations system (Chaudhary, 1977: 14–16: ILO, 1977). In much of Latin America, too, the sharp dualism between large and economically dominant enterprises and the very small concerns (for example 90 per cent of establishments in Argentina have fewer than ten employees) also helps explain the restricted role of employers' associations, another vital consideration being that industrialists are incapable of promoting 'their interests with ability and vigour' because of the circumscribed power of the industrial entrepreneurial class in the larger society (Form and Blum, 1965; Imaz, 1972).

Conclusions

This analysis of contrasting managerial strategies and 'styles' and the origins and varied influence of employers' associations completes an appraisal of one of the principal sets of 'actors' in the industrial relations system. Managers in particular are a rapidly expanding and integral group in modern industrial societies and their polymorphous attitudes and behaviour, while still only partially understood, are likely to feature prominently in future cross-national comparative researches, where the ultimate weights to be attached to culture and ideology, politico-economic conditions, power and institutional forces must be determined. Employers' associations are also vital though considerably dependent on politico-economic systems, the power of trade unions and the state, the structure of industrial relations and not least the organizationally based policies of professional managements in the large-scale corporations.

Chapter 4 Labour and trade unions

Productive workers have always been accorded a position of special prominence in the industrial relations literature. In part, this derived from an awareness of their role as the largest single group in industrial society, the foundation upon which the wealth of nations ultimately rests. But it has also arisen from the recognition that working people and their families have traditionally borne the brunt of adjustments in the labour market and the impact of advanced technologies. Even more, however, the association of workers through trade unions has been the focal point of analysis. As Korpi (1978) has observed, together with political parties, labour unions are the main power resource of working people, relatively close to their lives in the enterprise. Yet, while collective strength can promote the resolution of a variety of problems faced by the workforce, it ensures conflict with management and the state and, in turn, provides the *raison d'être* for the study of industrial relations in the first place.

Here, variations in the strategies of labour and in the patterning of trade unions amongst nations are assessed. After detailing an overall framework, trade unions relying on collective bargaining are examined with special reference to density, structure and government. This preludes an explanatory account of trade unions in which political and legislative methods are uppermost and of the integrative-type labour associations under socialism.

Theories of labour strategy and trade unionism

The strategies espoused by particular labour movements are shaped by choices and linked with distinctive orientations (especially instrumental and radical) and with the wider cultural and ideological environment in which they are formed. But these choices are subject, in turn, to a series of constraints of which, at the broadest level of analysis, those of economic and political structure, technology and, to some extent, the distribution of power in the larger society are most relevant. They are also interrelated with patterns of labour market segmentation and institutional structures. But, above all, the power and strategies of employers, managements and the state are crucial in influencing outcomes.

Trade unionism under collective bargaining is advanced by a high degree of industrialization, a market economy with a substantial private sector, a democratic political system, and pluralist institutional forms which ensure that trade unions are largely independent of state and management. Divergencies in trade union density amongst nations may be best explained by public policies which support collective bargaining and which, while partly a reflection of labour strategies, are also affected by managerial and state policies on trade union recognition.

Shifts in patterns over time depend upon such economic conditions as movements in prices, wages and levels of unemployment, but also upon diverse recognition policies linked with general political conditions. Meanwhile, variations in trade union structure are related to technology and industrial organization, the methods of trade union regulation, ideology, and white-collar employee attitudes. They also reflect broader 'subjective' influences, the extent of the public sector, and the conglomerate structure of the large corporation (and associated managerial strategies). Trade union government varies amongst nations according to political culture and system, ideology, economic factors (such as industrial concentration), legal provisions, voting patterns and practices of succession, and also the level at which collective bargaining is conducted.

Turning to 'disjunctive', or oppositional, trade unions with political, religious or nationalist objectives, a cultural or ideological background facilitating 'value' rather than 'instrumental' rationality is basic, but vitally important, too, are the stage of industrialism and a dominant role for the state in economic planning and industrial relations. Finally, integrative trade unionism in socialist countries is the outcome of historical choices guided by clear-cut ideologies in conditions of dominance by party and the state. Deviations reflect different sets of choices under decentralized economic and political structures. And finally, autonomous trade unions in the socialist state depend on broader cultural and ethical supports as well as on disparate sets of ideologies.

Strategies of labour: choices and constraints

The comparative study of workers and their associations must begin with the concept of labour rather than that of trade union. After all, though every industrial society is ultimately based on the productive powers of working people and has its largest single group in the employed population in non-managerial functions, not all societies have readily identifiable associations of labour, let alone trade unions which are engaged in collective bargaining. In general, it may be said that the bulk of strategic choices by members or representives of labour are directed at promoting the interests of working people in one or more of three primary areas: (1) the ownership of the employing enterprise; (2) the administration of work activities and the levels and systems of remuneration which apply to particular groups of workers; and (3) the legislative and other governmental actions which affect both the regulation of the employment relationship and macro-level policies on employment, social security and other redistributional concerns. Yet there are remarkable divergencies amongst nations in the degree of emphasis on each of these issues.

The first part of this chapter is designed to establish, largely at a theoretical level, the origins of these differences. The comparative analysis of trade unions then provides a vehicle for amplifying the main points of variation and highlighting a range of substantive themes.

Social 'action' and labour strategy

Taking first, then, the meanings and choices which guide action itself, it will be seen, in Figure 4.1, that these are again interpretable in terms of the general categories of social action. The essential distinction is between strategies focused by *instrumental-rational* concerns (these produce commitments to 'economism', 'pure and simple unionism' and trade unionism under collective bargaining) and those dominated by *value-rational* motives (in which political ('radical'), religious or nationalist objectives are uppermost). *Affectual* commitments to the solidarity of community, trade union or workgroup are also readily identifiable in labour affairs, but they are not strictly rational in the sense of linking motive and action together in a clear-cut means-end relationship (see Sahay, 1973). Moreover,

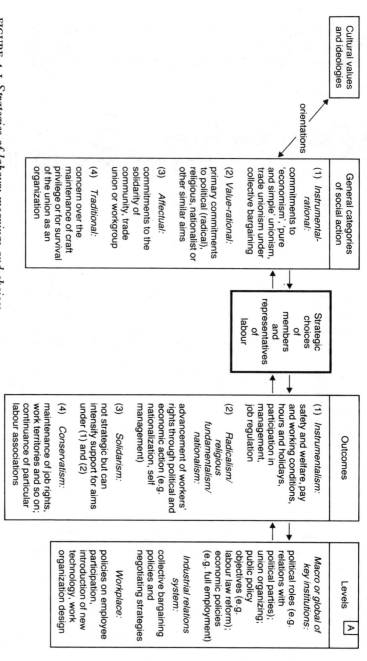

FIGURE 4.1 *Strategies of labour: meanings and choices*

Note: The bulk of the material in this figure is original but the items in the box marked A are derived from Kochan, McKersie and Cappelli (1984: 23)

much of *traditional* conduct (e.g. the maintenance of craft privileges or practices which secure the survival of, say, the union as an organization) is habituated and not formulated in terms of strategic choices at all.

With respect to outcomes, the categories of social action logically indicate the primary division amongst the world's labour movements in terms of *instrumentalism* and *radicalism*. The first covers the familiar attempts by members or representatives of labour to secure improvements in safety and welfare, pay and working conditions, hours and holidays, participation in management and aspects of job regulation generally. By contrast, the second embraces labour movements in which the focus is on the attempt to transform the employment relationship (for instance, through the public ownership of the means of production and/or workers' self-management). And it also encompasses the actions of labour associations in which religious or nationalist purposes are central. To exhaust the categories of social action, *solidarism* and *conservatism* have also been included amongst the outcomes (see again Figure 4.1) and the further distinctions of Kochan, McKersie and Cappelli (1984) have been added to cover labour strategies at: (1) the macro or global level of key institutions (focusing on political, public and legal policy issues); (2) the 'industrial relations system' (such as collective bargaining policies or negotiating strategies); and (3) the workplace (e.g. the objectives of employee participation in management).

Choices, culture and ideology

But why do strategies of labour vary in these ways? Part of the diversity must, of course, be accounted for by the nature of choice itself, but the anchorage of strategy in broader cultural and ideological conditions is also fundamental. For instance, the tendency for Anglo-Saxon countries to have predominantly (instrumental) labour movements is too pronounced to be a purely chance occurrence and, indeed, is associated with the displacement of value rationalities accompanying the rise of industrialism (Weber, 1930). But broad ideologies also underpin the primary distinction between 'instrumental' and 'radical' labour movements, the former indicating a materialist conception of social worth, and the latter being an offshoot of one or other of the varieties of socialism.

The constraints of environment

However, strategic choices are circumscribed by a series of constraints in the environment, including economic and political structures, technology and power in the larger society, together with patterns of segmentation and the conditioning effects of organizations and institutions (see Figure 4.2).

First of all, then, aspects of economic structure are relevant to labour strategies in at least three respects. To begin with, countries with high levels of public ownership may be expected to have politically conscious labour movements, because in such circumstances, industrial decisions are inexorably bound up with governmental policies. Secondly, high levels of industrial concentration are also generally conducive to radicalism (Banks, 1970), but this relationship does not apply universally (France thus has a greater proportion of small and medium concerns than Britain, but a more revolutionary trade union tradition). And thirdly, as we shall see, movements in prices, wages and unemployment certainly affect trade union attitudes and behaviour (Bain and Elsheikh, 1976).

But labour strategy is also intimately connected with the distinctive characteristics of political systems. Although, appropriately, these are examined in greater depth in Chapter 5, 'instrumental' purposes amongst trade unions are likely to have advanced in two- or multi-party democracies where: (1) the franchise has been secured for the bulk of the adult population prior to the emergence of trade unions; (2) a formal party of labour has emerged with a functional separation between political and economic objectives; and (3) political institutions have been decentralized, reducing pressure to develop 'peak' organizations to ensure effective influence over governments. Technology also relates to variations in labour strategy at given *stages of industrialism*, for traditional forms of craft consciousness cannot emerge in societies increasingly characterized by automated enterprises or, say, in the 'advanced' sectors of Third World economies. By contrast, for comparative analysis, the effects of social stratification on trade union 'character' appear to be weak because: (1) the changes in occupational strata upon which social position is based are fairly similar across different countries despite persistent, substantial variations in labour strategy and institutions; and (2) the prestige and social ranking of occupations in east and west are, in any event, not markedly disparate (see Abercrombie and Urry, 1983; Lane, 1982).

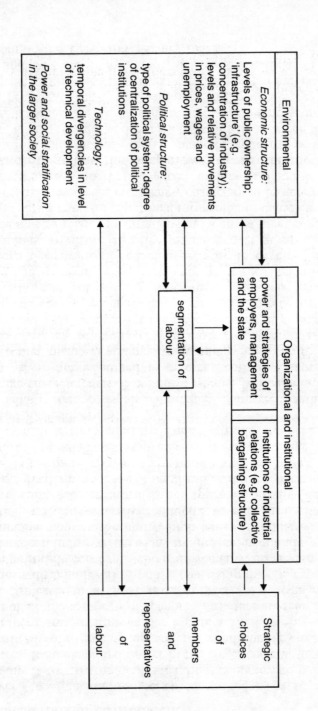

FIGURE 4.2 *Strategies of labour: constraints*

Labour market segmentation

However, the strategies of members and representatives of labour are almost certainly interlinked with patterns of labour market segmentation, a concept vital for understanding the divisions *within* the employed workforce in given countries. Yet, for the comparative analysis of industrial relations there are limitations to this type of explanation partly because of its focus on *intra* societal differences but also because segmentation is *to some extent a product of distinctive labour strategies themselves* (see Loveridge and Mok, 1979). Nevertheless, although it is difficult to find systematic support for such a proposition, high levels of segmentation may reinforce (in both developed and developing societies) exclusive forms of 'instrumentalism' amongst the dominant sections within labour and spontaneous but ill-organized forms of erratic and ill-focused radicalism on the part of the relatively underprivileged.

Power and strategies of employers, management and the state

But prominence is accorded to the power of the 'actors' in the industrial relations system in the genesis of labour strategies. Partly, this is related to the strength of the labour movement in different countries, but the role of employers, managements and the state is also decisive. For instance, militant employer strategies and a lack of willingness to recognize and deal in 'good faith' with trade unions promotes labour radicalism, while a powerful role for the state in the *industrial relations system* almost invariably fashions politically conscious labour movements. Moreover, as Clegg (1976) has argued, these conditions are embodied in institutional processes and, in consequence, have a sustained impact on the structure of collective bargaining.

Labour strategy and the formation of trade unions

The series of choices and constraints isolated so far in the genesis of distinctive labour strategies are now appropriately evaluated in more empirical detail through the comparative study of trade unions. Indeed, it should be emphasized that, throughout history, working people have strategically chosen to advance or to protect their interests through combination. A fallacy of all determinist arguments is to view labour 'as an abstract mass in the grip of an abstract force' (Perlman, 1928: 9–10), rather than composed of social 'actors' capable of shaping their own destiny and institutions. And while the distribution of power amongst the 'actors' in the industrial relations system is vital in affecting the extent and the independence of this role, employers and the state are seldom so overwhelmingly dominant that 'reciprocity of influence' is negated entirely.

But, for comparative purposes, it is by no means easy to establish a definition of a trade union which receives widespread support amongst industrial relations scholars and yet is sufficiently broad to include all the cases which merit analytical attention. Hence, rather than entering into sterile conceptual controversies, three principal types of trade union are identified here according to their strategic objectives and the extent to which oppositional (disjunctive) or integrative functions are uppermost. These are:

(1) *Trade unionism under collective bargaining:* predominantly 'instrumental' purposes, a high degree of independence from state and management and largely oppositional functions.

(2) *Disjunctive-type trade unions with political, religious or nationalist objectives:* 'value' rational purposes and, above all, a political (radical) character. Political and legislative means predominate in the accomplishment of objectives and, while usually oppositional, the extent of independence from state and management varies considerably (this is high in western countries such as France and Italy, but typically low in the Third World).

(3) *Trade unionism under socialism:* characterized by predominantly integrative functions, and a relatively limited independence from state and management (though there are several deviations here from the 'ideal type').

Trade unionism under collective bargaining

The strategic choice to establish and to maintain trade unions with predominantly collective bargaining functions is expedited by four conditions. Firstly, a high degree of industrialization is probable because young trade union movements are typically forced to adopt political methods, if only to ensure an adequate foundation for the propagation of collective bargaining machinery. Secondly, market principles of resource allocation and a prominent private sector will normally be present since, in their absence, it is virtually impossible for trade unions to be autonomous from the state. Thirdly, a democratic political system with two or multi-parties is a strong possibility, since this enables a meaningful separation of political and industrial means of representing the interests of working people. And finally, as will be detailed further in Chapter 5, pluralism rather than corporatism is the most appropriate institutional context for collective bargaining.

Trade union density

However, amongst countries in which collective bargaining is the overriding trade union function, conspicuous differences remain in the extent to which employees are members of trade unions (see Table 4.1). There are a number of countries with extremely

TABLE 4.1 *Trade union density in leading countries in which collective bargaining is the dominant union function* (percentages)

Country	Density (per cent of employees in trade unions)
Sweden	90
Finland	81
Belgium	70
Denmark	65
Norway	63
Australia	55
Great Britain	51
Netherlands	39–40
Canada	37
Switzerland	37
West Germany	36–37
Japan	35
United States	20

Statistical notes:

1 The table is based on the latest available figures from a variety of sources: Anderson and Gunderson (1982: 474); Bain and Price (1980); Kassalow, (1980: 47); Mills (1982: 217–19); and Price and Bain (1983: 47).

2 There are many different problems over comparability that reflect: (a) the slightly different dates referred to in the various studies; (b) whether professional and employee associations are included in official statistics; and (c) the precise populations used to obtain density percentages.

3 There are also variations in existing published sources. The density of unionization in Sweden is thus variously given as 90.5% (IDE, 1981a), 87.2% (Bain and Price, 1980) and 82.3% (Kassalow, 1980).

high union densities (notably Sweden, Finland and Belgium); others in medium range (e.g. Australia and the UK) and others again where union density is much below 50 per cent of the employed population (especially the USA). At any given point in time these variations may be best explained by the degree of public support for collective bargaining that, in turn, moderates managerial and state policies on trade union recognition, as well as labour strategies and the willingness of employees (particularly in the white-collar sector) to seek unionization in the first place. For comparisons over a lengthy historical period, public support for unions remains vital, but a series of economic variables (such as movements in wages, prices and unemployment) are important as well.

The diverse strategies of labour, management and the state linked with public policies on recognition are central to variations in union density. Clegg thus regards the *extent* and *depth* of collective bargaining and 'support for union security either from employers or through collective agreements' (1976: 27) as basic here. In the United States density figures are low because of the limited *extent* of collective bargaining in the public sector and amongst white-collar employees. By contrast, *depth* of bargaining and union *security*, occasioned by favourable public policies, largely explain Sweden's very high union density amongst all major employee groups and sectors. Nevertheless, such outcomes are also, in part, the product of diverse strategic choices of labour, which take place under distinctive sets of economic, political and ideological conditions. A characteristic of countries with high union densities is the successful functional separation of political and industrial objectives of labour and the use of Social Democratic parties to secure favourable conditions for recognition, while a concern for 'positive sum' policies and a focus on industrial objectives also ensures that employers are generally willing to accept trade unions as bargaining partners.

And at all events, for the examination of fluctuations over time, a number of economic variables must be added to the explanation. Leaving aside monumental upheavals (such as those which have occurred in Germany), the broad changes in union density in eight western countries are set out in Table 4.2. It will be seen that, while in some cases the patterns have not altered greatly (e.g. Australia) and while in others (e.g. West Germany) union density is now lower than in 1920, in others again (e.g. the

TABLE 4.2 *Trade union density in selected years in eight countries*

	1920	1930	1940	1950	1960	1970	1975
Australia	42.2	43.5	40.4	56.0	54.5	50.5	54.3
Canada	15.0	13.5	18.3	32.8	34.5	34.7	34.6
Denmark	35.1	32.0	42.4	51.9	59.6	62.5	66.6
Germany	52.6	33.7	n.a.	33.1	37.1	36.3	37.2
Great Britain	48.2	25.7	33.4	43.8	43.5	47.2	49.2
Norway	20.4	18.3	n.a.	n.a.	61.5	61.8	60.5
Sweden	27.7	36.0	54.0	67.7	73.0	80.4	87.2
United States	16.7	8.9	16.4	28.0	26.3	27.1	25.1

n.a. = not available

Source: Bain and Price (1980: 170)

Scandinavian nations) spectacular rates of increase have been recorded.

The approach favoured by Bain and Elsheikh (1976) is to view the determinants of the proportional rate of change of union membership as the proportional rate of change of retail prices, the proportional rate of change of wages, the level and/or the proportional rate of change of unemployment, and the level of union density. But, while it is clearly vital to add these economic variables to explain patterns of change over time, the very large differences in movement must be understood in terms of broader strategies of labour, managements and the state under distinctive sets of political and ideological conditions. Indeed, there is now broad agreement that it is 'a conjunction of favourable economic and political forces' (Price and Bain, 1983: 63) that is responsible for major fluctuations in union density.

Trade union structure

'Collective bargaining', as Clegg (1976: 39) has proposed, 'is compatible with any union structure'. However, when trade unions use collective bargaining as the foremost means of influencing the terms and conditions of employment, union structure is likely to reflect industrial or occupational divisions and not political or ideological principles. To explain variations amongst countries, the mode of technology and industrial organization at critical points of trade union development, methods of trade union regulation, ideology and white-collar unionists' attitudes are all relevant. But for a comprehensive explanation, these variables have to be supplemented by further 'subjective' influences (such as religious commitments), the extent of the public sector and managerial strategies in the large corporations.

In Table 4.3 the dominant types of trade union structure are set out and it will be seen that the most common single pattern is for *industrial* unions to feature prominently (these refer to unions which recruit all grades of employees in a single industry). This is the composition in Belgium, Canada, Finland, Norway, Sweden, the United States and West Germany. However, in many countries there are still *craft* unions based on skilled occupational groupings, and these include Australia, Denmark, Great Britain, Norway, Sweden and the United States. Again, in other cases, there are *conglomerate* unions (i.e. covering members in more than one industry, e.g. the Netherlands and the United

States) or *general* unions which are open to almost all employees in a given country (e.g. Australia, Denmark and Great Britain). Three other broad but restrictive categories which are commonly found are *white-collar or professional unions* (e.g. Australia, Denmark, Finland, Great Britain, the Netherlands, Sweden and West Germany), unions organized on *ethical* or *religious* principles (e.g. Belgium and the Netherlands), and unions with membership confined to *public sector* employees (e.g. Britain). Finally, although in Japan unions are largely autonomous of management, their structures are predominantly *enterprise*-based.

TABLE 4.3 *Trade union structure in leading western industrial societies*

Australia	general, craft, industrial, white-collar
Belgium	industrial, professional, religious, public sector
Canada	industrial, craft, conglomerate
Denmark	general, craft, white-collar
Finland	industrial, white-collar, professional and technical
Great Britain	general, craft, industrial, white-collar, public sector
Japan	enterprise
The Netherlands	religious, conglomerate, white-collar
Norway	industrial, craft
Sweden	industrial, craft, white-collar and professional
Switzerland	industrial, craft, religious, white-collar
United States	industrial, craft, conglomerate, white-collar
West Germany	industrial, white-collar

Sources: Anderson and Gunderson (1982); Clegg (1976); IDE (1981a); Kriesi (1982) and Sumiya (1981)

How are these variations to be explained? The most detailed and influential thesis in that of Clegg (1976), who focused to begin with on the state of technology and industrial organization at the time of birth and growth of a trade union movement. Although, on his testimony, the new skills of the industrial revolution led to craft and promotional unions; mass production favoured industrial and general unions. Furthermore, as white-collar employees have multiplied, so 'their unions have grown with the large-scale organizations of the present century' (Clegg, 1976: 39). But the methods of trade union regulation are also relevant. Before the advance of collective bargaining unilateral regulation required organization by *occupation*. But as collective bargaining proliferated, general unions expanded around the previously established crafts which had once relied on unilateral 'controls'. Similarly, if there are no strong occupational unions, industrial unions become pre-eminent. This type of union structure is also strongly favoured on ideological grounds and hence, where unions have been destroyed and when a subsequent reconstruction on a 'predetermined pattern' is feasible, industrial unionism typically emerges. Finally white-collar employees 'tend to perceive their interests as different from those of manual workers and to prefer their own separate occupational unions' (Clegg, 1976: 39).

For the most part this case is convincing, but requires supplementation in at least three respects. Firstly, some union movements which largely rely on the method of collective bargaining are still divided on ethical or religious counts and hence the wider 'subjective' forces which underlie these differences have to be included. Secondly, with the growth of the *public sector* accompanying state intervention in the economy in the post-Second World War period, another important principle of union structure has been reinforced. And thirdly, where large-scale conglomerate corporations have arisen, *enterprise* rather than *industry* may assume prominence as a logical basis to extend union structure (and this is especially so if, as in Japan, managements endorse this form of trade union).

Trade union government

The analysis of union government embraces wider issues of democracy and oligarchy within labour unions and, not surprisingly, has attracted considerable interest in the industrial relations literature. However, because it is not feasible to advance, in other than a superficial way, a systematic classification of variations in union government from one country to the next, it was decided: (1) to set out in general terms the principal sets of forces which are relevant for comparative analysis; and (2) from a substantive point of view, to focus on a more specific case study examination of contrasts between the UK and the USA.

In Figure 4.3, the main analytical assumptions for interpreting variability in union government amongst nations are detailed. As will be seen, these comprise a number of environmental conditions, the organizational structure of the principal trade unions, the power and organization of employers, management and the state in the industrial relations system and a series of

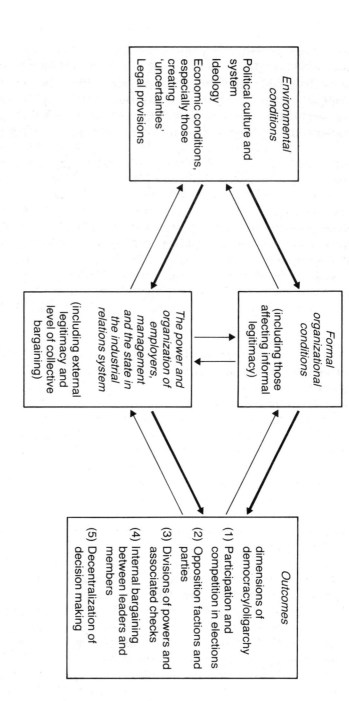

FIGURE 4.3 *Comparative trade union government: analytical assumptions*

Environmental conditions

Political culture and system

Ideology

Economic conditions, especially those creating 'uncertainties'

Legal provisions

Formal organizational conditions

(including those affecting informal legitimacy)

The power and organization of employers, management and the state in the industrial relations system

(including external legitimacy and level of collective bargaining)

Outcomes

dimensions of democracy/oligarchy

(1) Participation and competition in elections

(2) Opposition factions and parties

(3) Divisions of powers and associated checks

(4) Internal bargaining between leaders and members

(5) Decentralization of decision making

outcomes indicating relatively high degrees of democracy or oligarchy respectively.

Taking first of all the environmental factors, these are potentially numerous and complex (for reviews see Martin, 1968; Child, Loveridge and Warner, 1973; Strauss, 1977; Anderson, 1978; Poole, 1984), but those of greatest consequence are political culture and system and relate to the degree of pluralism or corporatism obtaining in individual countries. Ideology (and above all the commitment of activists to leadership principles based on socialist conviction) may well be relevant in some cases. Environmental uncertainty tends to favour oligarchy and is linked with economic conditions and social unrest (see Martin, 1968). And finally legal provisions on, say, union ballots are potentially decisive (see Undy and Martin, 1984).

But a range of intermediary or intervening conditions are of considerable significance as well, and encompass formal organizational patterns within the leading trade unions and the power and organization of the other 'actors' in the industrial relations system. The first relate to so-called *democratic potential* within the representative system, as well as to the various constraints of the union's administrative system (Child, Loveridge and Warner, 1973). Moreover, they include processes of power and legitimacy (the role of rule books, the principles of elections and the degree of solidarity and so on – see James, 1981). Meanwhile, the second cover power, structure and *external* legitimacy in the industrial relations system. In particular, powerful managements promote decentralization within trade unions and an enhanced role for the lay activist (see Clegg, 1976); while an influential state encourages the emergence of 'peak organizations' of labour and a relatively high degree of centralization and oligarchy. Finally, the various outcomes include a series of dimensions of democracy in trade unions, such as participation and competition in elections, opposition factions and parties, division of powers and associated checks, internal bargaining between leaders and members and decentralization of decision making (see Undy and Martin, 1984).

But to extend these arguments further, a comparison between the UK and USA is instructive. Indeed, a series of environmental conditions (different patterns of political development, political culture, ideology and legal intervention), formal organizational variables (voting systems and the presence or absence of a 'clear and logical' line of succession) and institutional factors (especially the power of management and the role of the state in industrial relations) all contribute to interpreting the principal contrasts.

Empirically, then, Edelstein and Warner (1975) have conducted the most impressive cross-national study of union government, so far, that covered fifty-one American and thirty-one British unions. They were able to demonstrate that, by comparison with the American situation, in British unions there were considerably closer elections to fill top or near-to-top vacancies. This, however, did not obtain for contests *against* incumbents where, in Britain, the absence of open factions and restraints on electioneering reduced the number of contests. In short, there was a greater extent of organized opposition in American unions.

To explain these differences, a series of interlocking political, cultural and ideological conditions are relevant. In the USA, these combine to ensure that the prevalence of the British system of 'permanent tenure' is less evident and that deferential values are less common. Moreover, the absence of a Labour Party prevents the channeling of political discontent away from the unions. The greater 'economism' and commitment to individual achievement may be of consequence in increasing the number of contests and, certainly, the British emphasis on procedure and constitutionalism ensures that 'the task of leadership is easier . . . because there is greater premium on authority' (Warner, 1981: 65). The legislative supports for union contests (and notably constitutional guarantees regarding the free circulation of campaign literature) also encourage greater opposition to incumbents in American unions.

But organizational variables such as a suitable voting procedure and open succession are also critical (Edelstein and Warner, 1975). *In other words, the greater degree of internal opposition in American unions could be attributed at least in part to the wider use of ballots and to the relative absence of the so-called 'clear and logical line of succession' through which top posts in British unions are frequently filled.* To be sure, such a position has been criticized by Undy and Martin (1984) on the grounds that no proper account is taken of balloting methods and that, in British unions, some members are not uncommonly defeated 'by candidates without experience at the higher levels of government', but the case remains a valuable checkweight to environmental determinism. Moreover, for Britain and America, it is also stronger than the argument from collective bargaining structure in which, although 'union constitutions and methods of administration' are seen to effect the distribution of power and the extent of factional conflict within unions, 'the level of bargaining is the primary explanatory variable' (Clegg, 1976: 54). The logic of this thesis is that 'decentralization presents opportunities to factions' and hence, whereas under industry bargaining opposition is less likely to emerge, it is to be expected where regions or branches have considerable autonomy. Yet, while this position clearly has substance in broader comparisons (including, for example, continental Europe), both the UK and the USA have relatively decentralized bargaining systems and hence the primary explanations for variations in union government in these countries has to be sought elsewhere.

Disjunctive-type trade unions with political, religious or nationalist objectives

But trade unions with predominantly instrumental purposes relying on the method of collective bargaining are only one of the main types of labour organization. Indeed, in many instances, a variety of 'value-rational' objectives (notably, political, religious or nationalist) are uppermost and this has pronounced consequences not just for trade union character but also for density, structure and government. Even in the west, many countries in which trade unionism under collective bargaining now predominates once had far more radical labour movements (e.g. Germany) and important examples remain in which trade unions are dominated by political parties and wider religious affiliations (e.g. France, Italy). For the bulk of trade unions in the Third World, too, political or legislative channels, rather than collective bargaining, are the foremost means for securing improvements in pay and working conditions.

Here, then, a second principal type of trade unionism is examined, characterized by: (1) a dominance of 'value-rational' over instrumental purposes; (2) a focus on political or legislative means; (3) a formally oppositional role; (4) a varied extent of independence from state and management. Most countries with labour organizations of this type have not insignificant private sectors, but above all, the strategic choice to establish and to persist with such arrangements rests on: (1) a favourable cultural or ideological background; (2) stage of industrialism; and (3) a dominant state role.

Culture and ideology

First of all, then, meanings linked with value-rational premises are almost invariably entwined with broader cultural or ideological conditions. Taking the cases of France and Italy, the main relevant forces for labour are a persistent revolutionary commitment and the significance of Roman Catholicism. In France, the revolutionary tradition encompasses the diverse strands of Leninism, Blanquism (in which the role of political parties in strategies for radical change is emphasized) and, to a lesser extent, syndicalism (see Gallie, 1983: 177–205). In Italy, too, there are enduring radical currents and close trade union-political party linkages. As the IDE (1981a: 205) researchers, for example, noted:

> The strong political orientation of Italian unionism . . . is both a cause and an effect of the close ties which existed between the confederations and the various parties. . . . The confederations were also dependent on the parties for financial support and for personnel at the national and local level which further strengthened the position of the parties in relation to the unions. As a result, the parties were in a position to influence and, if need be, determine union policies which often reflected purely party political concerns and ideologies.

These background conditions are indelibly imprinted on trade union character, density, structure and government (see Table 4.4). So far as character is concerned, this is most evident in the focus on mobilization rather than representation, a pattern evident at shop-floor as well as national levels. Hence, as Gallie (1983: 112–13) pointed out on the basis of his researches:

> it was clear from an examination of the way in which the French unions actually operated in the workplace that their underlying conceptions of the objectives of trade unionism had major implications for their everyday activity. The trade union activists laid a strong stress on ideological contestation. . . . Through the careful orchestration of an atmosphere of confrontation, they sought to underline the conflictual character of the system and thereby produce conditions under which it was likely that workers would be receptive to their wider ideological appeal.

Predominantly political objectives also produce low levels of union density (in France between 20 and 25 per cent). This arises

TABLE 4.4 *Trade unionism in France and Italy: character, density, structure and government*

Character	Density	Structure	Government
		(both part horizontal (geographical) part	
		vertical (industrial))	
France Revolutionary: infused by Leninism, Blanquism and syndicalism. Radical: ethically based assumptions	20–25%	Confédération Générale du Travail (CGT) Confédération Française Democratique du Travail (CFDT) Confédération Général-Ouvrière (CGT-FO) Confédération Française des Travailleurs Chrétiens (CFTC) Fédération de l'Éducation Nationale (FEN) Confédération Générale des Cadres (CGC)	'Democratic centralism', sectarianism, and factionalism
Italy Strong political orientation linked with Communist, Socialist and Christian Democratic views	38%*	Confederazione, Generale Italiana del Lavoro (CGIL), Confederazione Italiana Sindicati Nazional dei Lavoratori (CISL) Unione Italiana del Lavoro (UIL)	'Democratic centralism', sectarianism and factionalism

(mobilization rather than representation)

* Data derived from Clare Walter of UWIST Library, Italian Embassy and *Yearbook of Labour Statistics 1982* (ILO, 1971–82) (figures on economically active population). The percentage may be an underestimate because it leaves out the smaller Italian unions, being based on the CGIL, CISL and UIL only.

for three principal reasons: (1) employers oppose all positive policies for union recognition and hence reduce union security; (2) workers who have primarily instrumental goals find the trade unions unattractive; and (3) the unions themselves may be more interested in recruiting a committed elite rather than a mass membership (Clegg, 1976; Gallie, 1983).

Above all, however, ideological and ethical premises largely shape union structures. In both France and Italy the dominant labour federations (CGT and CGIL) are organically linked with their respective Communist parties; in each case, there are radical unions separate from the main federation (CFDT and UIL) and both have trade unions with strong links with the Roman Catholic Church and Christian democracy (CFTC and CISL) (for details see Table 4.4). Moreover, trade union government cannot be separated from the decisive impact of the Communist Party, the emphasis on 'democratic centralism' and tendencies towards schism and factionalism associated with the impress of ideology. Indeed, in France, the informal rule in the CGT is for 'the communists to constitute half of the *Bureau Confédéral* – the highest decision-making body in the union' (Gallie, 1983: 164) and in Italy the formal subordination of union government to political purpose in the CGIL is effected through a system of interlocking directorates (IDE, 1981a).

Stage of industrialism

Notwithstanding the crucial importance of culture and ideology in understanding the patterning of trade unions in which political ends are uppermost, stage of industrialism is also fundamental. Indeed, there would seem to be force in the case of Ross and Hartman (1960) that, at the early stages of industrialism, trade unions tend to focus on political means, if only to facilitate changes in the legal framework to enable collective bargaining itself to flourish. This argument also applies to developing countries, where political methods are particularly prominent in trade union activity. However, this is not to suggest that 'as trade unions mature' (cf. Lester, 1958), collective bargaining invariably replaces the method of legal enactment (indeed, as the Webbs (1897) proposed, the overall historical sequence may well be contrariwise). To illustrate these points, Sweden has been selected as an example of a country where radical trade unionism was characteristic *of the early period of industrialism* and where a series of historical strategic choices gradually brought about the predominance of collective bargaining, while cases from the Third World are examined in the next two sections.

Part of the reason for the early political radicalism of labour movements was the association with the struggle to secure the franchise. In many countries, the embryonic industrial working class had no effective means of political representation and viewed trade unions as a potent vehicle for achieving universal suffrage as well as collective bargaining rights. Certainly, in the case of Sweden, the early political struggles of labour centred on the franchise (this was legislated for in 1918 and became effective from 1921 onwards). From the beginning, the development of unions was intertwined with politics, with the Swedish Social Democratic Party not infrequently being involved in the establishment of particular labour organizations. But, gradually, the strategy of the labour movement altered and, in the catalytical historical compromise of 1932, political and economic power were separated, class conflict focused on 'positive sum' policies related to economic growth, economic concentration was encouraged, and not least, a welfare re-distributional effort was mounted (Korpi, 1978: 80–6). The separation of political and industrial objectives had a pronounced effect on patterns of strike activity (see Chapter 6), and, above all, the unions had 'access to a relatively efficient political alternative which they could use to achieve important goals, primarily through changes in employment, fiscal and social policies', ensuring that the 'new conflict strategy of the labour movement . . . moved the centre of gravity of distributional conflict from the industrial to the political arena' (Korpi, 1978: 99).

The role of the state

But there is no ineluctable evolutionary logic which ensures that all countries will develop along the lines of Sweden or indeed of other western countries in which trade unionism under collective bargaining gradually became ascendant. Indeed, the continued prominence of political, religious and nationalist objectives in the labour movements of the 'new' nations suggests, rather, that a pronounced role on the part of the state in economic planning and in industrial relations will ensure that such transitions are not always repeated.

A number of the issues raised in this section will be examined at greater length in Chapter 5 and hence lengthy treatment here is unnecessary. But it is clear that political objectives are usually paramount in trade unions in the developing nations and that this is linked with the omnipresent role of the state itself. Barbash (1984: 120–1) has thus cogently observed that

> Industrial relations in the developing societies – functioning in the context of intense nationalist feeling, anticolonialism, new nationhood, labour surpluses, rising expectations, illiteracy, polarized social structures, systematic planning, one-commodity economies and one-party states, and the absence of a mediating middle class – are necessarily producing industrial relations institutions that differ sharply from those of the West. In general, instead of more or less autonomy, industrial relations in the developing society become highly dependent on and almost completely attuned to the state's purposes.

Indeed, the association between political purposes in trade unions and an extensive role for the state has been observed in many developing countries. In his authoritative review of labour relations in southern Asia, Schregle (1982) thus demonstrated this relationship in all the principal countries covered (Pakistan, India, Nepal, Bangladesh, Sri Lanka, Thailand, Malaysia, Singapore, Indonesia and the Philippines) and observed, generally, that in nations where economic, social, political and cultural developments are subject to deliberate government planning, the state is never passive in the sphere of labour relations. Moreover, for Pakistan, as the International Labour Office (ILO, 1976a: 198) recorded:

> 'collective bargaining' in fact has become a misnomer since all major terms and conditions like working hours, leave and festival holidays, bonus, participation in profit, medical facilities through social security, retiring benefits, are being regulated by labour laws. Apart from fixation of minimum wages, the state is also legislating general wage increases to provide relief against the rise in the cost of living. Provision for setting up wage commissions to determine wages and other terms and conditions of workers in any industry has also been made in the Industrial Relations Law.

The situation in much of Latin America is similar; for instance, in Venezuela, the backbone of the labour movement is the Confederación de Trabajadores de Venezuela (CTV), with affiliates comprising 90 per cent of organized labour. But, as with other 'unions, federations and confederations', this organization has retained its political character and functions as much as an extension of a political party as a collective bargaining agent (Valente, 1979: 176).

Moreover, political objectives in labour movements in the Third World tend to produce low levels of union density (10–15 per cent is not untypical), structural divisions based on ideology (e.g. 'left-wing', 'right-wing' and 'neutral' as in Hong Kong; see Turner, 1980: 26) and limited internal democracy (partly because of the lack of a craft 'cadre' in the union; see Barbash, 1984: 123). On the other hand, religious and ethnic allegiances can be a source for linking together different trade unions in the Third World. For example, the International Confederation of Arab Trade Unions (ICATU) has a total membership of about ten million workers and, in 1979, it included representatives from fifteen Arab nations (see Table 4.5). Indeed, its founding was largely a political step in the direction of pan-Arabism (Shabon, 1981: 288–306).

Trade unionism under socialism

An examination of the third and final of the leading modes of trade unionism involves an assessment of labour organizations in socialist countries. Trade unionism under socialism is characterized by predominantly integrative functions and by a relatively close organic link with state and management, the origins of the main Soviet model being best understood as a strategic choice in the context of an ascendant party and state, focused by clear-cut ideologies.

Ideology, strategic choice and compromise

According to the dominant Soviet ideology, trade unions in western countries emerged 'to protect the worker from the oppression of capital', but antagonistic interests are assumed to be absent 'in a society where the means of production are nationalised and controlled by the state' and 'where the state in the last analysis is answerable to the people' (Lane, 1970: 303). The formative model of trade unionism under socialism was the outcome of a compromise in the USSR at the Tenth Communist Party Congress in March 1921. The first proposal of Shlyapnikov, Kollontai and Medvedev emphasized trade union independence and advocated a syndicalist approach in opposition to bureaucratic domination of the economy of the party and the state. The

TABLE 4.5 *National affiliates of the International Confederation of Arab Trade Unions (ICATU)*

Algeria	Union Générale des Travailleurs Algériens
Bahrain	Preparatory Committee of the Workers' Movement
Egypt	General Federation of Workers, Egyptian Federation of Labour
Iraq	General Trade Unions Federation of Workers
Kuwait	General Trade Unions Federation of Workers and Employees
Jordan	General Federation of Jordanian Workers[a]
Libya	General Federation of Trade Unions
Mauritania	Union des Travailleurs de Mauritanie
Morocco	Union Marocaine du Travail
Palestine	Palestinian General Federation of Workers
Somalia	General Assembly of Workers, Somali Workers' Council
Syria	General Trade Union Federation of Workers
Tunisia	Union Générale Tunisienne du Travail
Yemen Arab Republic	Federation of Yemen Trade Unions
People's Democratic Republic of Yemen	General Confederation of the Republic Workers' Trade Unions
Lebanon	General Federation of Maritime Transport Workers of Lebanon;[b] National Federation of Trade Unions of Workers and Employees in Lebanon[b]
Eritrea	Eritrea Workers' Federation[c]
United Arab Emirates	Peoples' Front for the Liberation of the Arabian Gulf[d]
Sudan	Sudanese Federation of Workers' Trade Unions[e]

a = in exile
b = listed as member before the Lebanon War of 1975
c = overseer status
d = attended the 5th congress
e = former member

Source: Shabon (1981: 297)

second, recommended by Trotsky, Bukharin and Frunze, urged 'complete subjugation of the unions to Party and State authority' (Ruble, 1981: 10) with 'military'-type organization to implement production plans and to maintain discipline. The third, successful, position, put forward by Lenin and Tomsky, 'allowed for some independence but within the strict confines of broader party and government policies' (Ruble, 1981: 10–11).

The Leninist conception was consistent with the principles of 'democratic centralism', with the dangers foreseen of craft-conscious unionism producing 'labour aristocracies', and with the use of labour organizations as 'transmission belts' from state to worker, acting as 'schools of administration, economic management and communism' (Wilczynski, 1983: 67). Yet the compromise nature of the trade unions in the Soviet Union ensured certain ambiguities in their role and contributed to their dual-functioning character. As Littler and Lockett (1983: 32) have observed:

> On the one hand, policies, especially those concerning economic development, planning and production targets, were to be determined by the party and state and transmitted to the workforce via the unions. But, on the other, unions were to defend workers against bureaucratic or unscrupulous managers who pursued short-term objectives at the expense of workers' health and safety.

Be this as it may, the historical compromise linked with ideologies is etched on trade union density, structure and government. The integrative and educational functions of trade unions thus contribute to very high levels of union density. Currently, Soviet trade union leaders claim to have organized 98 per cent of the total workforce, or 128 million people, who are members of 31 industrial unions, 70 regional councils, 700,000 factory organizations, 500,000 shop committees and 2.5 million union groups (Ruble, 1981: 2). Trade unions, moreover, are structured according to the production principle (i.e. on industrial lines), reflecting the rejection of territorial-type military organization and syndicalist-type craft or occupational unions. And finally, the Leninist precept of 'democratic centralism' in union government is indicated in Figure 4.4. The main 'deliberative organs' (the USSR (All-Union) Congress of Trades Unions) and the principal 'executive organs' (the USSR (All-Union) Central Council of Trade Unions (AUCCTU)) are thus at the apex of a governing structure in which influence spreads downwards from the highest to the intermediate and lower tiers.

Decentralization: economy and polity
However, there are important deviations from the dominant

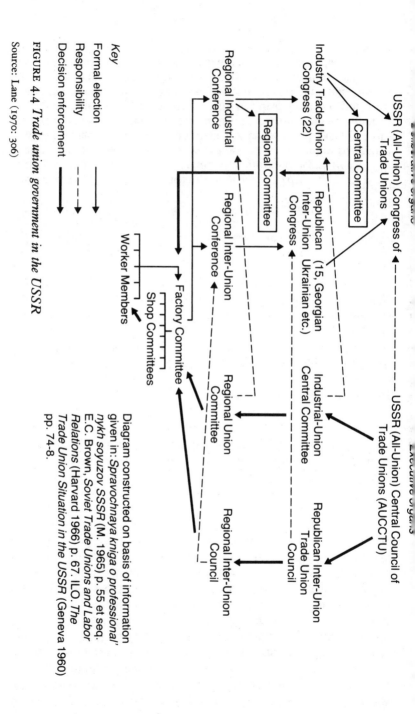

FIGURE 4.4 *Trade union government in the USSR*

Source: Lane (1970: 306)

Key

Formal election

Responsibility

Decision enforcement

USSR (All-Union) Congress of Trade Unions

USSR (All-Union) Central Council of Trade Unions (AUCCTU)

Industry Trade-Union Congress (22)

Central Committee

Regional Industrial Conference

Regional Committee

Republican Inter-Union Congress (15, Georgian Ukrainian etc.)

Regional Inter-Union Conference

Industrial-Union Central Committee

Republican Inter-Union Trade Union Council

Regional Union Committee

Regional Inter-Union Council

Factory Committee

Worker Members

Shop Committees

Diagram constructed on basis of information given in: *Spravochnaya kniga o professional' nykh soyuzov SSSR* (M. 1965) p. 55 et seq. E.C. Brown, *Soviet Trade Unions and Labor Relations* (Harvard 1966) p. 67. ILO. The *Trade Union Situation in the USSR* (Geneva 1960) pp. 74-8.

Soviet model of trade unionism in socialist societies that are connected with the degree of decentralization of economic and political activity. *Ceteris paribus,* there is no doubt that greater reliance on markets and local political decision making enhances the autonomy of trade unions and, conversely, any shift towards tighter planning controls in either or both spheres reduces the freedom for manoeuvre of labour organizations. Moreover, this thesis would seem to apply both to changes within a single country over time and to comparisons at any given historical juncture between two or more nations. Here, these arguments are illustrated by a brief review of developments in the USSR and China. The effects of a more comprehensive programme of economic and political decentralization are examined in the Yugoslav case.

In the USSR, changes in the role of trade unions are clearly combined with broader shifts in economic policy and structure. The original Leninist conception was thus circumscribed in the Stalin era when, during the first Five Year Plan (1928–32), the central planning agencies largely reasserted full control over labour. The increasing autonomy of the Soviet trade unions from the 1950s onwards was intimately associated with the programme of economic reforms and, indeed, by the 1970s, union leaders in the plant were negotiating collective agreements with management (Ruble, 1981: 63). Moreover, although Soviet trade unions still bear responsibility for labour discipline and for stimulating the fulfillment of work norms, as Zukin (1981: 284–5) has documented:

> During the Khrushchev and Brezhnev eras, labour unions assumed a more benevolent – almost a corporatist – role in conjunction with the state. Soviet unions had never lost a residual right to express the workers' social-welfare concerns and to participate in job-related grievances. In this period the law was changed to deepen these rights. Now labour unions are allowed to introduce legislation affecting social welfare. Housing is allocated in each enterprise by a joint management-union committee. The pension and social-security systems are administered by the unions. Inspectors from the union examine work sites for conformity with health and safety regulations and can make binding recommendations for their upgrading. Unions continue to represent workers in collective as well as individual grievance cases, about half of which are resolved in the plaintiffs' favour.

In China, the effects of shifting political and economic ideologies and structures on adaptations in trade union functions over time are also pronounced. Historically, there was a crisis in 1951 in the relationships between the Chinese Communist Party and the trade unions, union structures partially collapsed during the Great Leap Forward and were swept away completely during the Cultural Revolution. Recently, however, they have been revitalized (in 1978 the Ninth National Trade Union Congress (the first for twenty-one years) was convened) and have received a particular boost since February 1983, when, as part of a programme of economic reform, a nationwide experiment in labour contracts was introduced (Littler and Lockett, 1983).

Indeed, the current focus on labour productivity and decentralization through workers' congresses (see Chapter 7) has enhanced both the productive and protective functions of trade unions in China. The first are admittedly based on integrative purposes but would be unlikely to occur at all if the central administrative authorities envisaged no role for trade unions whatsoever. Moreover, the increased activity of trade unions enshrined in current economic policy certainly provides scope for the enhancement of protective functions (e.g. workers' treatment by managerial and supervisory personnel). And the upshot has been rising levels of trade union density (1967 = 0 per cent; 1979 = 52 per cent; 1982 = 62 per cent), a structure with industrial as well as territorial or regional characteristics and, increasingly, the tendency for elections to take place in unions (rather than the use of the so-called nomenklatura system in which the list of appointments is controlled by the party) (Littler and Lockett, 1983).

But the role of trade unions in Yugoslavia is indicative of the possibilities for autonomy when more radical decentralization of political and economic institutions is effected. Indeed, if anything, the limitations on Yugoslav union development have stemmed more from the workers' councils and from management than from the state itself. The programme of decentralization in Yugoslavia from 1950 onwards thus embraced political and economic as well as industrial institutions (Riddell, 1968). Earlier, during the 'administrative period', trade unions had been essentially 'transmission belts' for state policy but, after the break with Stalin, their role changed, to be designated as subordinate to the workers' councils.

Nevertheless, the considerable *extent* and *depth* of union organization in Yugoslavia has presented opportunities for an enhanced role from the mid-1970s onwards. Over 90 per cent of the Yugoslav industrial workforce is unionized and the trade unions themselves are organized, on 'production lines', in six principal federations, according to the main branches of the economy. Moreover, they are established on a territorial basis as well and brought together in commune and city-wide associations with representatives elected to republican and national federations (Zukin, 1981). In a decentralized political economy this depth of coverage has enabled gains for the unions to be made at three levels: (1) they are now formally equal partners with government in concluding social compacts on issues of broad social significance; (2) the 'middle' range geographical federations of unions have become most influential; and (3) in the enterprise, they have recently acquired the functions of proposing candidates for all self-management and administrative origins, safeguarding the new system of workers' control, and criticism and initiatives with respect to self-management agreements (IDE, 1981a; Zukin, 1981).

Culture, autonomy and 'Solidarity'

No study of trade unionism under socialism, however, could afford to ignore an assessment of the conditions which have given rise to the strategic decisions to establish fully autonomous associations of labour of which 'Solidarity' in Poland is by far the most significant. Indeed, the principal background influences tend to be culturally based nationalism, Christian ethics and the labour movement objectives of local autonomy and self-management. 'Solidarity' itself emerged in Poland in late 1980 and lasted until it was suppressed by Martial Law imposed on 13 December 1981. Other examples of autonomous unions in socialist countries include the Free Trade Union Association of Workers in the Soviet Union (a short-lived Ukranian initiative in 1978), the attempt in Wuhan in China in 1981 to form independent unions and the Free Labour Union formed in Romania after the strikes in the Jiu Valley in 1977 (Wilczynski, 1983).

The objectives of 'Solidarity' reflected the continuing strength of Polish cultural identity, the vitality of the Roman Catholic Church and its provision of an alternative set of ethics to the predominant ideology of the Communist Party and, not least, the commitment of rank-and-file workers to local autonomy and self-management (workers' councils have indeed periodically surfaced in Poland). These were reflected in trade union character and most notably in the series of demands which were voiced by the leaders of 'Solidarity' itself, including: (1) free trade unionism, independent from the party and from employers; (2) the right to strike; (3) the appointment of managerial staff according to qualifications and not party membership; (4) the abolition of special shops and other privileges; (5) the revision of censorship laws; (6) the release of political prisoners; (7) access of all religious denominations to the mass media; (8) automatic wage increases to compensate for price increases; (9) priority to supplying the domestic market over exports; and (10) other industrial, economic and political demands, including the long-run objective of workers' self-management (Wilcyznski, 1983: 76).

The mass appeal of 'Solidarity' was demonstrated in trade union density. At its height it had recruited nearly ten million members, comprising 90 per cent of the country's working population outside agriculture and being proportionately the largest 'free labour union' in the world (see e.g. MacDonald (ed.), 1981; Ascherson (ed.), 1982; Persky and Flam, 1982; Singer, 1982; and Weschler, 1982). In organizational terms, it was divided into thirty-eight regions, with craft or professional principles being subordinate to a territorial structure. There were thus at one time 531,000 workers in the Gdansk chapter, 1.4 million in Upper Silesia and 916,000 in Lower Silesia (see e.g. Singer, 1982 and Weschler, 1982). Moreover, it sought to establish long-term collective agreements in the enterprise, to fulfill collective bargaining functions, and ultimately to accomplish workplace democracy. Furthermore, its governing principles were democratically based with local unions grouped into strong regional fraternities and affiliated to the national body called the National Co-ordinating Commission and headed by the policy-making Presidium. Hence, while the greater power of the Polish state was ultimately to occasion its demise, 'Solidarity' was to provide a vital working model of an autonomous trade union in a socialist country.

More theoretically, too, in this chapter the case has been confirmed for developing a series of explanatory propositions in a variety of substantive areas rather than attempting to establish a single general comparative theory. After all, not only is it essential to differentiate the principal strategic objectives of labour that produce fundamental divergencies in density, structure and organization, but it is also necessary to conduct separate analyses of trade unions under collective bargaining, labour unions with predominantly political, religious or nationalist objectives and labour organizations under socialism. Moreover, as will now be demonstrated, this argument applies no less forcefully to a comparative assessment of the state's role in industrial relations.

Chapter 5 Governments, political parties and the role of the state

'In a generation,' as Barbash (1984: 14) has observed, 'the state has advanced from the periphery to the centre of the economy' with industrial relations being 'profoundly affected by the pervasiveness of its presence'. Despite considerable problems in identifying the personnel, locating its various segments and reaching an acceptable definition, the state is indisputably the 'third force' in the industrial relations system. Even in laissez-faire political economies of the nineteenth century, there was some legal regulation of hours and conditions of work and the behaviour of trade unions. But subsequently, with governments assuming overall responsibility for the economy and links being forged between specific political parties and either employers or labour, the activities of the state have appreciably expanded. Socialism and corporatism (the two most powerful political movements of the twentieth century) have amplified this influence. And more latterly, its global ubiquity has been ensured by a 'late-development' effect which has the consequence that, in the 'new' nations of the Third World, the overall impact of the state is on a far greater scale than at the dawn of industrialism in the west.

A theory of the state

But a non-reified account of *diversity* in the state's role in industrial relations must proceed again on the basis of the concept of strategic choice. Members of governments and their agencies may be seen to formulate distinctive policies on labour issues linked with *the problem of control*, which arises in such areas as employment, enterprise decision making and the distribution of economic rewards and at a number of levels (e.g. macro-institutional, 'industrial relations system' and workplace). In the west, the types of state intervention that are assessed are: (1) *pluralism* (a circumscribed state influence in a largely fragmented and decentralized political economy); (2) *'societal'* *corporatism* of the so-called corporatist democracies (in which centralized or moderately centralized governments reach agreements with strongly organized and usually centralized interest groups; see Wilensky, 1983); and (3) *'state' corporatism* (where strongly interventionist governments are unchecked by independent organizations of labour).

The establishment and maintenance of pluralist industrial relations institutions is fostered by: (1) a wider culture in which there is an enduring commitment to 'freedom of association' and a 'moral duty' to seek compromises and concessions; (2) broad ideologies which are in opposition to 'monist' forms of government and in which consensus is seen to rest on deeply rooted political beliefs and not on the performance or output of the system; (3) an economic structure which has evolved from a pronounced laissez-faire stage; (4) a democratic political structure comprised of a two- or multi-party system; (5) 'countervailing' powers amongst the other 'actors' in the industrial relations system (the independent strength of labour being vital); and (6) at an institutional level, the durability of collective bargaining institutions and a willingness, by managements in particular, to recognize and to bargain in 'good faith' with representatives of labour.

But corporatism in industrial relations is the most common form of state role in countries in which governments have always been active in economic planning. Frequently ushered in by public pressure in 'control crises', it is also nurtured by a commitment to harmony and identity of interests at a cultural or ideological level, reflected in a range of ethical and political philosophies that include Catholicism, Conservatism and Social Democracy. 'Societal' corporatism is the logical outcome of powerful, centrally organized interest groups and of open, competitive political systems. By contrast, state corporatism is facilitated by the concentration of powers in government, monopoly forms of capital, the absence of independent associations of labour, and political systems with a single party. Moreover, so far as the more specific links between particular political parties and trade unions are concerned, the predominant variations in the west are explicable by distinctive historical power struggles, sharply focused by coherent ideologies.

In the east, there are also pronounced variations in the state's role in industrial relations, encapsulated in the divergent experiences of 'command' and 'market' systems. In all cases, the patterns of industrial relations are affected by single-party government and by the public ownership of the means of production, ensuring the absence of an independent body of employers and a largely integrative function for trade unions. But command systems stem from conscious, ideologically informed strategies, focused by a commitment to political purpose and a lack of autonomy of managers and workers in the enterprise. By contrast, the decision to introduce market forms of socialism based on self-management can be ascribed to radically different, historically grounded ideologies linked with specific political forms, a concern for economic purpose and the decentralization of the overall regulation of the political economy.

In developing societies the role of the state in industrial relations is almost invariably substantial, suggesting that divergencies amongst nations stem in part from the *timing* of industrialism. Thus, in the predominantly corporatist countries of the Third World, laissez-faire policies in the economy and in industrial relations are seldom considered and pluralism lacks a bedrock. Moreover, in the developing socialist nations, moderately decentralized planning ensures that the state's impact is more substantial than at a comparable stage of industrialism in the west, but far less than in the 'command period' of control in the Soviet Union.

Definitions

The state is not easy to define unambiguously, comprising a shorthand expression for 'a set of institutions or apparatuses comprising the legislature, the executive, central administration (the civil service), the judiciary, the police and local government' (Hill, 1981: 239). To be sure, it is an *institutional system of political domination* which encompasses 'both modes of political representation *and* means of intervention' (not least in capital accumulation and in industrial conflict) (Jessop, 1977). But in no sense should it be regarded as the product of capitalism (on the contrary it is in command-type socialist countries that its impact is particularly pronounced) and, indeed, only becomes capitalist in so far as 'its structural connections with the capitalist economy secure the conditions for capital accumulation' (Jessop, 1977). Moreover, its cohesiveness varies substantially, to some extent in relation to the degree of formal separation of judicial, executive and legislative 'powers' (Montesquieu, 1977).

Strategies of members of the state

The strategies of members of the state are addressed either directly or indirectly to *the problem of control* (see Shalev, 1983a). But to explain the main variations requires a more sophisticated analysis in terms of strategic choices set within the context of power struggles which arise historically under distinctive politico-economic structures and ideological conditions.

In Figure 5.1 a framework for analysis is presented that, in addition to strategic choices, encompasses: (1) the general categories of social action; (2) problematic areas of control and typical policy outcomes; and (3) the levels at which action typically occurs. Fundamental decisions by members of the state (focused by the problem of control) are thus interpreted in terms of a series of choices which are linked to *instrumental-rational action* (reflecting goals such as 'system' performance, low levels of industrial conflict and so on), *value-rational action* (in which ideological or cultural purposes focusing on control are uppermost), *affectual conduct* (inconsistent and irrational reactions) and *traditional action* (based on a commitment to maintaining an established structure of institutional domination). Following Shalev (1983a), the framework has been extended to comprise *problematic* areas of control that include employment, work and the distribution of economic rewards. Varied policies may be expected in each case (e.g. in employment, industrial democracy and income redistribution). Finally, the levels of action may again be at a global level of institutions (e.g. macro-economic or social policies), in the industrial relations system itself (e.g. on labour and employment standards law) or in the workplace (e.g. covering regulation of workers' rights or employee protection) (cf. Kochan, McKersie and Cappelli, 1984). But these categories have to be reinforced, at the level of meaning, by the guiding influence of different cultures and ideologies and by structural environmental *constraints* (notably, those arising from divergent political economies and political systems). Moreover, the intervening effects of organizational and institutional factors (such as the power and strategies of the other 'actors' and degree of centralization and associational monopoly of the principal interest groups) have also to be accommodated (see Figure 5.2).

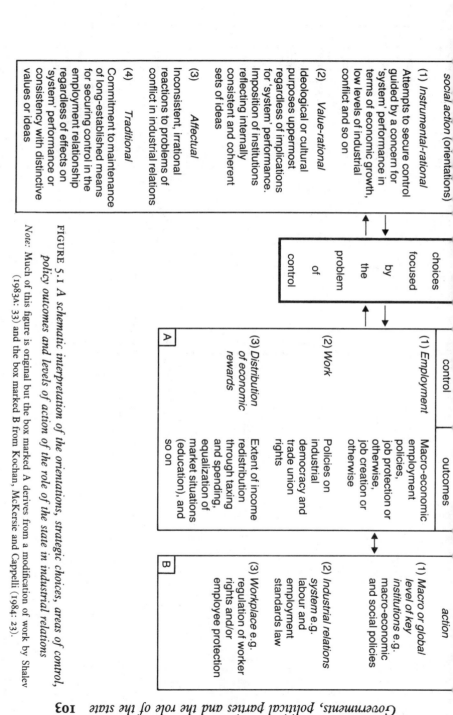

social action (orientations)		control	outcomes	action
(1) *Instrumental-rational* Attempts to secure control guided by a concern for 'system' performance in terms of economic growth, low levels of industrial conflict and so on			**A**	**B**
(2) *Value-rational* Ideological or cultural purposes uppermost regardless of implications for 'system' performance. Imposition of institutions reflecting internally consistent and coherent sets of ideas	choices focused by the problem of control	**(1)** *Employment* Macro-economic employment policies, job protection or otherwise, job creation or otherwise	**(1)** *Macro or global level of key institutions e.g.* macro-economic and social policies	**(1)** *Macro or global level of key institutions e.g.* macro-economic and social policies
(3) *Affectual* Inconsistent, irrational reactions to problems of conflict in industrial relations		**(2)** *Work* Policies on industrial democracy and trade union rights	**(2)** *Industrial relations system e.g.* labour and employment standards law	**(2)** *Industrial relations system e.g.* labour and employment standards law
(4) *Traditional* Commitment to maintenance of long-established means for securing control in the employment relationship regardless of effects on 'system' performance or consistency with distinctive values or ideas		**(3)** *Distribution of economic rewards* Extent of income redistribution through taxing and spending, equalization of market situations (education), and so on	**(3)** *Workplace e.g.* regulation of worker rights and/or employee protection	**(3)** *Workplace e.g.* regulation of worker rights and/or employee protection

FIGURE 5.1 *A schematic interpretation of the orientations, strategic choices, areas of control, policy outcomes and levels of action of the role of the state in industrial relations*

Note: Much of this figure is original but the box marked A derives from a modification of work by Shalev (1983a: 33) and the box marked B from Kochan, McKersie and Cappelli (1984: 23).

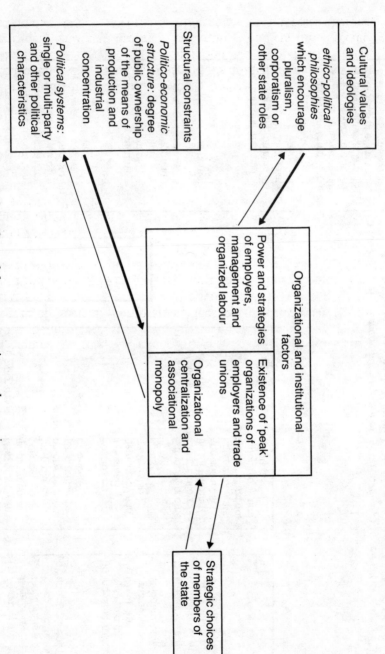

FIGURE 5.2 *Strategic choices of members of the state: meanings and constraints*

Western industrial societies

Taking the west first of all, the predominant strategies of the state in industrial relations are usually classified on the basis of four 'ideal types': liberalism, paternalism, pluralism and corporatism. These stem from two dimensions involving the external control of industrial relations by the state (laissez-faire or interventionist) and the degree of freedom of trade unions (autonomous or heteronomous). *Liberalism* represents the minimum of direct intervention with respect both to regulatory laws and to the conduct of trade unions. Under *paternalism,* there is a low degree of control by the state over employment relationships, but trade unions are typically enmeshed in governmental decision-making processes. In the case of *pluralism,* the role of the legislature can be considerable so far as defining general terms and conditions of employment is concerned, but trade unions maintain a high degree of autonomy. And finally, in *corporatism,* the state is heavily involved in general legal regulation of industrial relations *and* in the incorporation of labour unions (see Strinati, 1979; 1982: 26–7).

Turning now to assess pluralism and corporatism in the light of empirical cases, it is first worth gauging the main variations. While Schmitter's (1981) ranking of countries according to their degree of 'societal' corporatism does not directly relate to the strategic policies of 'actors' in the state itself, it is closely linked with industrial relations phenomena and is thus adopted here. Based on two structural characteristics of the trade union movement (the degree of organizational centralization and the extent to which a so-called 'single-national central' organization enjoys a representative monopoly), from Table 5.1 it is reasonable to suggest that the most pluralist countries are Italy, Britain, France, Canada, the Republic of Ireland and the United States, with the most corporatist nations being Austria, Norway, Denmark, Finland and Sweden.

Pluralism

Pluralist institutions and political processes were, of course, celebrated in the 1950s and early 1960s on the grounds that they comprised 'a system of representation that supported political legitimacy and stability by fragmenting conflicts into specific, pragmatic, hence negotiable differences of interest' (Berger,

TABLE 5.1 *'Societal' corporatism: simple rank order and combined rank order of western nations*

	Simple rankings		Combined ranking
	Organizational centralization	Associational monopoly	Societal corporatism
Austria (A)	I	3	I
Belgium (B)	3	(9)	7
Canada (CDN)	(13)	(9)	(11)
Denmark (DK)	8	(1.5)	(4)
Finland (FL)	(5)	(4.5)	(4)
France (F)	10	(14)	13
Germany (D)	9	6	8
Rep. of Ireland (IRL)	(13)	(9)	(11)
Italy (I)	(13)	(14)	15
Netherlands (NL)	2	(9)	6
Norway (N)	(5)	(1.5)	2
Sweden (S)	(5)	(4.5)	(4)
Switzerland (CH)	(7)	(14)	9
Great Britain (GB)	(13)	12	14
United States (USA)	(13)	(9)	(11)

Source: Schmitter (1981: 294)

1981: 20). The existence of 'countervailing powers' in the modern political economy was seen to be conducive to raising the material well-being of the population and ensuring a degree of justice in the actual distribution of rewards. Moreover, individuals who were able to combine into organized interest groups (and, above all, trade unions) were able to obviate an otherwise weak position in respect either of the market or of the bureaucracy (cf. Galbraith, 1952).

But the choice of arrangements of this type is in practice encouraged by no less than six conditions: (1) a cultural commitment to freedom of association; (2) ideological support for the notion of 'countervailing' powers and the distrust of all 'monist' political systems; (3) an economic structure once based upon laissez-faire principles; (4) a democratic polity; (5) substantial independent 'powers' vested in the trade unions; and (6) in the actual system of industrial relations, a collective bargaining structure which is deeply rooted and sustained not least by management's willingness to recognize and to bargain in 'good faith' with trade unions themselves.

First of all, then, members of the state may refrain from incorporating trade unions if this is consistent with wider cultural pressures. In the exigencies of wartime and in other circumstances of national crisis, more or less corporatist institutions may find favour. But, in general, pluralism is encouraged by a commitment to freedom (and particularly freedom of association) in the 'larger' society and 'a moral imperative' in the duty to make compromises and concessions with other groups (Flanders, 1970; Clegg, 1975). Its primary ideological basis is so-called 'interest group' democracy in which organized associations within the polity are actively promoted as crucial intermediary power centres between the state and the individual. Both liberal and social democracy can provide supporting political tenets, but the first is linked with laissez-faire economic policies and the second frequently presages 'societal' corporatism. Moreover, pluralism originally arose (particularly in the UK) in opposition to the 'political doctrine of sovereignty' and to 'monist' political systems (see Clegg, 1975).

The underlying structure of the economy contains a number of elements which, singly or in conjunction, engender pluralist industrial relations institutions. Historically, pluralism evolved within countries which once experienced a pronounced laissez-faire stage (e.g. USA, Ireland, UK). Meanwhile, oligopolistic industries, a mixed economy and an adequate material base to enable all parties to achieve some at least of their interests, are also consistent with this development (cf. Clegg, 1975).

A democratic polity, with a two- or multi-party system and a body of rules that enable interest groups to function effectively, is vital. At one level this is obvious (i.e. in the antinomy between monism and pluralism and the distinction between laissez-faire and pluralist systems), but to contain corporatism, the political channel of representation must be sufficiently robust to ensure that ordinary citizens do not turn away entirely from conventional forms of representation (Wilson, 1982). Moreover, pluralism works well 'in political systems where consensus depends on common and deeply rooted political beliefs and not primarily on assessment of the system's performance and output' (Berger, 1981: 21), for otherwise pronounced pressures develop to revert to either laissez-faire or corporatist structures.

The independent power of trade unions is critical to effective pluralism. Of all the 'actors' in the employment relationship, labour leaders have the greatest interest in promoting collective bargaining (see Strinati, 1979, 1982). By contrast, a concentration of power in the state favours corporatism; where it is spread amongst a substantial number of private employers but largely confined to this group, a laissez-faire outcome is likely; and strong managements institute 'unitary', not 'pluralist' decision-making processes. A fragmented structure of trade unions and the inability of national labour officials to make binding commitments on behalf of the membership are also advantageous (the obverse situation makes trade unions attractive for corporatist initiatives). Finally, institutional processes sustain commitments to collective bargaining machinery and embody mechanisms for socializing new recruits into established patterns of pluralist decision making. Managerial recognition of trade unions and their 'rights' to negotiate, coupled with a willingness to bargain in 'good faith', are paramount here (see Brown (ed.), 1981), for without this support, workable pluralist institutions are difficult to sustain.

To illustrate these points, Britain represents a country with one of the lowest rankings for 'societal' corporatism (for the US case see Wilson, 1982). A number of 'corporatist' elements (notably in the social contract and in incomes policy) emerged in the 1970s and a neo-laissez-faire strategy involving limited governmental intervention in the economy but a number of restrictions on trade unions has been prominent in the 1980s. But the overall tendency has been for the underlying structure of collective bargaining to check 'societal' corporatism (Fishbein, 1984).

A favourable cultural and ideological background for pluralism in Britain is reflected in early public support for collective bargaining. This can be traced to the final report of the Royal Commission of Labour in 1894, to the Whitley Committee in 1917–18 and later to the Donovan Commission in 1968. Moreover, even the Conservative Party's Industrial Relations Act of 1971 and, less surprisingly, Labour's Employment Protection Act of 1975 contained broad commitments to collective bargaining (Clegg, 1979: 415). A gradual evolution from a laissez-faire stage of economic development is also relevant (indeed, the emergence of pluralist institutions involved an attempt to correct the imbalances and injustices of the earlier period), while democratic institutions are generally supported and employers' associations and trade unions are hardly ever the focal points of their members' *political* identities. To be sure, concern over the performance of the economy is a significant handicap, but despite substantial recent reversals and a loss of membership, trade unions have remained fairly strong and fragmented with the national leadership unable to guarantee incomes policies. Finally, experience with collective bargaining is long-standing, and from the mid-1960s to the late 1970s, management even facilitated the growth of workplace bargaining by developing plant-level dispute procedures and agreements (Brown (ed.), 1981).

Corporatism

Yet, pluralist relations between the state, employers and trade unions are by no means universal in the west. The rather different but widely implemented strategic choice of corporatism is rooted in other types of cultural and ideological philosophy (such as Catholicism, Conservatism and Social Democracy) which emphasize harmony and the identity of interests of interdependent functional groups. In general, too, corporatism is facilitated by a crisis in pluralist institutions, 'concentrated' industrial infrastructures, the predominance of national, privately owned 'monopoly' capital and a long history of the state having been responsible for ensuring capital accumulation (see Strinati, 1979, 1982).

'Societal' corporatism

But, for comparative purposes, finer distinctions are necessary in which 'societal' corporatism of the so-called 'corporatist democracies' has to be contrasted with 'state' corporatism in which there are 'monist' political forms and no effective separate organization of labour interests. Apart, then, from the conditions which favour corporatist strategies overall, the 'societal' variant depends greatly on: (1) a democratic political system with two or multiple parties in contention for office; and (2) above all, centrally organized interest groups with considerable organizational control over the membership (see Schmitter, 1981). Political systems in which 'societal' corporatism flourishes are thus not appreciably dissimilar from those which encourage pluralism, but they differ markedly from the supportive political environments of 'state' corporatism. Schmitter (1974: 93) has thus observed that 'societal' corporatism is characterized by 'relatively autonomous, multilayered territorial units; open, competitive electoral processes and party systems; ideologically varied, coalitionally based executive authorities – even with highly "layered" or "pillared" political subcultures.' It is, therefore, the institutional structure of organized interests that underlies 'societal' corporatism, with employers' associations and trade unions being: (1) formally independent of the state, but highly centralized; and (2) having limited fragmentation and considerable organizational control over the behaviour of the membership. By contrast, if collective bargaining is decentralized, employers' associations weak, trade unions strong at 'local' levels, and widespread factionalism and internal dissidence prevents unified and cohesive policies, state initiatives are inevitably circumscribed.

Illustrations from Austria and Switzerland are instructive here. In the first case, the centralization of the large interest groups has furthered the organization of chambers (statutory public corporations with compulsory membership), *Sozialpartnerschaft* has been institutionalized since the 1950s by agreements between business and labour leaders, and the Chambers and interest groups are entitled to give their opinion on all government bills *before* they are submitted to Parliament. More specifically, the trade unions are represented by the *Österreichische Gewerkschafstbund* (ÖGB), with this Federation dominating the Chambers of Labour, as does the Federal Chamber of Business *(Bundeskammer der gewerblichen Wirtschaft)* those of the other side (Lehmbruch, 1979). By contrast, in Switzerland, although the organizational structure of interest associations 'is characterised by a limited number of peak associations which are hierarchically structured and recognised by the central state in very specific ways . . . the peak associations are neither altogether singular nor compulsory nor functionally specific with respect to the categories of members organized' (Kriesi, 1982: 133). Hence, the organizations of labour, in particular, are fragmented and include the Federation of Labour (SGB), the Christian-National Federation of Labour (CNG), the peak Association of White-collar Workers (VSA), the Federation of Free Workers (LFSA) and the Federation of Protestant Workers (SVEA). The employers are more organized along corporatist lines, but again there are sharp institutional divisions between the VORORT and the Zentralverband (ZVA). Moreover, in

Switzerland there is 'virtually no centralized bargaining between capital and labour', incomes policy is 'almost non-existent' and 'wage-bargaining is highly decentralised' (Kriesi, 1982: 134).

'State' corporatism

Although it is no longer a dominant pattern in western Europe, 'state' corporatism is also of considerable analytical interest and merits a brief examination. The product of monist political systems in which organized interests (particularly of labour) have been suppressed, it occurs when 'territorial subunits are tightly subordinated to central bureaucratic power; elections are non-existent or plebiscitory; party systems are dominated or monopolized by a weak single party; executive authorities are ideologically elusive or more narrowly recruited and are such that political subcultures based on class, ethnicity, language, or regionalism are suppressed' (Schmitter, 1974: 93).

Franco's Spain provided an interesting example of 'state' corporatism in a western European country, but it deviated somewhat from the ideal type because the organizations of labour were never fully incorporated. Following their victory in the Spanish Civil War, the new military authorities assumed 'full representation of the collective interest' and, in a proclamation in 1936, outlawed political and interest group activity. The objective was to create 'a corporative system to integrate the defeated working class, disciplining it and at the same time giving it more symbolic than real participation in the new state' (Linz, 1981: 387). Although never fully achieved, it was also the strategy of members of the state to integrate the professional, technical and middle classes, as well as the employers, into the service of the national economy. For labour, the charter Fuero del Trabajo (1938) was designed to ensure that all elements of the economy were 'organized in *sindicatos verticales* by branches of production or service and hierarchically ordered under the direction of the state' (Linz, 1981: 389). But, again, this was never fully accomplished and, by contrast with the German Nazis and the Italian Fascists, the Spanish Falange was never able to ensure the development of its own Central Obrera Nacional Sindicalista (CONS). Above all, welfare state activity was conducted through the Ministry of Labour and not through the *sindicatos*, a situation which ensured that social security was based on citizenship and not membership of the appropriate labour organization (hence depriving the state-sponsored unions of a critical function). To reinforce its distance from the 'pure-type', a law of 1958 later allowed for the development of collective bargaining (even though this was not favoured by the employers) and broke the vertical structure of the *sindicatos*. Moreover, a gradual diffusion of industrial relations institutions from other advanced industrial countries led to a greater freedom in syndical elections (and a form of limited pluralism) long before the reforms of 1976–77 (see Linz, 1981: 365–415).

Political parties, labour and the state

In theoretical terms, political parties are vital because they give organized expression to interests, make them politically effective and link 'democratic pressures and the policy outcomes of state activity' (Hill, 1981: 243). There are thus frequently parties conjoining both business and labour organizations to the polity and, in the case of trade unions, three main patterns may be identified. The most common form, typified by the Scandinavian countries, Australasia and the UK, is the close institutional link between trade unions and either Labour or Social Democratic parties and for the two to represent identifiable wings of a labour movement, functionally specialized along industrial and political lines. In other cases (as in France and Italy), the leading trade union has been incorporated by dominant Communist parties. And in the third, characterized by so-called US exceptionalism, there is no Labour party at all and the unions lack any effective organic link with an existing political party. To explain these variations, distinctive historical power struggles between labour and particular political parties, closely linked with focused ideologies, are basic.

Taking Norway to exemplify the first case, the relationship between the Norwegian LO and the Labour Party (DNA) has always been close, facilitated from the beginning by a variety of institutional arrangements. As the IDE (1981a: 22) has recorded, the Labour Party has, since the start in 1887, been based mainly on collective membership and, indeed, 'two members of the party's Central Committee' have traditionally been 'members of the LO's Secretariat, and the LO [has] had two members on the party's Central Committee'. Moreover, while the decision on compulsory Labour Party membership for LO's members is left to individual unions, the close connections between political and industrial wings of labour have long been characteristic. Hence, the Norwegian Labour Party came to prominence in the 1930s, when it launched a 'work for all' policy and 'created a strong alliance between industrial workers, small independent farmers and fishermen' (IDE, 1981a: 13). Except for the period 1965–73 (and later in the 1980s), it has held office since that time and has been able to win more of the popular vote than any other single party in virtually all post-war elections. The stable political base for labour has also had repercussions in the industrial sphere and helps to explain the very high levels of union density in Norway (see Chapter 4).

By contrast, France provides an example of a western European country in which the principal political connection of the trade unions is with the Communist party, a phenomenon which, we have seen, encourages inter-union divisions and a low level of overall union density. At its inception in 1895, the CGT (especially after its fusion with the more vigorous Federation of Bourses) was committed to the doctrine of revolutionary syndicalism and hence eschewed all links with political parties (Lorwin, 1954; Gallie, 1983). Its chief focus of action was the local trade union and, in particular, the 'classic issue of craft versus industrial unionism was debated for years' (Lorwin, 1954: 25). Not surprisingly, the CGT tended to favour the latter organizations and decided, at its 1906 convention, 'to admit no more craft unions and to promote the amalgamation of its existing craft affiliates into industrial unions'. Following a reformist period after 1909, the subsequent domination of the CGT by the Communist Party was largely a product of the turmoil of the Second World War and its aftermath. As Lorwin (1954: 108–9) has observed:

> The communists succeeded in identifying anti-Communist with anti-national and anti-working class behaviour. They used the trade union purge commissions to purge the union movement not only of collaborationists but also of potential opposition leaders.
>
> By March 1945, at the first CGT National Committee meeting since liberation, the Communists were strong enough to change the distribution of seats on the Executive Board, to acquire nominal parity with the reformists, instead of the three-to-five ratio of the 1943 reunification. In September they were in clear control of the Federation. . . .
>
> For the first time since its foundation in 1895, a political party was in command of the General Confederation of Labour.

Moreover, this situation also reinforced the decision of the CFTC to remain separated from the CGT and hence prevented the formation of an integrated French trade union movement (for a detailed analysis see Gallie, 1983).

But, if internal struggles within labour and between trade unions and political parties focused by coherent ideologies, partially explain the main variations, a more complex analysis is required for cases in which no linkages of this type have been forged. Ever since the publication of Werner Sombart's (1906) influential treatise, *Why is There no Socialism in the United States?*, there has been considerable interest in American 'exceptionalism' or the failure of US labour to develop working-class politics on the western European model. This is not to say that American labour is apolitical (even if it may be primarily job-conscious) and still less that it does not vigorously engage in pressure group politics. But it is to note its distinctiveness in the limited appeal of socialist ideology to leaders and rank-and-file members, in the absence of a US socialist political party and in the inability or unwillingness of the trade unions to establish a political wing as part of an integrated labour movement.

The principal causes of American exceptionalism are usually traced, to begin with, to environmental conditions in US society. Chief among these are the cultural commitments to liberalism and freedom; the high degree of social fluidity and opportunities for upward social mobility; the cleavages in American society on ethnic and religious lines that diminish the saliency of class divisions; and the subtle status differences that again serve to deflect attention away from issues of class and class consciousness (for a review see Laslett and Lipset (eds), 1974). But also relevant is the actual behaviour of trade union leaders at crucial historical junctures, the factionalism and splitting within the early socialist political groups and their failure to capture the imagination of labour (ultimately being themselves absorbed in job-conscious unionism) (see Laslett, 1974 for a review).

Nevertheless, above all other contributory factors, the political structure and institutions of American society and the fact that universal adult suffrage had been introduced long before the rise of influential trade unions have probably been crucial. As Lipset (1971) has shown in a US-Canadian comparison, the presidential system tended to block the so-called third-party route, which is encouraged by the parliamentary system, and favour direct political lobbying rather than the formation of a new political force. Moreover, the fully fledged democratic polity which existed prior to mass unionism blunted radicalism's edge by depriving it of a potent political rallying call (i.e. the attainment of full adult suffrage), while the established political parties were also able to incorporate a number of the demands of labour into their own programmes and hence head off the growth of an influential socialist party.

Socialist countries of the Second World

So far, then, we have seen that, in the west, the impact of the state on industrial relations is generally greater now than in the nineteenth century, but variations persist in the extent and form of this influence. In the developed east, the role of 'central administrative organs' is usually substantial, though (and this cannot be emphasized too strongly) there remain pronounced differences both currently and historically. Indeed, four main types of state-industry relations in the economically advanced socialist countries may be traced, all of which have consequences for the employment relationship. These are: (1) the Stalinist command model of the Soviet Union between 1928 and 1962; (2) reformed, centralized directive planning (as in the German Democratic Republic and the USSR at present); (3) moderately revisionist planned socialism (Bulgaria, Czechoslovakia); and (4) market socialism (Hungary, Yugoslavia) (for a more detailed analysis see Wilczynski, 1983).

Contrasting command and market models, a theory of the role of the state under centralized socialist planning must begin with the public ownership of the means of production. But command economies should in no way be regarded as the outcome of inevitable structural conditions over which the 'actors' themselves have no control, but rather as stemming, in distinctive historical circumstances, from strategic choices, focused by clear-cut ideologies, and guided by the consciously formulated policies of the elite of a single pre-eminent political party. In the meanings which inform action, political purpose is uppermost, and the state, directed by the party, has dominance over all other social groups. In the industrial relations sphere the state is the employer, management is dependent, trade unions have integrative structures and functions and there is no self-management, no workers' control and no power to the 'soviets'.

In essence, then, the role of the state in industrial relations in command economies reflects the dominance of political strategy and the associated web of institutions designed for its fulfillment. As Lane (1976: 75) has indicated, this is reflected in the impact of the five major groups 'charged with guiding and managing the overall system:' the Communist Party and associated organizations, the government executive or bureaucracy, popularly elected soviets, 'pro-regime', mass organizations such as trade unions, and organizations which are in one way or another non-socialist. The key role is played by the Party which, because it is the leading political institution, 'seeks to control administrative bodies by determining policy at the highest level and enforcing it at lower levels' (Lane, 1976: 75). This is accomplished by the method of 'democratic centralism' which endeavours 'to promote the election of leading committees from the bottom to the top, dual subordination of executive bodies both to higher bodies and to bodies which elect them, the subordination of minority to majority decisions, and the subjection of lower bodies to higher ones' (Lane, 1976: 75).

With respect to industrial relations, we have already seen the extent to which the structure and policy of management and the traced to 1926, when, in the first five-year plan, it was Soviet Union, but, to illustrate the pattern further, manpower planning, restrictions on labour mobility and work discipline are analysed. In the USSR, the origins of manpower planning can be traced to 1926, when, in trhe first five-year plan, it was introduced on a systematic basis. Subsequently, it has become 'a rather sophisticated instrument of economic policy and management' with plans typically covering enrolment in education and training institutions, job placements, labour transfers, organized *ad hoc* recruitment drives, the creation of new jobs and wages and other forms of personal income. Furthermore, 'manpower plans for enterprises and institutions include ceilings on the number of employees, mandatorily expected increases in labour productivity and perhaps labour releases, wage funds, incentive funds and average wages' (Wilczynski, 1983: 22). The direction of labour is also subject to the strategic policies characteristic of a command political economy. In the USSR, there was conscription of labour in 1919–20, and there are still limitations on labour mobility for the first appointments of graduates, the allocation of members of the Communist Party and communist youth organizations, the transfer of certain highly skilled workers, recruiting in rural areas for industry and, conversely, the temporary transfer of workers to rural areas (Wilczynski, 1983: 41). Furthermore, work discipline in a command economy is regulated by the state through a *labour code*. This typically encompasses elements such as punctual attendance, active performance of tasks, maintenance of 'social property' in the works, compliance with safety and security regulations, co-operation at work and the duty to work. Moreover, the labour codes may be enforced through personal labour books, barriers to freedom of movement, comrades' or social camps, financial penalties, corrective and penal labour and even scientific management schemes (Wilczynski, 1983: 48–50).

Nevertheless, to emphasize the diversity and range of possible choices under socialism, changes have occurred in the Soviet Union in the past quarter of a century in the behaviour of trade unions, the influence of management, participation by workers in decisions at enterprise level, the allocation of workers to enterprises, the application of labour codes, labour mobility and 'differentials'. For instance, Grossman (1979: 42–3) has observed that Soviet planners now rely largely on market forces to place personnel in given enterprises and that individual workers are free to select their place of employment. To be sure, the government still has a number of 'levers' available to influence this choice (e.g. plans, policies, regulations and employment agencies) but, since the mid-1950s, it has come to depend more 'on incentives rather than compulsion' (Grossman, 1979: 43).

Under market socialism, state-industry relations are characterized by limited overall regulation of the economy, self-management, a confined role for the Party, an enhanced influence of management and the enterprise director, relatively independent trade unions, restrictions on centralized forms of manpower planning, freedom of movement of labour and the determination of labour codes locally through the workers' councils (IDE, 1981a; Wilczynski, 1983).

In the case of Yugoslavia, the policy of decentralization and the use of market mechanisms arose from the deliberate, conscious choice of a political elite under distinctive historical and social conditions at the end of the 1940s. It was nurtured by sharply focused ideologies, which emerged from the clash between Tito and Stalin and resulted in the abandonment of bureaucratic planning mechanisms. An important base was the 'liberation front', which had been active in freeing the country from Nazi rule without the assistance of the Red Army and which was pluralist and decentralized in structure as opposed to the Party which was ideologically homogeneous and centralized (Riddell, 1968; IDE 1981a: 219–20). Indeed, its successor, the Socialist Alliance, not only continued with such policies but was also a principal target of Stalin's opposition. Above all, it fostered an ideological commitment to *social* rather than *state* ownership, the recognition of the alienation of the worker under bureaucratic socialism and the necessity of effecting the 'withering away of the state', not least in the industrial relations sphere. In sum, the introduction of self-management, which is the enduring monument of the Yugoslav experiment, was characterized by a process of 'liberalization' which involved 'the separation of the Party from the state apparatus, the transformation of the Party into the League of Communists, the abolition of Party organizations in work organizations, the decentralization of state management, the development of the market, the transformation of imperative planning into indicative planning, and the incorporation of the Yugoslav economy into the international division of labour' (IDE, 1981a: 219).

Developing countries

Variations in patterns of state involvement in industrial relations in the Third World and the contrasts with the developed west and east may also be examined in temporal terms by reference to the thesis of late development, the evidence again supporting the overall argument that substantial diversity of experience may be expected to stem from the spread of industrialism in the 'new' nations. Despite universally high levels of state intervention, there are pronounced differences from one developing nation to another, occasioned not least by the distinctive state strategies that arise in the main types of political economy. In general, too, an increasingly rich array of 'hybrid' forms of involvement have emerged.

Of all the 'late-development' effects isolated by Dore (1973), none is more fundamental than the likelihood of the state being involved in economic and industrial relations activity. The thesis is broadly sustained in the case of Latin America, where, as Wiarda (1981) has noted, although aspects of politics and 'personality' are relevant in explaining the high level of state intervention and the inter-country differences, the phase of industrialization and the level of economic development are basic. Generally, then, the pattern of Latin American labour relations has a number of corporatist elements, although the situation is complicated by the variety of ethical and ideological influences, diverse levels of economic and industrial development and the distinctive periods during which key legislation has been enacted. Moreover, there has been, if anything, a gradual shift away from corporatist forms since the Second World War.

State intervention in industrial relations in Latin America overall is thus described as neo-corporatist (see e.g. Morris and Cordova, 1962; Alexander, 1965; Alba, 1968; Malloy (ed.), 1977; Stepan, 1978; Wiarda, 1981), not least because the ethical and ideological codes that have affected management-worker relations do not all stem from a common corporatist source. Indeed, although, by 1950, seventeen out of twenty Latin American countries had adopted constitutions containing articles dealing with labour's rights and responsibilities, the majority were of a mixed type and reflected 'the long influence of liberal and republican forms now coupled with corporative features' (Wiarda, 1981: 160). To be sure, the restrictions were as prominent as the freedoms, but while the labour ministries were key instruments maintaining the status quo, the labour codes had liberal and social democratic as well as 'corporative' characteristics.

So far as state regulation of and control over trade unions is concerned, six major areas can be identified in Latin American labour 'codes': (1) the requirements that must be met to form a union; (2) the 'prerequisite' to obtain government recognition; (3) permissible union functions; (4) requirements 'that make the labour organizations dependent on government funds'; (5) regulations on internal union procedures; and (6) labour-management relations generally (Wiarda, 1981: 166). Understandably, these contain certain 'corporative' characteristics, but there are marked dissimilarilities in terms of the degree of autonomy vested in the labour organizations themselves. Again, there are substantial differences from the corporatist democracies of Europe, on account of contrasts in political economy, varying material infrastructures, influence of trade unions and employers' associations, and level and timing of development itself.

The case of China is instructive on divergencies in state involvement in socialist countries, the pattern being influenced not only by 'late development' effects, but also by changing political policies, reflecting diverse ideologies and deeply rooted historical and cultural traits, focused in the notion of a geographically balanced pattern of economic development (see Lardy, 1978: 189). Substantial alterations have thus occurred in the degree of enterprise autonomy from the state and in the impact of workers on decision making in distinctive periods (notably the centralization of economic and financial planning (1949–57), the 1958 decentralization, the 'cultural revolution' and the recent period of 'modernization') (see Lin, 1966; Wheelwright and McFarlane, 1970; Myers, 1980; Rosenberg and Young, 1982). But the current policy is to give enterprises more autonomy on the basis of authority shared between managers and workers in order to promote 'grass roots' participation and efficient economic management. The arrangements for industrial democracy will be highlighted further in Chapter 7, but here it is worth pointing out that, under the new constitution, worker/staff congresses have been rejuvenated and up to 30 per cent of company profits can be used for workers' welfare, thereby introducing a substantial degree of group incentive at local levels and reducing dependency on the state.

Summary

This analysis of the role of the state in industrial relations brings to a close the second section of this volume in which the three main 'actors' in all industrial relations systems have been examined. Substantial variations in state involvement have been documented and a wide range of influences on the patterns of diversity have been isolated. Throughout, the case for avoiding single, unidimensional theories has been sustained and the necessity for developing complex explanations in each substantive area, embodying historical or temporal as well as current insights, has been reaffirmed. It is now appropriate to focus attention on basic themes which derive from our overall approach to comparative industrial relations. These cover industrial conflict, industrial democracy (focusing on production relationships) and the distribution of economic rewards (covering the distribution sphere).

Part 3

Key themes in comparative industrial relations

Chapter 6 Industrial conflict

That conflict is basic to industrial relations is a proposition echoed by scholars of diverse disciplinary backgrounds and normative conviction. The systems analyst views it as ubiquitous, but ultimately as a form of deviant behaviour, and hence focuses upon rule-making processes for tension management and grievance resolution. Pluralists and Marxists see it as endemic in industrial societies with substantial private sectors (the former stress interest-group divisions and the latter the cleavages based on social class). And most would concur with Faucheux and Rojot (1979: 36) that 'conflict is the motive force of the industrial relations system', since its various processes are essentially designed to contain labour unrest. To commence the account of comparative themes with industrial conflict is thus scarcely contentious and involves an explanation of strike patterns and a number of other forms of worker protest.

A theory of industrial conflict

The heterogeneous conflict strategies of employers and managers, labour and trade unions, and governments and members of the state are formed within instrumental or value rationalities that encourage a series of high or low dispute outcomes. These are reflected in conspicuous variations in the incidence of strikes amongst nations and, above all, in distinctive profiles or 'shapes' of stoppages, characterized by the dominance of *duration*, *breadth* or *frequency*.

The meanings which inform given strategies are linked first of all with culture, which affects a number of *qualitative* dimensions of strike activity, even though, except in the Third World, its consequences for *quantitative* aspects of disputes are more circumscribed. The influence of ideology is difficult to disentangle from broader political conditions, but the strategy of 'mobilization' is connected with radical or revolutionary movements and with strikes of unusual breadth.

So far as constraints on strategic choices are concerned, different political systems are associated with the relative emphasis on organized or unorganized conflicts respectively. Political 'exchanges' between organized labour and governments explain low levels of conflict in a number of countries. Moreover, in their absence, the strike is widely deployed as a form of political protest (especially where there are strong Communist Party-trade union ties). However, since the Second World War, a series of economic conditions such as movements in real wages, unemployment and inflation have been at the heart of strike activity in the west. These not only account for a number of variations amongst countries at a given point in time, but also the longer-term movements (notably the main cycles of conflict).

At an intermediary level of analysis, the organizational strategies of management designed to secure job control are consistent with strikes of long duration. Furthermore, amongst institutional variables, the degree of consolidation of collective bargaining agreements underlies dispute profiles dominated by frequency of stoppage. A long duration of disputes is also associated with the constitutional nature of strikes, the level of bargaining, long-term contracts, legally (or morally) binding no-strike agreements and the scope of issues covered by collective bargaining. Finally, the distribution of power amongst the 'actors' largely explains which conflict strategies are ascendant at any given moment in time. And, above all, in eastern Europe, the pervasiveness of the state ensures that conflict is predominantly unorganized (even though recent relative trade union autonomy has resulted in higher strike propensities).

Conflict strategies

Notwithstanding a common interest amongst the parties in ensuring that the wealth of a nation is not undermined completely by internecine strife, conflicts in industry occur in both the production and the distribution spheres. But whether or not these deeply rooted, *latent* tensions become *manifest* in strike activity and other forms of discontent reflects the diverse strategic choices of all the 'actors' set within wider meanings and constraints.

Conflict strategies are interpretable through distinctive orientations associated with instrumental and value rationality respectively (see Table 6.1). Taking employers and managers first of all, an overriding commitment to profitability, productivity and economic performance or the defence of private enterprise against militant trade unionism can be expected to produce a high incidence of disputes (a priority for human relations policies or for benevolent paternalism being usually accompanied by industrial peace). In the case of labour and the trade unions, conflict stems either from its perceived tactical advantage for securing improvements in pay and conditions or from its connection with policies of political mobilization and radical societal transformation. Discord is less probable, however, if instrumental goals can be achieved through established institutional channels or there is a political commitment to maintaining, say, a 'sympathetic' party in office. For governments and members of the state, policies which centre on economic criteria for 'system' performance, or which seek to secure the dominance of given political creeds (regardless of the implications for social order), will generate industrial unrest. Conversely, an emphasis on the social accomplishments of a society or on wider citizenship strategies rooted in industrial democracy and high welfare spending can be presumed to advance harmony.

Strategies and industrial conflict: outcomes

To be sure, the choices outlined so far and their outcomes are set within broader meanings and are constrained in practice, not least by the distribution of power. But the upshot is an intricate and diversified pattern of industrial conflict amongst nations. Moreover, although, for analytical purposes, our focus will be largely on strike activity, at the outset the many aspects of conflict should be affirmed through the trenchant statement of Clark Kerr (1964: 170–1):

> The manifestation of hostility is confined to no single outlet. Its means of expression are as unlimited as the ingenuity of man. The strike is the most common and most visible expression. But conflict with the employer may also take the form of peaceful bargaining and grievance handling, of boycotts, of political action, of restriction of output, of sabotage, of absenteeism, or of personnel turnover. Several of these forms, such as sabotage, restriction of output, absenteeism and turnover, may take place on an individual as well as on an

TABLE 6.1 *Choices and conflict strategies: the main variations based on 'action' categories*

The 'actors' in the industrial system	Conflict strategy (high or low)	Orientations	
		Instrumental rationality	Value rationality
Employers and managers	High	overriding concern for profitability, productivity and economic performance regardless of 'human resource' implications	threats perceived to, say, private enterprise through militant trade unionism; opposition to recognition of such unions
	Low	human relations priority for employee welfare and morale as well as production	focus on organizational cohesiveness and benevolent paternalism on moral or ethical grounds
Labour and trade unions	High	perceived advantages in terms of improving pay and conditions: tactical strikes and manifestations of conflict	radical or revolutionary use of trade unions as a means of political mobilization and societal transformation

	Low	fulfillment of instrumental goals seen as possible through existing institutional channels	commitment to the maintenance of a 'sympathetic government' (e.g. Social Democratic) via 'responsible unionism'
Governments and members of the state	High	perception of 'system' output and performance in exclusively economic terms regardless of social implications	determination to maintain control regardless of implications for the 'problem of order' to ensure the dominance of strongly held political or ethical creeds
	Low	view of 'system' performance in social terms and concern over social implications of high rates of economic growth	emphasis on 'citizenship' rights of the population; social and system integration through industrial democracy and high welfare spending

organised basis and constitute alternatives to collective action. Even the strike itself is of many varieties. It may take the form of refusal to work overtime or to perform a certain process. It may even involve such rigid adherence to the rules that output is stifled.

Moreover, strikes themselves are not homogeneous events. Rather, as Gouldner (1954: 65–6) has observed, they involve a cessation of work, a breakdown in the flow of consent and an open expression of 'aggression' and remain 'a social phenomenon of enormous complexity, which, in its totality, is never susceptible to complete description, let alone complete explanation'. Indeed, leaving aside problems of validity and reliability of data (for detailed reviews see Turner, 1969; Ingham, 1974; Shalev, 1978b; Creigh, Donaldson and Hawthorn, 1982), the experience of particular countries is by no means consistent on every measure of strike activity. The disparate measures of strikes used in comparative analysis yield four main dimensions: (1) *frequency* – the number of work stoppages in a given unit of analysis over a specified time period; (2) *breadth* – the number of workers who participate in work stoppages; (3) *duration* – the length of stoppages, usually in man-days of work lost; and (4) *impact* – the number of working days lost through stoppages (see Stern, 1978). And, as Table 6.2 reveals, these are typically measured in terms of: (1) number of stoppages per 100,000 wage and salary earners; (2) involvement per 1,000 wage and salary earners; (3) average duration of stoppages in working days; and (4) number of working days lost per 1,000 wage and salary earners. Moreover, although great caution is required in their interpretation and use (see Creigh, Donaldson and Hawthorn, 1980), if the USA is taken as an example, fairly low scores in terms of *frequency* and *breadth* of stoppage sharply contrast with an unusually high average *duration* of disputes and a figure close to the median for *impact*.

Diversity in strike activity reflects varied strategies of the 'actors' and also the specific *functions* of strikes, which are revealed in pronounced differences amongst countries in dispute profiles or 'shapes'. As is shown in Figure 6.1, the overall structure of strikes can be determined by combining the measures of duration, size and frequency (for a review of changing profiles over time, see Shalev, 1983b). On this basis, it will be noted that five main types of strike pattern for leading 'western' countries are discernible, with the fundamental contrasts

TABLE 6.2 *Strike comparisons: leading 'western' industrial societies (averages for years 1972–81 inclusive)*

Number of stoppages per 100,000 wage and salary earners (frequency)*		*Involvement per 1,000 wage and salary earners* (breadth)	
Australia	47.1	Italy	741
New Zealand	38.2	Australia	265
Italy	22.3	Spain	246
Spain	22.0	Finland	214
Ireland	19.6	Israel	156
France	18.9	Portugal	114
Portugal	13.8	New Zealand	111
Israel	12.5	France	85
Canada	10.5	United Kingdom	68
United Kingdom	9.9	Canada	60
Finland	8.9	Denmark	47
Denmark	8.5	Ireland	44
Belgium	6.7	Japan	37
Japan	6.3	Sweden	26
United States of America	5.5	Belgium	22
Sweden	2.6	United States of America	21
Norway	1.2	Federal Republic of Germany	7
Netherlands	0.5	Austria	6
Austria	0.3	Norway	5
Switzerland	0.3	Netherlands	5
*Data for Federal Republic of Germany not available.		Switzerland	0

Average length of stoppages in working days (duration)		*Number of working days lost per 1,000 wage and salary earners* (impact)	
United States of America	18.19	Italy	1382
Ireland	16.05	Spain	956
Canada	14.67	Canada	880
Norway	9.40	Ireland	706
Belgium	9.36	Australia	660
United Kingdom	7.80	United Kingdom	531
Denmark	6.21	Finland	529
Sweden	5.53	Israel	429
Federal Republic of Germany	4.43	United States of America	382
Netherlands	4.40	Denmark	292

TABLE 6.2 (*cont.*)

Average length of stoppages in working days* (duration)		Number of working days lost per 1,000 wage and salary earners (impact)	
Spain	3.89	New Zealand	289
Israel	2.75	Belgium	206
New Zealand	2.60	Portugal	188
Japan	2.59	France	187
Australia	2.49	Sweden	144
Finland	2.47	Japan	96
France	2.20	Norway	47
Italy	1.87	Federal Republic of Germany	31
Portugal	1.65	Netherlands	22
Austria	1.50	Austria	9
Switzerland	—	Switzerland	2

*Working days lost ÷ worker involvement

Source: International Labour Office, *Yearbook of Labour Statistics 1973–1982* inclusive. Tables on Industrial Disputes and Employees in the Active Population

between the United States, Italy and Australia being especially worthy of attention. These are:

Type 1: Long *duration* of stoppages is dominant: characteristic of the United States of America, Canada and Ireland.

Type 2: Considerable *breadth* of disputes largely determines overall 'shape': exemplified by Italy and, to a lesser extent, Finland, Spain and Israel.

Type 3: The structure of strikes is determined principally by the relatively high *frequency* figures: the case of Australia and New Zealand and, to a lesser extent, France and Portugal.

Type 4: A similar ranking in terms of frequency, duration and membership involvement produces the characteristic strike 'shape' of the United Kingdom and Japan.

Type 5: A typically low incidence of strike activity, but the *duration* of the few stoppages is not insignificant: characteristic of Belgium, Denmark, Netherlands, Norway and Sweden.

Patterns of industrial conflict: meanings and constraints

But to avoid an excessively 'voluntaristic' analysis of industrial conflict it is vital to take account of various meanings and constraints. These are elaborated in Figure 6.2 which depicts diverse outcomes (overall patterns of strike activity, dispute 'shapes' (duration, breadth, frequency) and other types of industrial conflict), stemming from strategic choices, but informed by general meanings (culture and ideology) and the broader effects of political and economic conditions, organizational variables, the institutional structure of industrial relations and the distribution of power amongst the 'actors' themselves.

Meanings, culture and ideology

The pervasiveness of broad meanings in the interpretation of strikes is evident first of all in the consequences of culture for variations in *qualitative* aspects of disputes (see Edwards, 1979). For illustration, the Organization for Economic Cooperation and Development has suggested that, in respect of Japan, there are three unusual constituents of strikes: the societal pressure towards consensus which places a 'heavy responsibility' on the parties to resolve disputes 'without resort to overt conflict'; the tendency for industrial action to take a demonstrative form (e.g. vacations being taken *en masse,* banning overtime, pasting posters or 'wearing head or armbands bearing the unsatisfied demands'); and the preference of the unions for 'harassment' rather than 'damage' because of their close structural ties with the enterprise (OECD, 1977: 25–6).

To be sure, the more specific effects of culture on *quantitative* diversity are more contentious in the west, the case here being usually advanced by way of a rather superficial contrast between northern and Latin European countries. For example, Faucheux and Rojot (1979) have proposed that the assertion of individualism (reflecting Protestant rather than Catholic values) militates against collective forms of action and hence strike activity and, in turn, accounts for the lower strike propensities in, say, Scandinavia rather than in Italy and Spain. Against this, however, in studies in which culture has been measured (cf. Hofstede, 1980), Sweden and Norway have been found to be more 'collectivist' than countries like the USA in which strike activity is far more common. Typically, too, the density of unionization (also

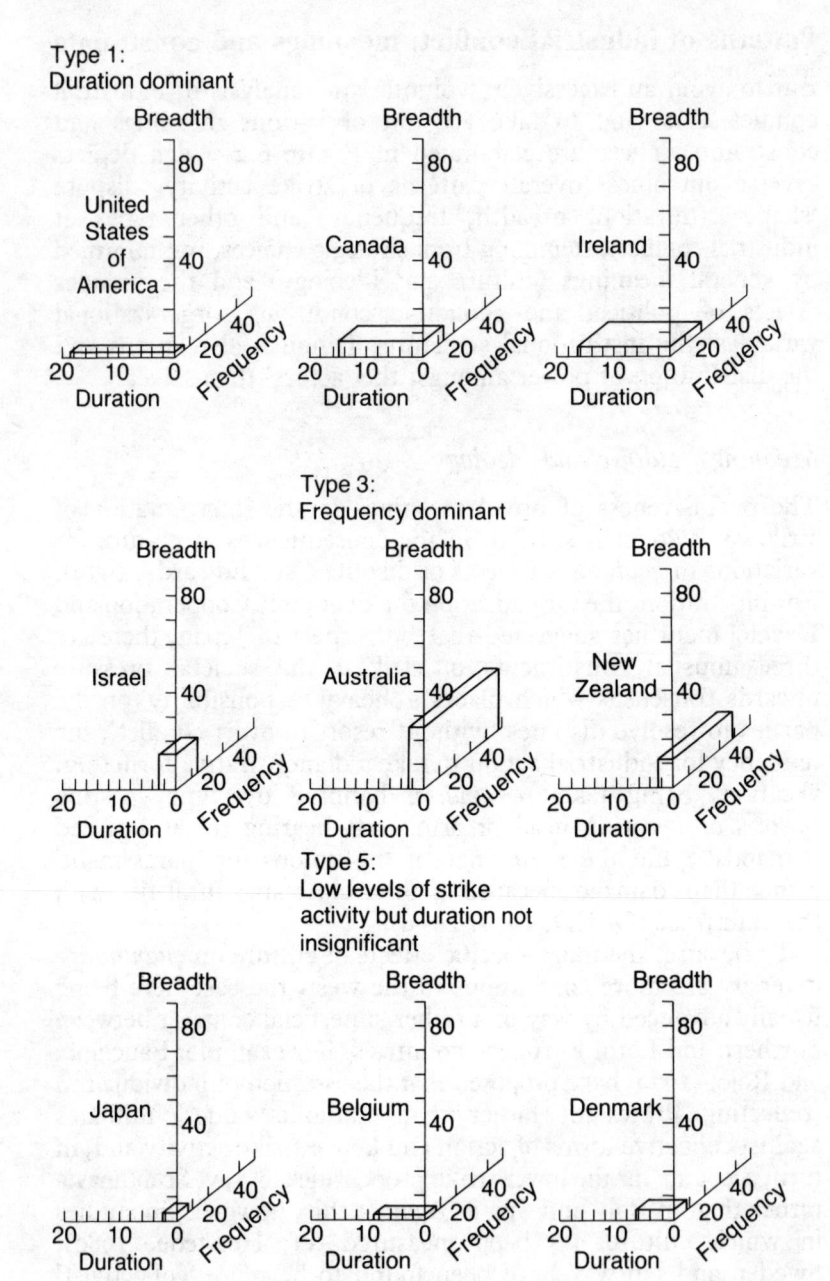

Type 1:
Duration dominant

Type 3:
Frequency dominant

Type 5:
Low levels of strike
activity but duration not
insignificant

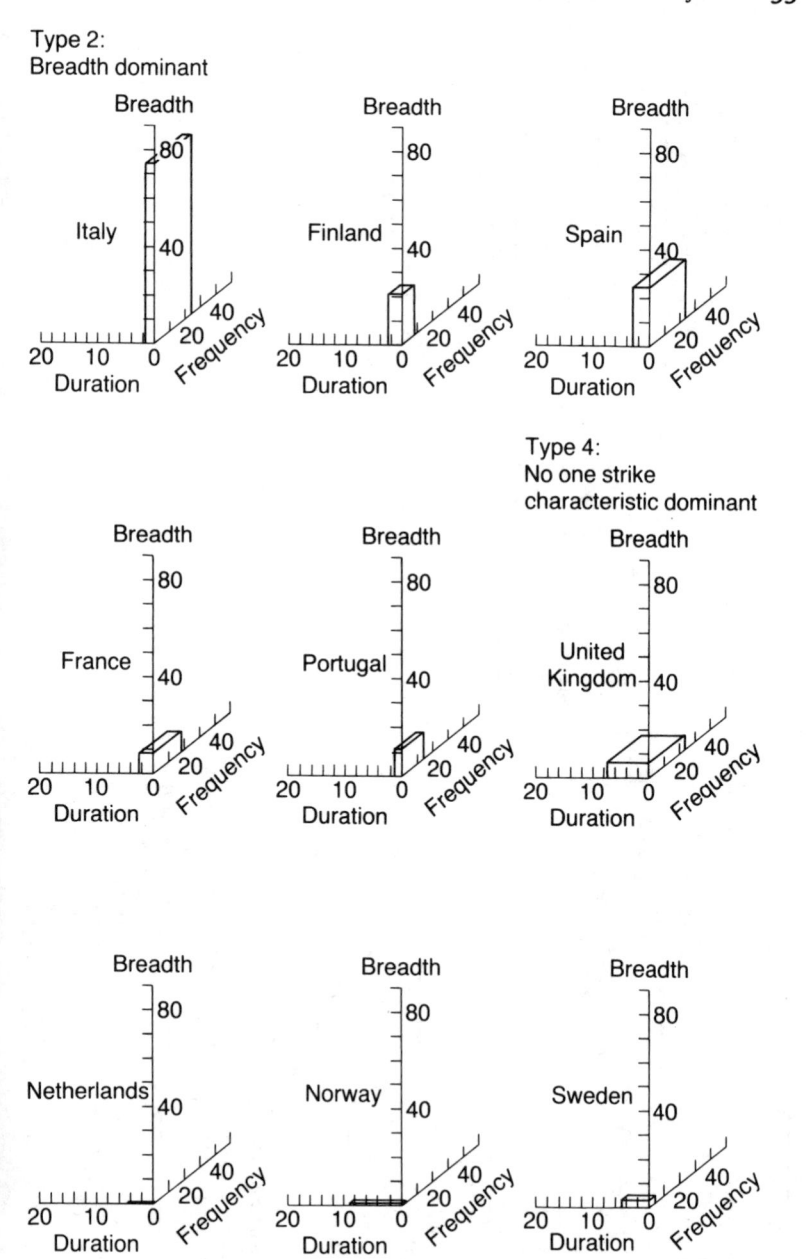

FIGURE 6.1 *Strike profiles: leading western countries*

Notes: (1) Data incomplete for Federal Republic of Germany
(2) Strike activity in Austria and Switzerland negligible

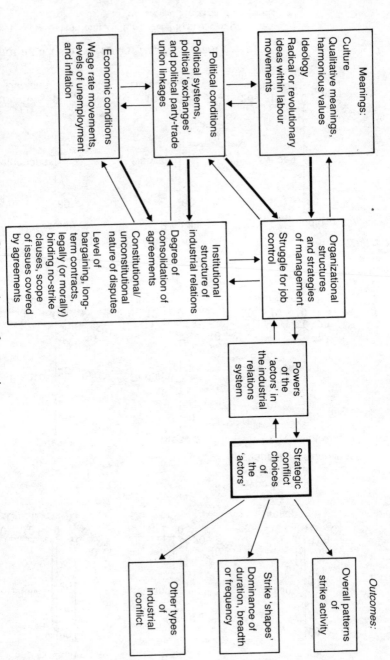

FIGURE 6.2 Patterns of industrial conflict: meanings and constraints

reflecting collectivism) is much higher in northern than in Latin Europe. And, as we shall see later, the major historical shifts in pattern (Norway and Sweden were once highly strike-prone) are almost impossible to explain on the basis of cultural traits.

But there is evidence to suggest that variations in strikes in the Third World are related to cultural differences since the neo-Confucian countries are characterized by emphasis on harmony of interests and are virtually free of stoppages. To assess the experience of developing countries, data are available in the International Labour Office's *Yearbook of Labour Statistics*, but questions remain over comparability, and essential material on employment (particularly on wage and salary earners) is incomplete and subject to considerable error. However, using the measure of working days lost as the least vulnerable to problems of reliability and validity, indications are that in Far Eastern countries (e.g. Hong Kong, Singapore, South Korea and Indonesia) strikes have only a limited impact. By contrast, a low-moderate incidence of disputes occurs in most African countries (although the sample here is both selected and small); while India and a number of Latin American and Caribbean countries are unusually strike-prone (see Table 6.3). But, although fundamental, culture is not the sole explanation for these disparities. Other factors include the historical circumstances surrounding the rise of organized labour (particularly its part in colonial struggles) and the organizational and institutional structure of trade unions themselves (overlapping jurisdictions contribute to a high strike propensity; see Poole, 1982a).

The effects of *ideologies* are difficult to disentangle from those of political systems, but there are strong grounds for concluding that they are closely entwined with strike 'shapes' and especially those dominated by *breadth* of stoppage. For example, in his comparative studies of France and the UK, Gallie (1978, 1983) has established that, by contrast with their British counterparts, French trade unionists are more committed to 'mobilization' than to 'representation' and have more combative, politically conscious and oppositional orientations corresponding to radical and revolutionary ideologies. Moreover, while the overall strike rate is not decisively higher on every measure in France than in Britain, the varying *profiles* can be readily interpreted by ideological diversity. Indeed, even allowing for dissimilar recording methods, varied objectives of labour are clearly reflected in the breadth and frequency of strikes in France by comparison with

TABLE 6.3 *Variations in strike patterns amongst selected developing countries (working days lost per 1,000 wage and salary earners) (averages for years 1972–81 inclusive)*

Country	Working days lost (1,000's)
India	856
Peru	855
St Pierre et Miquelon	719
Jamaica	605
Trinidad and Tobago	578
Guatemala	403
Bermuda	387
Costa Rica	367
Malta	339
Puerto Rico	330
Panama	203
Cameroon	111
Pakistan	93
Thailand	57
Philippines	56
Barbados	50
Tunisia	48
Egypt	32
Venezuela	22
El Salvador	20
Hong Kong	13
Singapore	8
Korea	4
Indonesia	1

Source: International Labour Office, *Yearbook of Labour Statistics* 1973–82 inclusive. Tables on Industrial Disputes and Employees in the Active Population

Britain, where disputes are typically of longer duration and have a noticeable economic impact. In general, too, although wider political elements are also relevant, the mobilization strategy of trade union leaders in Italy (and to a lesser degree, Spain) are indelibly imprinted on the national strike 'profile'.

Constraints
Political conditions
But a comprehensive explanation for variations in strike activity

amongst nations (covering overall propensities *and* divergent strike 'shapes') has to encompass the constraints of environment, organization, institution and the distribution of power (for a review of approaches see Strauss, 1982). Indeed, the political systems of individual countries, the 'exchanges' between organized labour and governments and the relationship between Communist parties and trade unions are all relevant here.

The effects of political system will be examined in more detail in connection with the role of the state in eastern Europe, but it is worth mentioning that integrative one-party regimes tend to reduce the level of organized conflict at the expense of appreciable problems of spontaneous workers' actions, including job changing, absenteeism and occasionally more violent uprising. However, in the west, the adoption of strategic 'political exchanges' is basic to the explanation of the relatively strike-free character of some countries. Indeed, successful institutionalization of conflict depends in large measure on labour abandoning strike action in return for full participation in the national polity and a just distribution of economic rewards, accomplished through appreciable levels of welfare-state spending (see Pizzorno, 1978b; Korpi and Shalev, 1979). By contrast, where strike activity remains high, disputes typically retain their significance as instruments of political action which are designed to compel government intervention in disputes, to impress on public consciousness the force and vigour behind workers' demands and 'to exact political pressure on the centre' (Shorter and Tilly, 1974: 343–4).

The political 'exchange' thesis applied well to long-term movements in patterns of strike activity in the west in general up until the Second World War and to the north and central European experience thereafter. At risk of oversimplification, during the first half of the twentieth century, there were parallel movements in strike activity in all these countries. The growth of unions and working-class political action resulted in a mobilization that 'generated everywhere a great wave of strike activity', which, in the words of Shorter and Tilly (1974: 306), produced an 'essential similarity of patterns of conflict among countries with similar modes of worker representation in the central polity'. However, following the Great Depression and the immediate post-war period, the 'fundamental identity' of strike activity gave rise to major divergencies. The first comprised the *west European pattern* of Italy and France of strikes of great size and brevity reflecting the determination of 'the politically impotent working classes' to participate in national politics. The second was the *post-war north European pattern* of Scandinavia, the Netherlands and West Germany in which the strike largely withered away following the entry of the working classes into the polity through the political success of the Social Democratic or Labour parties. And the third was the *North American pattern*, in which significant levels of industrial conflict remained but the 'strike shape' (involving long duration) was dissimilar from that of western Europe (Shorter and Tilly, 1974).

Taking the case of Sweden, (which, despite a rise in disputes in the 1980s is in the bloc of countries with a low level of stoppages), a dramatic alteration in strike proneness closely followed the accession to power of the Social Democratic Party in 1932, an event which encouraged labour first to defer and then to abandon its earlier strategy of wholesale industrial militancy. In other words, 'the primary cause of the record low level of industrial disputes in Sweden in the post-war decades' was the shift in power distribution in the society and 'the changes in the conflict strategies of the parties which this induced' (Korpi and Shalev, 1979: 174). Moreover, in countries where the strike remains a primary weapon of working-class political action (e.g. Italy), frequent and broad-based stoppages predominate.

In some countries without successful institutionalization of industrial conflict, the situation is compounded by the relationship between dominant Communist parties and trade unions for, in these circumstances, disputes retain their significance as a form of political action and this has ramifications for both overall strike propensity and the shape of stoppages. Hibbs (1976: 1058) has thus shown that 'strike activity varies (inversely) with the relative size of Communist party membership', and this further endorses the proposition 'that Communist parties in advanced industrial societies remain important agencies for the mobilization of latent discontent and the crystallisation of labour-capital cleavages'. For instance, a high incidence of disputes in countries such as Italy is attributable in part to the presence of a strong Communist party with links with the leading trade union (CGIL). Moreover, the Italian strike profile, with relatively large, brief and frequent stoppages, reflects the dominance of so-called 'Leninist' trade union organization principles with fairly small memberships (in terms of density) and slender financial resources (Hibbs, 1976).

Economic conditions

For much of the post-war period, however, economic conditions (such as wage rates, unemployment and inflation) have been more elemental than political exchanges to the explanation of varying strike activity amongst western nations. Hence, in a three-country comparison of France, Italy and the USA, Snyder (1975) showed that the political model (coupled with labour's organizational capacity for collective action) was a significant predictor of the frequency and size of conflict in all countries up *until* the Second World War. In the post-war years, however, on account of a greater success in institutionalizing industrial conflict, *economic* rather than *political* forces became dominant.

The main variations in strike patterns since the Second World War are set out in Tables 6.4 and 6.5 which cover, respectively, changing patterns of: (1) involvement and duration; and (2) the number and impact of stoppages (since 1955). The first reveals divergent movements in Italy and France (together with Australasia, Finland and Japan), the northern European countries, North America (together with Ireland) and Belgium, Denmark and the UK. The second highlights further complexities associated with the wave of disputes which swept across most western nations in the late 1960s and early 1970s. It also shows that while the *number of stoppages* increased after the mid-1950s in North America, Australasia, Japan, Finland, France and Italy, there was no similar acceleration in the Netherlands, Norway, Switzerland and the UK. In the same period, the *impact of disputes* became more severe in Australia and New Zealand, Italy, France, Canada, Ireland and the UK; but in the USA, Austria and Germany there was a more varied and fluctuating pattern.

The primary conditions underlying these complex movements are economic factors such as shifts in real wages and levels of unemployment. Hibbs (1976, 1978) thus showed that short-term fluctuations in strike activity in the leading western nations reflected a rational economic calculation and working-class sophistication in relation to movements in these economic variables. Real rather than money wages were critical because of their effect on the gap between the worker's level of aspiration for a particular standard of living and its actual achievement. And, although there is no constant relationship between these variables (see Shalev, 1983b), allied with labour's attempt to 'capitalize on the strategic advantages of a tight labour market',

TABLE 6.4 *Trends in involvement and in duration in strike activity in the post-war period in the west*

	Characteristics of industrial conflict		
	Long-run change in involvement	Post-war involvement	Post-war duration
Sweden	Decline	Low	—
Norway	Decline	Low	—
Austria	Decline	Low	—
Germany (Fed. Rep.)	Decline	Low	—
Netherlands	Decline	Low	—
Switzerland	Decline	Low	—
Denmark	Stable	Low-medium	Low
United Kingdom	Stable	Medium	Medium
Belgium	Stable	Medium	Medium
United States	Stable	Medium	High
Canada	Stable	Medium	High
Ireland	Stable	Medium	High
Finland	Increase	Medium	Medium
Japan	Increase	Medium	Low
New Zealand	Increase	Medium	Low
Australia	Increase	High	Low
France	Increase	High	Low
Italy	Increase	High	Low

Note: based on Korpi and Shalev (1979: Table 2: 178)

an inverse association obtains for the volume of industrial conflict and the rate of unemployment (Hibbs, 1976: 1057).

Moreover, looking at the long-term changes in patterns of conflict, in conjunction with economic movements, there is strong support for a cyclical rather than linear interpretation. Ross and Hartman (1960) of course noted that a decline in strike activity and an alteration in dispute practices accompanies the integration of the working class into the political system. And, while the typical stoppages at the initial phases of industrialization were restricted in size (because of the absence of large-scale enterprises), and low in frequency (on account of weak union organization), but long-drawn out (reflecting visible employer hostility to embryonic unions); the mid-twentieth-century pattern was one in which the size of strikes increased (higher levels of industrial concentration), stoppages became more frequent

TABLE 6.5 *Trends in the number of strikes and in working days lost through strikes in leading western countries 1955–77*

| | Number of strikes | | | | | |
	1955–9 (average)	1960–4 (average)	1965–9 (average)	1968–72 (average)	1970–4 (average)	1975–7 (average)
Australia	1,159	1,145	1,537	2,333	2,557	2,192
Austria	n.a.	n.a.	n.a.	n.a.	n.a.	n.a.
Belgium	101	46	67	137	187	248
Canada	234	309	563	577	730	1,004
Denmark	33	40	29	42	96	193
Finland	60	57	90	431	946	2,121
France	2,040	2,001	1,885	3,233	3,651	3,846
Germany (Fed. Rep.)	n.a.	n.a.	n.a.	n.a.	n.a.	n.a.
Ireland	63	72	108	132	160	153
Italy	1,896	3,522	3,080	4,338	4,694	3,205
Japan	784	1,215	1,467	2,123	3,164	2,608
Netherlands	60	69	25	37	33	12
New Zealand	58	75	132	245	335	492
Norway	20	10	6	9	12	24
Sweden	15	18	18	57	74	65
Switzerland	4	3	1	4	4	11
United Kingdom	2,530	2,512	2,380	2,825	2,885	2,334
United States	3,884	3,446	4,742	5,322	5,458	5,428

| | Number of working days lost per thousand people employed | | | | | |
	1955–9 (average)	1960–4 (average)	1965–9 (average)	1968–72 (average)	1970–4 (average)	1975–7 (average)
Australia	154	144	201	400	596	509
Austria	24	60	18	5	14	1
Belgium	415	80	72	194	241	194
Canada	341	192	663	757	763	900
Denmark	96	206	30	20	358	76
Finland	788	151	84	364	590	600
France	120	144	126	149	166	201
Germany (Fed. Rep.)	36	18	6	38	48	8
Ireland	115	256	541	540	430	492
Italy	277	632	821	1,110	1,054	1,200
Japan	121	98	68	85	114	81
Netherlands	21	28	5	23	48	19
New Zealand	38	63	105	158	182	317
Norway	174	104	8	13	48	33
Sweden	14	5	25	59	55	39
Switzerland	—	6	—	1	1	3
United Kingdom	199	132	156	494	576	264
United States	529	273	491	592	530	400

n.a. = not available   Source: Clarke (1980: 16,18)

(greater union organization and mobilization) and in which each dispute was of 'markedly reduced duration' (Ross and Hartman, 1960; Shorter and Tilly, 1974; Hibbs, 1976). More generally, too, those adopting the 'withering away of the strike' hypothesis identified three leading supporting conditions: the creation of a web of institutional rules, the institutional isolation of industrial conflict from political struggles, and improved material prosperity (see Reynaud, 1980).

But the case for a long-term decline was effectively destroyed by the upsurge in disputes in western Europe in the late 1960s and early 1970s. Moreover, to explain the occurrence of strike waves, the strategies of 'actors' in a period of high inflation are paramount. Much of the unrest of the early 1970s was induced by government policies implemented to reverse an inflationary spiral. Increased conflict was in part a reflection of the growth of unofficial action, but it also represented the militant strategies of previously quiescent groups which had borne 'much of the brunt of the counter-inflation policies' (Soskice, 1978: 221). Specifically, a number of 'frustration factors' came into operation in the three-to-four-year period prior to the strikes: '(1) moderation of real wage growth, with a complementary reduction in labour's share and increase in the share of profits; (2) compression of differentials between skilled and semi-skilled workers *and/or* public and private sectors *and/or* different industries; and (3) rationalization of production, via mergers *and/or* increasing workloads *and/or* disadvantageous changes in plant payment structures' (Soskice, 1978: 246). The growing intervention of the state in overall economic planning, as well as more directly in industrial relations, also ensured that the institutional isolation of labour disputes (i.e. their separation from political struggles) was difficult to sustain. Finally, an inflationary background led to the disruption of established procedural and substantive norms and was reflected, most obviously, in the rise of plant-level bargaining and the multiplicity of overlapping negotiational units and levels.

Organizational strategies of management

But economic conditions can also impact on strike activity through the organizational strategies of employers. Above all, in highly competitive environments with pressure on product markets, managements pursue 'unitary' industrial relations strategies which are reflected in appreciable levels of *intensity* in the struggle for control (Edwards, 1981). And the consequence is a high level of strike activity, together with a willingness of the parties to engage in long battles. Hence, if breadth of stoppage is rooted in the ideologies and strategies of labour, managerial policies and actions are firmly stamped on strike profiles characterized by long duration.

This so-called 'job control thesis' receives strong support from North America, where the conventional shape of disputes reflects extensive employer hostility to trade unions and to encroachments on managerial 'prerogatives', coupled with a willingness to carry through such convictions in actual behaviour. However, the case is only partially valid because, in the USA, 'business unionism', with a substantial dues-paying membership, enables labour to countenance 'trench warfare'. Moreover, in Ireland, where there are a small number of extensive and protracted stoppages, managerial industrial relations strategies are more similar to the UK, which has a different strike profile, than to the USA. Indeed, the pattern in Eire is largely explicable through the pronounced tendency for the parties to interpret disputes in terms of conflicts about *rights* rather than interests, for this produces a limited number of very fundamental struggles which the processes of compromise and concession that typify collective bargaining are ill-adapted to resolve (McCarthy, 1973).

In sum, the thesis emphasizing managerial strategies for job control requires further validation to be sustained outside the North American continent. Yet it remains a valuable corrective to the one-sided focus on working-class and trade union behaviour of the 'political' school and it reinforces the case that explanations for strike activity are complex, not least because disputes have different *meanings* and *functions* in individual countries.

Industrial relations institutions

But the institutional structure of industrial relations is also both a significant explanation for overall strike propensity and a primary determinant of variations in strike 'shape'. Not all the variables isolated here are of equal explanatory moment (consolidation of bargaining structure would thus appear to be especially critical) and most are, in their turn, rooted in deeper economic, political and social movements. But the institutional thesis is vital for understanding dispute profiles typified by high *frequency* of stoppage. The earliest proponents of this argument were Ross and Hartman (1960) who, in addition to labour political activity (defined as the existence/tenure of office of a Labour Party), traced variations in strike patterns amongst countries to the combined effects of organizational stability (the age of the labour movement and stability of membership), leadership conflicts in the labour movement (factionalism, rival unions and rival federations coupled with the strength of communism in unions), the status of union-management relations (degree of acceptance by employers and consolidation of bargaining structure) and the role of the state (in defining the terms of employment and in dispute-settlement problems and procedures). Clegg (1976: 82) has also identified a limited number of the dimensions of collective bargaining structure as decisive: 'plant bargaining leads to a relatively large number of official strikes', industry or regional bargaining is conducive 'to a smaller number of larger official strikes', while the number of strikes is also 'likely to be high where dispute procedures are absent or defective'.

The degree of consolidation of bargaining structure (reflecting the extent to which plant, industry, regional or national bargaining predominates) correlates well with variations in strikes. Hibbs (1976) thus contrasted decentralized systems of collective bargaining (e.g. Canada and the United States) with centralized systems (e.g. the Netherlands) and highly centralized systems (e.g. Norway and Sweden) and demonstrated a strong covariance between the mean level of strike activity and the degree of centralization of bargaining systems. And, as Edwards (1981: 226–7) has pointed out, there is a virtually automatic tendency for centralized systems to incorporate into one dispute what would otherwise be several separate strikes under plant bargaining and hence to reduce the overall number of stoppages.

Considerable caution is obviously necessary in comparisons of *frequency* (because this measure is seriously affected by different recording methods), but profiles in which it is dominant are explained not only by the prevalence of plant-level negotiations but also by the variable *functions* of strikes. For example, the large number of stoppages in Australia and France can be interpreted as brief demonstrations which put pressure on negotiators (in Australia to affect the outcome of arbitrated wage awards, in France to influence the political 'centre') (Edwards, 1981). Moreover, in the USA and Canada, the prolonged duration of stoppages reflects: (1) the constitutional nature of disputes (such strikes are typically long); (2) the level of bargaining (that few resources are at risk in local disputes reduces pressure to reach an early settlement); (3) long-term contracts; (4) legally and morally binding no-strike clauses; and (5) the wide range of subjects covered in agreements (a wide scope of issues increases the risk of a breakdown in negotiations) (Clegg, 1976; Edwards, 1981).

However, other aspects of institutional structure, such as organizational stability and leadership conflicts, have only a restricted impact. Britain and the United States thus have comparatively mature labour movements but the strike clearly shows no sign of withering away in either of these countries. The impact of leadership conflicts is more difficult to assess but may be expected to apply to variations amongst particular unions or industries rather than to country-by-country differences. For instance, as Edwards (1981) has pointed out in the United States, even the healing of the AFL-CIO rift had no appreciable affect on the strike pattern. Moreover, while the different modes of third-party intervention can be relevant, it is hard to demonstrate any direct links between, say, arbitration machinery and the overall incidence of conflict. Australia thus remains highly strike-prone despite the presence of the Federal Australian Conciliation and Arbitration Commission (AC & AC) and its reinforcement through a series of State tribunals and wages boards (Frenkel (ed.), 1980).

The power of the 'actors'

The relative strength of the parties in the industrial relations system (and 'larger' society) underlies a number of variations in industrial conflict, and, in particular, explains which conflict strategies become ascendant. Managerial strength permits strategies aimed at securing job control at the expense of 'constitutionalism', while labour weakness accounts for the dominance of breadth of stoppage in a given strike profile, reflecting 'demonstrative' acts of protest rather than the sustained pressure at the centre of a successful 'political exchange'. But the effects of the distribution of power are best exemplified by eastern Europe, where a dominant role for the state ensures not only formally integrative functions for trade unions, but also that conflict is typically unorganized.

There is no systematic and reliable evidence on industrial conflict in the Soviet Union or other countries in eastern Europe, but strikes and a wide range of unorganized forms of protest do occur. However, by comparison with the 'average' level for the west, organized conflict has almost certainly been reduced by a 'belief system in which homogeneity of interests and social harmony is emphasised' and by the 'lack of any tradition of unions organizing strikes to improve pay and conditions' (Lane, 1970: 314). To be sure, disputes in the 1920s were a serious problem in the Soviet Union; so much so, indeed, that by 1929, Party leaders had 'declared strike actions to be anti-proletarian and counterproductive' (Ruble, 1981: 15). Recently, too, strikes have occurred in Moscow, Leningrad, Baku (Azerbaidzhan), Kaments-Podolshii (Ukraine), Temir-Tau (Kazakhstan) and Kaunas (Lithuania). Again, despite official denials, in 1980, for instance, there were reports of major work stoppages involving between 70,000 and 200,000 auto workers in Togliatti and Gorki (Ruble, 1981: 102). Nevertheless, while the data presented in Table 6.6 unavoidably understate the total, there are probably no more than a 'few dozen' strikes per year in the USSR (Pravda, 1979: 349).

TABLE 6.6 *Workers' strikes, demonstrations and riots 1956–73 in the Soviet Union by main issue involved*

Issue	1956–9	1960–4	1965–8	1969–73
Changes in work norms and pay	3	4	1	5
Inadequate pay	—	—	1	2
Management conduct	1	1	—	1
Food prices/supply	—	10	1 (riot)	3
Housing and living conditions	2	4	—	2
Militia or police conduct	—	—	2 (riots)	1 (riot)
Unspecified in reports	1	9	—	7

Source: Pravda (1979: 349)

To explain the low incidence of organized conflict in the Soviet Union and allied states, the official ideology and political-economic structure of centralized forms of socialism are relevant (in particular, strikes and other measures to protect the employee are deemed unnecessary on the assumption of an identity of interests amongst workers, management and the state). But power relations within industry and the wider society are more fundamental. Indeed, an omnipresent state ensures that industrial disputes invariably have political implications and, because trade unions in most of eastern Europe still have integrative structures and functions, conflict is predominantly unorganized (working-to-rule, labour turnover, absenteeism and so on). In a valuable review of 'spontaneous' workers' activities in the Soviet Union, Pravda (1979) has thus listed four main types of behaviour which indicate dissatisfaction: job changing, lack of discipline, writing critical letters and collective protest. The most widespread form of action is job turnover which, following the removal of labour controls in 1956, has run at a rate between 19 and 22 per cent per annum. Violation of work rules is also a 'serious form of workers' spontaneity' and involves the loss of 'tens of millions' of man-days annually. The writing of critical letters to the press is very common and, even in the Stalin era, received official approval. Again, despite problems of editorial selection and of identifying the correspondents, in a study of those who wrote letters to *Komsomolskaya Pravda,* workers were found to have penned more than any other complainants (Pravda, 1979: 343). Moreover, protest action itself is not confined to strikes, but is also reflected in appeals to higher authorities, public demonstrations and dissident activity. A common form of industrial action by Soviet workers is also to slow-down production (Pravda, 1979: 333–66). And finally, although these are rare, rioting and violence accompanying spontaneous uprisings do occur (e.g. Romania (Jiu Valley) 1977 and Poland 1980–1).

Indeed, to reinforce the link between the degree of autonomy and influence of trade unions and the likelihood of disputes taking an organized form, the case of Yugoslavia is instructive. In Chapter 4, we observed how trade unions there have become prominent and it is thus scarcely surprising that strikes have proliferated as a consequence. The first known strikes in Yugoslavia under socialism took place in 1958, but up to 1969 a further 1,900 work stoppages were recorded and from 1973 'more than 200 occurred in Slovenia alone' (Wilczynski, 1983: 184). Moreover, because of the widespread use of market mechanisms, as in the west, disputes have typically centred on distribution and production issues which arise *in the actual enterprise* rather than on, say, the price of consumer goods (see Table 6.7).

TABLE 6.7 *Strikes in Yugoslavia: predominant issues* (survey of 512 cases)

Demands	No. of strikes	No. of workers
(1) Improved basis of payment	141 (29%)	14,968 (23%)
(2) Higher pay	139 (29%)	15,578 (24%)
(3) Change of norms and basic wages	70 (15%)	10,710 (16%)
(4) Observance of self-management rights	68 (14%)	12,281 (19%)
(5) Dismissal of managers	34 (7%)	4,383 (7%)
(6) More dynamic management	21 (4%)	2.895 (7%)
(7) Reduction of social differences in the enterprise and in society	8 (1%)	5,054 (8%)
Total	479 (100%)	66,869 (100%)
No answer	33	976
Grand total	512	67,845

Source: Wilczynski (1983: 188)

Conclusions

In general, then, there is no uniformity in the patterns of industrial conflict amongst nations, neither is there any appreciable tendency for strikes to have diminished but rather for widespread differentiation, punctuated by pronounced strike waves, to feature in the west; for a focus on unorganized conflict in the east to be gradually reinforced by increasing strike activity accompanying the greater autonomy of trade unions; and for a fairly low but varied impact of disputes to be evident amongst Third World nations. Moreover, explanations for the origins and subsequent reinforcement of a distinctive national experience of strikes require a subtle analysis of varied strategies, set within diverse cultural and ideological meanings and interlocking political, economic, organizational and institutional constraints, and the conditioning effects of a given distribution of power amongst the 'actors' themselves.

Chapter 7 Industrial democracy

A belief in the virtues of democratic control is anchored in fundamental human values which pervade most industrial societies. Widely advocated as a solution to alienation, for optimizing individual freedom in a collective context, and as a means of obviating the undesirable effects of asymmetrical distributions of power (Poole, 1978), it has captured the imagination of the reformer seeking to eradicate latent and manifest conflicts in the work process itself. But common pressures have had multiple institutional consequences, for the machinery for industrial democracy (designed to accommodate interests in the production sphere) is richly heterogeneous in type.

A theory of industrial democracy

Variability amongst nations is interpreted, first and foremost, as the outcome of strategic choices, focused in different preferences of the initiating 'actors'; and patterned by broad cultural and ideological meanings, public policies and legislative enactments. Culture is reflected in cohesive national values, which have diverse consequences for institutional innovation in industrial democracy. Ideology is also critical to the experiences of nations, for the types of institution, their initiating agents and principal objectives diverge fundamentally on the basis of the precepts of modern capitalism, managerialism, corporatism, liberal pluralism and social democracy, democratic socialism, state socialism and syndicalism. Moreover, at the level of meaning, ideologies and cultural values are mediated by public policies and reflected in given types of legislative enactment on industrial democracy.

Unlike economic and technological conditions, the institutional structure of industrial relations shapes some national practices (for instance, plant-based machinery for works councils and co-determination is likely in pluralist societies where negotiations between employers and trade unions are conducted at industry, regional or national levels). Again, the processes of institutionalization largely account for the continuation of a characteristic national pattern of industrial democracy and are interlinked with a general evolutionary trend towards greater experimentation encompassing countries in the Second and Third Worlds as well as in the west.

But, if the overall 'shape' of institutional machinery can be substantially accounted for by ideology and other 'subjective' meanings, power explains which forms of industrial democracy predominate. Historically, across the nations, a trend towards a greater degree of institutionalization is apparent, but cyclical movements within this very broad long-run change are no less fundamental. Indeed (and this cannot be stressed too strongly), times of institutional innovation closely parallel the 'waves' of industrial conflict analysed in the previous chapter, typically occurring immediately following periods of heightened tension and reflecting *diverse* attempts at accommodation under highly variegated distributions of power.

Strategic choices, rationalities and preferences

In the first place, then, the emergence of given forms of industrial democracy is intimately connected with the overall preferences (based on diverse interests) of the 'actors' themselves. In Table 7.1, the main patterns are elaborated on the basis of the premises of instrumental and value rationality, with the disparate objectives of employers and managers, labour and the trade unions and governments and members of the state being readily apparent.

In the case of employers and managers, the aims of raising profitability, productivity and efficiency (together with employee morale and satisfaction) are associated with a preference for shop-floor participatory programmes and consultative practices; while the search for harmony and organizational cohesiveness underlies profit sharing, co-partnership and commonwealth ventures (see Poole, 1978). When labour goals are job regulation and improvements in wages and conditions, trade union and workgroup controls, coupled with collective bargaining, are sought (by contrast, an interest in radical social transformation favours workers' control, syndicalism, industrial unionism, producer co-operatives and self-management; for definitions, see

TABLE 7.1 *Strategic choices, rationalities and preferences for given forms of industrial democracy*

	Orientations and preferences			
	Instrumental rationality	Preferences	Value rationality	Preferences
Employers and managers	Aims to raise profitability, productivity, efficiency, employee morale and satisfaction	Shop-floor participatory programmes, consultative practices	The search for harmony and organizational cohesiveness	Profit sharing, co-partnership and commonwealth ventures
Labour and trade unions	Objectives are to secure shop-floor level controls, increased job regulation by employees, and the improvement of wages and working conditions	Trade union and work group controls, collective bargaining	Desire for radical social reconstruction based on an 'irreversible shift' of power to workers and their families	Workers' control, syndicalism, industrial unionism, producer co-operatives, self-management
Governments and members of the state	Concern to enhance both economic and social performance (e.g. reducing the levels of industrial conflict)	Facilitative legislation, a range of practices encouraged depending on their success	Purpose is to secure 'system' and 'social' integration through 'blueprints' for the reconstruction of institutional relationships	Legislative enactments on works councils, co-determination and workers' self-management

Poole, 1978). Finally, for governments and members of the state, a concern to enhance economic and social performance is associated with a preference for facilitative legislation and for the introduction of diverse practices depending on their success (if more elaborate 'blueprints' for 'system' and 'social' integration are envisaged, comprehensive enactments are likely on works councils, co-determination, workers' self management and so on).

Strategies and diverse institutional forms

The strategic choices of the 'actors' and their manifold preferences are not always reflected in actual outcomes, not least because the commanding forms in a given country are the product of disparate meanings and constraints and, above all, the distribution of power in the industrial relations system and wider society. But, while there is no universally agreed meaning of industrial democracy (a minimum definition covers institutional arrangements that facilitate or enhance the influence of workers and/or their representatives over decision-making processes in the places of their employment), its permutations are reflected in at least six main institutional arrangements worldwide: workers' self-management, producer co-operatives, co-determination, works councils and similar institutions, trade union involvement and shop-floor level programmes (see Table 7.2).

To be sure, while there are notable disparities in institutional practice, *influence* and *involvement* are less varied amongst nations. Thus, as the Industrial Democracy in Europe International Research Group (IDE, 1981b) revealed, with the exception of Yugoslavia, a hierarchial pattern of involvement with a typically limited degree of participation by workers is characteristic in Europe. Moreover, with the partial exception of Yugoslavia and Scandinavia, the influence of workers and representative bodies is universally lower than for the highest echelons of management. But for comparative purposes, the thrust of the analysis must concentrate principally on explanations for *institutional* diversity. And, as is indicated in Figure 7.1, a series of broad cultural values and ideologies, public policies and legislation, the distribution of power in the 'larger' society, aspects of the institutional structure of industrial relations, and power and power conflicts amongst the 'actors' themselves are all relevant here.

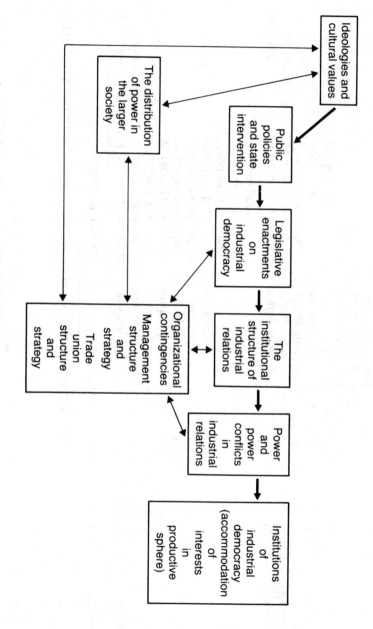

FIGURE 7.1 A comparative explanatory model of industrial democracy

TABLE 7.2 A comparative analysis of the main types of industrial democracy

Type	Defining characteristics	Structural properties	Range of incidence	Key examples
(1) workers' self-management	occurs in decentralized socialist economies. A substantial degree of workers' participation on the main decision-making bodies and the overall right of the workforce to use but not to own the assets of the enterprise	typical organs of administration include workers' assemblies, workers' councils and representation on management committees	Algeria, Peru, Poland, Yugoslavia and various Third World and eastern European societies	Yugoslavia
(2) producer co-operatives	occur in a variety of political economies. Workers' ownership with market mechanisms	many workers own stock, ownership is widely distributed, workers participate in enterprise management and control and share in the distribution of the surplus (profits)	very wide-ranging, including many Third World countries, France, Italy, Spain, USA and UK	Mondragon (Basque provinces of Spain)

(3) co-determination	rights of workers' representatives to joint decision making on actual enterprise boards in predominantly private enterprise economies	single- or two-tier boards (supervisory and management), varying rights to veto and proportion of workers' representatives on main board(s)	widely practised in western Europe (e.g. Italy, Norway, Sweden, West Germany) Africa (e.g. Egypt) and South America (e.g. Argentina)	West Germany
(4) works councils and similar institutions	varying political economies, bodies which regularly meet with management on enterprise issues	representatives of workforce elected, varying degree of legalism or voluntarism and extent to which committees are constituted solely by employees and are joint bodies	broad-ranging including Finland, Indonesia, Netherlands, Spain, Sri Lanka, West Germany, Zambia	Netherlands, West Germany
(5) trade union action a. disjunctive via collective bargaining	pluralist societies, acknowledgment of conflicting interests accommodated through trade union-management negotiations	trade union channel of representation on workers' side, varying degrees of legalism and voluntarism and levels at which bargaining is conducted	the most common form of participation in pluralist societies. Examples include Australia, Canada, USA and UK	USA UK

TABLE 7.2 (*cont.*)

Type	Defining characteristics	Structural properties	Range of incidence	Key examples
b. integrative	State socialism or corporatism. Trade union rights to determine various issues within a framework of harmoniously conceived interests of management, trade union and the state	trade unions have responsibility for areas such as holiday arrangements and influence decisions over dismissals, safety, welfare and working conditions but are integrated into both management and the state	the typical role for trade unions in a planned economy whether under state socialism or corporatism	USSR Eastern Europe
(6) shop-floor programmes	workers' initiatives and new concepts of work organization. Participation by employees in the organization of work in various political economies (e.g. autonomous workgroups and quality of work life programmes)	influence of workers varies depending on programme, though usually task-based	very wide-ranging worker practices and accommodative management techniques in First, Second and Third Worlds	Scandinavia USA

Meanings: culture and ideology

Throughout history, Utopian thinkers have argued passionately the feasibility of social and economic organization founded on mutual co-operation for the social good, with the respective talents of all men and women being released and developed to the full in an unconstrained and non-exploitative association with their fellows (Poole, 1978). These ideals have been frequently nurtured by broad cultural values, with commitments such as these being most likely to flourish in countries in which once again: (1) positive views on human nature and 'high trust' relationships prevail; (2) innovation is encouraged; (3) a future orientation facilitates strategic planning involving the workforce; (4) there is an emphasis on 'being' as well as 'doing'; and (5) hierarchical relationships between people are minimized (Hofstede, 1981; for an extended review, see Poole, 1985). Taking a number of examples, the industrial democracy framework in West Germany reflects a pronounced 'inclination to resolve differences by integrating opposing forces into an institutional organization', because 'accommodation and integration, as well as order and authority, occupy an important place in the national system of values' (Schregle, 1978: 88). There has thus been a long history of interest in workers' participation in Germany (the first germs of enthusiasm for works councils' legislation could be detected as early as the 1830s and 1840s), which persuasively points to a 'culturalist' explanation rather than one rooted in technology or economic conditions, which have altered substantially over the same period of time. Again, the development of the Yugoslavian system of self-management was facilitated by a heterogeneous and decentralized culture, coupled with certain agricultural co-operative practices, including the Balkan phenomenon of *zadruga*, in which two or three related families jointly owned their means of livelihood and produced and consumed communally (Riddell, 1968; Adizes, 1971; Blasi, Mehrling and Whyte, 1984). Again, the Mondragon producer co-operatives are closely interconnected with wider cultural and institutional supports (the educational system, the league of education and culture and credit union) and with the strong 'associative spirit' within the Basque region as a whole (even though this had to be built on to convert its closed character into an open one) (Johnson and Whyte, 1977; Oakeshott, 1978; Blasi, Mehrling and Whyte, 1984). And, while the IDE (1981b) researches found that a north-south cultural division within Europe had only a limited impact on levels of influence, it did affect the 'ways in which this influence is achieved' (Teulings, 1984: 240). In a sense, too, basic democratic values and practices, by definition, underlie all systems of workers' participation.

Furthermore, no serious analyst of industrial relations would dispute the proposition that the characteristics and objectives of particular types of industrial democracy are infused by general ideologies. The formal arrangements emerging under modern capitalism, managerialism, corporatism, liberal pluralism and social democracy, democratic socialism, state socialism and syndicalism are thus contrasting in institutional structure and conception, if not always in terms of actual effectiveness and practical outcomes (see Table 7.3). Hence, on the basis of disparate ideological assumptions, radically different varieties of participative machinery have been constructed (e.g. modern capitalism has engendered autonomous workgroup experiments, employee shareholding and co-partnership ventures; liberal pluralist and social democratic conceptions may be identified in collective bargaining, co-determination and works councils; while democratic socialism tends to be consistent with a self-management framework). A fuller account of the main examples has been presented in Table 7.2, but the Yugoslavian system is inseparably linked with highly explicit ideologies that emerged in opposition to state and bureaucratic modes of socialism (Riddell, 1968). The tendency towards 'absolutism' in the French industrial relations system (attributable to the accentuation of the concepts of ownership and individualism amongst employers and the polarized pattern of ideologies in management-worker relationships) has inhibited reformist moves in the direction of participatory democracy (Gallie, 1978; Greyfié de Bellecombe, 1978). And, although cultural values have clearly been pervasive in the emergence of participatory institutions in selected eastern European countries (e.g. Poland), moves in this direction have also been justified in ideological terms (the equation of industrial democracy with workers' power) (Rybicki, *et al.*, 1978: 2–4).

Public policy and legal enactment

But the highest meanings encompassed in cultures and ideologies are also fused at a public policy level and reflected in diverse legal provisions underpinning various institutional arrangements for

TABLE 7.3 *The main institutional forms of industrial democracy*

Various ideological positions	Modern capitalism	Managerialism	Corporatism	Liberal pluralism and social democracy	Democratic Socialism	State Socialism	Syndicalism
Initiating agents	Employers, management	Management	The state	Trade unions, political parties	Political party	Political party and the state	Trade unions, workers
Principal objectives and operational concepts	Productivity and efficiency	Human growth and development	System integration	Representative industrial democracy, power sharing, workers' rights	Limited self-management	Organizations for fulfillment of plans	Workers' ownership and self-management
Institutional forms	Co-partnership and employee shareholding	Employee involvement and joint consultation	Planning agreements, incorporation of unions at enterprise and society levels via integrative machinery	Worker directors, co-determination, works councils and producer co-operatives	Yugoslav workers' management and other self-management organs	Participation in management and union organization in USSR and most eastern European countries	Workers' control programmes (often delegative rather than representative)

Note: Adapted and modified from Poole (1981: 28)

industrial democracy, the IDE (1981b) researchers revealing that, in Europe, formal provision for workers' participation is greatest in Yugoslavia, Italy, Norway, Sweden, Denmark and West Germany and lowest in Great Britain and Israel (see Table 7.4) Indeed, four characteristic shapes were discovered: (1) the low-profile pattern, typical of Belgium and Great Britain, in which, with the partial exception of management and representative bodies, all groups have limited participative rights; (2) the hierarchical one-peaked pattern of France, Norway and Sweden, in which the focus of decision making is the level above top management; (3) the hierarchical two-peaked pattern of Denmark, Finland, West Germany, Italy, the Netherlands and Israel (where management and, to a lesser extent, the representative bodies have the highest scores amongst the various groups); and (4) the representative peaked pattern, which is confined to Yugoslavia (IDE, 1979, 278–80; IDE, 1981b).

Yet, while it has always been appreciated that the public and legal policies are basic to the different types of institutional machinery (and especially to the formulation of detailed specifications for committee structure, voting rights and so on), until recently it was not fully understood that these also underlie effective participation in terms of influence and involvement. Hence, as the IDE (1979: 292) researchers themselves noted:

> high levels of employee participation are a function of an intricate interrelation of internal managerial practices and externally promoted support systems based on formal laws or collective bargaining agreements.
> Further, both these variables together do a better job of predicting influence and power distributions than 'objective' technological or structural conditions such as organizational size, internal differentiation, or levels of automation. This last finding underscores the 'voluntaristic' nature of industrial democracy in the sense of being a system which is more the outcome of socio-political factors than of structural opportunities or constraints.

And, above all, 'codification' of participative rights through *de jure* provisions is an insistent centralized pressure, rooted in public policy and political power, that ensures that a measure of influence passes from top management to the representative

TABLE 7.4 *Formal participatory provisions in western Europe – extent of overall formal provision of participation by country (average number of decisions – out of 16 – with a formal source)*

Country	Workers (A)	Supervisors (B)	Middle management (C)	Top management (D)	Level above bodies (E)	Representative groups (F)	Outside groups (G)	Total	Country rank
				Level or group					
Norway	9.0	7.6	7.5	15.9	16.0	6.4	8.9	71.3	3
Sweden	8.2	10.1	10.1	13.6	12.4	12.7	1.7	68.8	4
Denmark	5.9	6.9	8.8	14.8	14.8	9.3	2.2	62.7	5
Finland	10.7	10.7	10.7	16.0	—	4.9	1.7	54.7	8
Great Britain	3.7	3.4	3.3	4.0	4.1	4.0	1.3	23.8	11
Germany	10.0	9.0	9.0	16.0	2.0	14.0	1.3	61.3	6
Netherlands	5.0	—	—	16.0	7.0	13.0	3.0	44.0	10
Belgium	6.4	9.8	10.8	11.8	5.9	10.8	4.5	60.0	7
France	4.7	4.6	4.4	6.9	12.6	11.0	3.0	47.2	9
Italy	11.6	9.4	10.7	14.3	7.9	12.6	7.0	73.5	2
Yugoslavia	15.3	12.6	14.6	14.1	7.2	13.8	8.4	85.6	1
Israel	—	—	—	10.6	2.0	13.8	10.2	19.6	12

Source: IDE (1979: 279, Table 2)

channels and which further defines the characteristic institutional shape of given national experiments.

Constraints: structures and institutionalization

However, for the *comparative* analysis of industrial democracy institutions, economic and technological constraints have limited explanatory consequence. Of course, if these forces are analysed historically, then, as Maurice and Sellier have pointed out, the *mode of industrialization* may be 'visible in the system of industrial relations' (1979: 324), and certainly in countries such as Sweden, the concentrated structure of industrial firms may have a bearing upon the institutional structures of collective bargaining and hence upon the patterns of participation (Ingham, 1974). Similarly, in France, the existence of a substantial number of small and medium-sized enterprises could have checked institutional developments in participatory democracy (Greyfié de Bellecombe, 1978). But, at any given point in time, there are obvious restrictions to this type of explanation because, *in countries with roughly equivalent economic and technical bases, radically divergent patterns of industrial democracy have been established.* For instance, amongst the most successful of the predominantly private enterprise economies, the West German system of co-determination has no obvious parallels in, say, the American or Japanese contexts. Again, in eastern Europe, independent workers' councils have periodically surfaced in Poland and Czechoslovakia (self-management being confined to Yugoslavia) and display few similarities with practices in East Germany or the Soviet Union.

Moreover, at an intermediary analytical level, the role of organizational variables in shaping divergencies in national experiences is circumscribed (Wilpert, 1975; IDE, 1979, 1981b; MPIO, 1980). Factors such as size and various dimensions of organizational structure as well as the 'cognitive attitudinal' orientations of managers, trade union representatives and workers have very little impact when set against the far greater effects of legal and other institutional supports (IDE, 1981b). Nevertheless, the structure of *industrial relations* institutions does account for some national differences. Collective bargaining at plant level thus tends to be the principal form of industrial democracy when the structure of negotiation is organized at that point but, in its absence, as Clegg (1976: 97) has observed, 'there are demands for alternative arrangements to allow workers to exercise some influence over those matters which concern them and which cannot be adequately regulated in industry or regional agreements'. Again, an 'inward shift in the locus of collective bargaining' can have profound repercussions for the characteristics of participatory machinery, which is demonstrated particularly in the transformation of works councils machinery to incorporate trade union representatives (Dufty, 1975: 17–72). Moreover, in the West German case, legally based works councils and co-determination reflect not only 'the traditional recourse to juridical regulations' but also the centralized structure of collective bargaining, the organization of trade unions on industry lines and the preference of trade unionists for exerting a strategic influence at national level over large-scale social and economic policy, rather than being concerned with the minutiae of plant-level agreements (Fürstenberg, 1978: especially 3).

On a long-term basis, institutional processes are also vital to the continuation of given practices and are associated with a progressive evolutionary expansion in the machinery of industrial democracy. Hence, as will be seen in Table 7.5, as the twentieth century has progressed, there has been a predilection for greater institutional innovation in leading western European countries. The data cover periods when there was either the introduction of a new institution or an essential extension of the rights of an existing one or the reform of an existing institution and, in addition to facilitative changes, three separate modes of introduction are identified (informal, collective agreement or statutory law). Fundamentally, too, once the first type of plant-level institution is established, the processes of institutionalization ensure the stability of distinctive machinery and hence a *continued* diversity of pattern amongst nations.

A broad evolutionary trend is also underlined by the institutionalization of industrial democracy in much of eastern Europe, even though, globally, this is likely to *reinforce* disparities in the structure and functions of machinery. Plant or factory committees have thus been created or given more extensive powers since 1976 in Bulgaria, the German Democratic Republic, Hungary and the USSR, while more ambitious systems based on 'collective management' and workers' councils machinery have emerged in Romania and Poland (in the former country assisted by legislation passed in 1968, 1971, 1973 and 1978) (see Wilczynski, 1983: 106–7).

TABLE 7·5 Introduction of industrial democracy institutions in principal European countries

Country	1900	1910	1920	1930	1940	1950	1960	1970	1980	1990
Belgium					délégations XX syndicales (C) (S)	works council law	general agreement (C) (S) on delegations	I I I extensions (C) (S) (S) to works councils law	I amendments to company act to provide worker representation on boards	
Denmark					co-operative committees X (C)					
Finland					labour agreement X act (S)	agreement on shop stewards		XX agreement on (C) (C) information	agreement on boards	
France				Matignon X agreement (S) general X agreement (C)		X enterprise sections committees syndicales (C)	works sections syndicales act (S) (S)	X X X act encouraging plant-level bargaining (S) (S) (F) Sudreau Report		
Germany		works council X act (S)				co-determination: XX Montan industries (S) (S) works constitution (S) act	works constitution act (C)	works constitution I co-determination constitution (S) law (S)		
Ireland	shop stewards X (I)					X joint consultation committees (I)		I worker participation (S) law		

Italy		commissioni interne (I)	factory councils (I) (S)		XX collective agreement act
Netherlands	labour act X (S)	works council X act (S)	co-determination IX (S) (S) agreement act		collective agreement act
Norway	workers' councils X (S)	extension of basic agreement (C)	works councils (C) agreement	act X I X on (S) (S) (S) public representation	co-determination act
Sweden	basic agreement X (F)	X works councils (C) agreement	I company act (S) changed to give minority representative rights		
United Kingdom	shop stewards X X (I) (I)	Whitley committees	joint production, (I) consultative and advisory committees	extension of shop stewards system (I)	X Bullock report (F) joint consultation (I)

Key

X = introduction of a new institution

I = reform of existing institution

(I), (C), (S), (F) = mode of introduction, informally (I), by collective agreement (C), by statutory law (S), or facilitative (F)

Sources: Includes modifications of Sorge (1976: Figure 1, 286–7) and additional material from IDE (1981a) and other national studies

Variety is also currently being encouraged by institutional developments in the Third World with some practices being both imaginative and radical (for instance, in Algeria, provisions in 1971 for the 'socialist management of the enterprise' were contained in Ordinance no. 71–4 (Zeffane, 1981) and, in the Co-operative Republic Act of 1980 in Guyana, the long-run transformation of both state and private enterprises to workers' co-operatives is envisaged (Poole, 1982a)). Above all, workers' congresses have proliferated in Chinese enterprises and are designed to buttress self-management in the factory. As it happens, the influence of these bodies has oscillated over time but, by June 1982, they had been instituted in 95 per cent of the big and medium-sized enterprises in China's major industrial cities (Ng, 1984: 56), their growth being closely linked with policies on decentralization and the move towards a greater degree of 'market socialism'. The formal powers of the congresses include the discussion, examination and initiation of production targets and plans, the formulation and administration of enterprise policies on labour protection and welfare and a new capacity to elect the factory management. To be sure, their effectiveness depends greatly on the willingness of the Party to reduce its influence on enterprise management and union, and it is certainly arguable that they are no more advanced as forms of industrial democracy than the western European institutions (see Ng, 1984: 73). Nevertheless, for our purposes, what is important to note is the marked acceleration of interest in workplace democratization in Third World countries, reinforcing global variety and indicating an appreciable late-development effect in the attempt to secure the accommodation of interests of the industrial relations parties in the production sphere.

The 'power' of the 'actors'

But if the overall shape of particular institutions for industrial democracy can be largely accredited to distinctive cultural values and ideologies (coupled with the structure of industrial relations institutions) and the extent of formal rules to legislative intervention (linked, in turn, with public policy and state intervention), power is decisive in determining which type emerges as dominant (Poole, 1978). Hence, although it should be emphasized that major initiatives in workers' participation have almost invariably required a strong presence of workers' associations or a legislature committed to such objectives, substantial divergencies in *practice* are largely based on the distribution of power (see Table 7.6). A strong presence of the state thus encourages a highly legalistic and regulated mode of participation (Porket, 1978). When associated with corporatism (as in the case of Japan), the pressure for social and system integration tends to encourage non-oppositional, consultative modes of participatory machinery at enterprise and workgroup levels (Odaka, 1975; Cooper and Kuniya, 1978). By contrast, in the USA and other countries in which the role of the state has been circumscribed and trade unions are on the decline, many of the most important initiatives have stemmed from human relations-oriented managers (e.g. the shop-floor participatory programmes) (Coleman, 1978; Strauss, 1980). Where trade unions are strong (as in Britain up until the 1980s), the development of participative machinery has

TABLE 7.6 *The relative power of the parties in industrial relations systems and the patterns of participation and industrial democracy machinery*

Types of institution and examples	State and legislature	Independent power of: Trade unions and workers' associations	Management and employers' associations
Highly formal (e.g. USSR and selected east European societies)	+	−	−
Corporatist and integrative pattern (e.g. Japan)	+	−	+
Managerial programmes of an *ad hoc* character and little institutional provision (e.g. USA)	−	−	+
Disjunctive institutions based on collective bargaining machinery (e.g. Great Britain)	−	+	−
Varied programmes and initiatives both central and local (e.g. Norway)	+	+	−

been typically grounded in collective bargaining and organized on the basis of a single channel of representation (Bullock, 1977). And finally, in cases such as Norway, where the labour movement is powerful, and governmental intervention through social and labour legislation has been marked, experimentation in a range of participative forms has occurred (IDE, 1981a).

Moreover, the distribution of power in the industrial relations system and wider society is basic to the explanation of the *origins* of institutional diversity. As is shown in Figure 7.2, at certain historical junctures, abrupt economic or technological changes or social breakdown or upheaval (e.g. following wartime) have occasioned widespread industrial unrest. But such exigencies have been met with varying responses in particular countries, reflecting not only diverse *strategic choices* but, above all, *distinctive patterns of power and interaction between the dominant political parties, the state, organized labour and employers.* Moreover, so far as institutional processes are concerned, machinery established at an early point in a nation's history constitutes a traditional reference point for solutions to industrial unrest and, even after a period of dormancy, may be reactivated in a similar or modified form at a subsequent period of reconstruction. Indeed, the distribution of power underpins 'cyclical' interpretations of the development of industrial democracy (see Ramsay, 1977, 1983), the historical experience being for the genesis or reform of industrial democracy institutions to occur when labour movements are strong and there has been a crest in a wave of industrial conflict.

In detail, leaving aside the wartime agreements, the upsurge of disputes in the later 1910s and early 1920s was met with various attempts at accommodation (by statute in Finland, Germany and Norway and informally in Ireland and the UK). But with the onset of the inter-war depression there was a sharp decline in institutional innovation and, in some cases (as in the UK engineering industry), employer lock-outs to reverse earlier gains by labour. Moreover, it was only when the depression eased in the later 1930s and when a series of Social Democratic and Popular Front governments emerged to mock the seemingly irresistible advance of Fascism and National Socialism, that the situation began to alter appreciably (the Scandinavian agreements covering collective bargaining and the Matignon Agreement of 1936 in France are obvious cases in point).

Following the Second World War, the rising influence of

labour in a full employment economy again triggered a number of interesting changes and an appreciable advance in the establishment of machinery for industrial democracy. In some countries (such as Ireland and the UK) this was associated either with the trade unions (the recognition of collective bargaining rights and the growth of shop stewards' systems) or with joint consultation. But other nations experienced major programmes of legislative reform encompassing either co-determination or works councils or both (e.g. Belgium, Sweden and West Germany). After the apparently successful institutionalization of industrial conflict between 1950 and the early to mid-1960s, the enthusiasm for institutional reform receded. But this situation altered dramatically following the outbreak of strikes which swept Europe in the late 1960s and early 1970s. In almost every European nation there was thus a major attempt at reinstitution-alization which covered both factory-level recognition of trade union activities (as in Belgium, France and Italy) and major reforms of company decision-making processes to include co-determination by employee representatives (as in Denmark, Norway, Sweden and West Germany). There were also a number of facilitative milestones (such as the Sudreau report in France and the Bullock Committee proposals in the UK), before this era of advance ended in the 1980s with the weakening of labour by economic depression and high unemployment.

Moreover, amongst the countries of western Europe, the degree of statutory intervention in industrial democracy depends greatly on power relationships in the wider society and particularly on the different reactions by governments in the nineteenth century to the rise of organized labour and to the new employment relationships which emerged when industrialism destroyed the system of medieval guilds. Indeed, Bendix (1964) and Rokkan (1970) have noted that there were three strategies here: (1) to withhold from workers the freedom of association and the right to combine; (2) to grant the right to form associations but to withhold the right to combine; and (3) to grant both the right to form associations and the right to combine. The state in most countries of continental Europe adopted the first policy, while the second was followed in Ireland and the UK and the third in Scandinavia and Switzerland. Moreover, as Sorge has observed, the predominant pattern was for 'a higher degree of repression to be associated with a *higher probability of a legal system of works councils emerging*' (emphasis added) (Sorge, 1976: 284). This is shown in Table 7.7 in which the Bendix/Rokkan scale of state repressiveness is combined with the three different types of institutions which, in Europe, evolved as the *first* types of representative machinery at plant level (legal works councils, contractually and informally recognized shop stewards or their committees, or contractual works councils). Plainly, then, if the right to form associations was denied to trade unions, plant level non-union organs were likely to develop, and conversely, if collective bargaining emerged in the enterprise, additional institutional channels became superfluous. Moreover, when the battle for industrial democracy had to be fought by organized labour against governments *as well as* against the employers, the upshot was that 'it became likely that the avenue for industrial democracy would be sought with the help of the state's legal machinery, either by the penetration of the state by workers' movements, or by attempts of the state to placate workers by introducing statutory councils, or by a mixture of both' (Sorge, 1976: 284).

TABLE 7.7 *The first plant level industrial democracy institution*

	Legal works council	Shop steward, shop stewards' committee	Contractual works council
country of 1	Germany, France, Netherlands Luxembourg		Italy
category on the Bendix-Rokkan scale of 2 state or repressiveness 3 (high = 1)		Denmark, Ireland, Norway, Sweden, Switzerland and the UK	

Note: Based on Sorge (1976: 284)

These historical conditions also underlie the vital distinction recently drawn by Teulings (1984) between 'corporatist' and 'syndicalist' approaches to industrial democracy in western Europe, the first being highly 'codified' and the second based on worker mobilization through unionization. All these countries have a centralized system of codification, but while three (the Netherlands, Sweden and West Germany) rely almost exclusively on legal procedures, others (Belgium, Italy, the UK and Yugoslavia) have a decentralized system as well. And, above all, these twin strategies of labour reflect deeper temporal patterns of struggle designed to wrest power away from top management, with 'the strength of political pressure, and of trade union activity at the company level', being 'responsible for the present degree of industrial democracy in Europe' and, in important respects, for its principal variations (Teulings, 1984: 239).

Conclusions

The resolution of conflicts of interest in the production sphere through industrial democracy has thus occasioned a rich range of institutional practices worldwide. The origins of this variability have to be sought in the nature of strategic choices informed by wider cultural and ideological meanings, transmitted through public policies and legislative enactments, distinctive institutional practices and given 'constellations' of the distribution of power in the 'larger' society and amongst the 'actors' themselves. Moreover, the limited significance of environmental structures in the overall explanation of the main institutional forms underscores the unequal impact of the main conditions isolated in the overall framework of analysis in each substantive area. Indeed, it is an elemental truism, no less applicable to the social sciences in general than to industrial relations, that the patterning of behaviour is intricate and multi-faceted, requiring sophisticated multi-causal explanations in order to establish the various origins of given phenomena.

Chapter 8 The distribution of economic rewards

Power and material possessions have always been focal points of antagonism and opposition amongst human populations. In industrial relations, these potent sources of conflict have been expressed in a continuing struggle for control within the workplace, in perennial disputes over ownership, income and pay, and in the search for a lasting accommodation of interests by industrial democracy and distributive justice. Here the division of income between specific groups in the population, pay differentials, the rank order of occupations in terms of remuneration and the redistribution of income and wealth through welfare state expenditures are all assessed amongst nations in terms of the unified conceptual approach of the investigation as a whole.

A theory of the distribution of economic rewards

The maintenance of a given distribution of economic rewards in any individual society is based on the extent to which economic efficiency or egalitarianism dominates the principles of allocation. But although variability is ultimately attributable to strategic *choices*, these are essentially shaped by 'subjective' meanings which focus orientations and outcomes (notably culture and ideology), coupled with the constraints of the wider environment (economic, political and socio-demographic), organizational structures (the impact of multinational corporations) and the distribution of power amongst the 'actors' and 'larger' society.

Culture underlies the extent of certain differentials in countries roughly matched for politico-economic system and level of development, together with the rank order of a number of occupations (e.g. engineering); while the ideology of socialism is related to the comparative pay of routine white-collar workers in east and west. But economic conditions (and, above all, the supply and demand for labour) remain the most reliable guide to what will happen to pay in the long run (though these, in turn, correspond with socio-demographic structures including ethnic composition and levels of education and training). Labour theory largely explains the well known curvilinear or 'U'-shaped pattern of income distribution (in which, following a period of intensification of inequalities in pay structure, as industrial development proceeds, there is a progressive movement towards greater equalization), while political conditions are interfused with disparities in income amongst the top percentiles of the population in east and west, and with diverse welfare state practices and ideology. The corporatist democracies in which the authority of central over regional or local government is strong have the highest levels of welfare state spending, while the role of the multinational corporation in the global economy modifies the effects of the curvilinear relationship between inequality in the distribution of economic rewards and level of development. Finally the relative power of 'actors' in the industrial relations system and 'larger' society is also consequential, for trade union density can affect the pay ranking of given groups, differentials, the degree of egalitarianism of income distribution, labour's share of the national income and welfare state ideology and practice. Governments also impact upon the dispersal of pay through incomes policies although, paradoxically, the greater the success here, the more likely it is for wage and salary controls to be abandoned.

Strategies, choices and constraints

Varying patterns of distribution of economic rewards (including income, pay differentials and the rank order of occupations) are thus to be interpreted analytically as the outcome of the strategies of 'actors', set within broader cultural and ideological meanings, and constrained by a variety of economic and political conditions, organizational structures and the distribution of power amongst the parties in the industrial relations system and 'larger' society (see Figure 8.1). At the heart of strategic choices in the sphere of distribution is an underlying tension between *economic efficiency* and *equality,* with the former encapsulating the premises of *instrumental rationality* and the allocation of rewards according to economic contribution (as assessed by the market, by employer or by the state). If left unchecked, disparity in income shares and industrial discord are typical eventualities. By contrast, the latter stems from *value rationality,* with criteria such

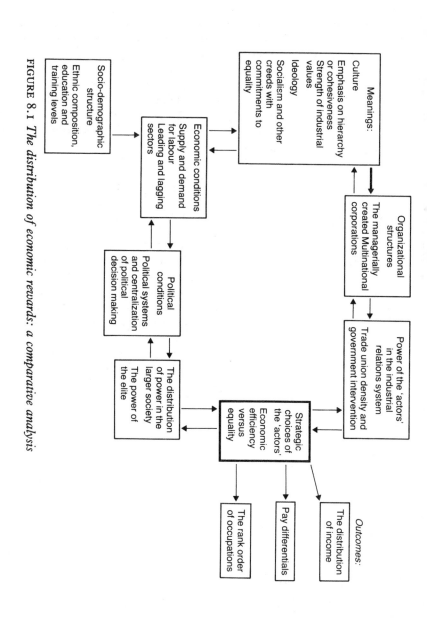

FIGURE 8.1 *The distribution of economic rewards: a comparative analysis*

as need, fairness, social cohesion and justice being dominant, with social harmony being engendered at the expense of economic growth. There are several hypothetical relationships here, but employers and managers typically espouse efficiency, the labour movement strives for equity, and members of the state (partly depending on its political composition) will variously weigh up these objectives, reflecting the extent to which 'system performance' is assessed on economic or social criteria or both.

Culture

The broad 'subjective' meanings which guide strategic choices on the distribution of economic rewards are inseparably linked with cultural traits and ideologies. Above all, this is evident in the ways in which a relative emphasis on hierarchy or cohesiveness in a national system of values and industrial ideals shape differentials and the rank order of occupations.

Pay structure, of course, refers to comparisons of pay in different occupations, which are arranged in a hierarchy encompassing both pay and social standing. Moreover, for analytical purposes, to focus on occupations is legitimate because, despite the wide spread of remuneration, this accounts for the largest differences in earnings (see Phelps Brown, 1977: 29). At first sight, regardless of country, uniformity is apparent. After all, with the sole exception of the relative position of technicians and lower administrative occupations, in a sample of seven western countries (Denmark, France, West Germany, Italy, Norway, the UK and the USA), Phelps Brown (1977: 32) revealed a common rank order in the structure of earnings with higher administrative occupations and engineers and professional grades all better remunerated than any of the manual groups. However, the *distances* between ranks are by no means identical and these disparities are in part a product of culture. Hence, for France, Belgium and Italy, manual-non-manual differentials in monthly earnings in industry are pronounced (at 156.5, 145.8 and 141.2 respectively), but they are less in Great Britain (111.6), the Federal Republic of Germany (137.6) and the Netherlands (137.7) (Saunders and Marsden, 1981). This also applies to the differentials of higher management and executives over other non-manual and manual groups (see Table 8.1); while in France and Germany, disparate 'national styles of organizing production and ordering human relations within the firm' (Phelps Brown,

TABLE 8.1 *Pay differentials by occupational grades in industry 1972; average earnings by occupation as a percentage of the average for all workers in industry; full-time, all ages*

Occupational grade	Great Britain	West Germany	France	Italy
Non-manual men				
1B & 2 higher management and executives	169.8	164.8	247.1	246.4
3 Assistants	111.8	120.2	142.2	155.0
4 Clerical	94.9	90.1	105.3	107.1
5 Foremen	126.1	135.0	140.6	135.6
All	132.2	134.9	162.1	171.6
Manual men				
1 Skilled	107.6	107.1	99.1	105.1
2 Semi-skilled	99.4	94.6	79.3	90.2
3 Unskilled	87.6	86.5	73.9	78.6
All	101.3	100.7	89.6	94.0
Non-manual women				
1B & 2 higher management and executives	105.4	131.9	188.3	171.7
3 Assistants	75.5	95.0	127.5	133.4
4 Clerical	61.1	69.2	84.0	89.6
5 Foremen	81.2	93.4	102.5	102.2
All	64.0	83.3	94.0	106.2
Manual women				
1 Skilled	53.8	71.1	75.6	71.2
2 Semi-skilled	56.1	64.5	66.5	69.7
3 Unskilled	52.2	62.3	66.4	72.1
All	54.1	63.8	67.8	71.0
All workers in industry	100.0	100.0	100.0	100.0

Note: Derived from Marsden (1981: 310); see also Saunders and Marsden (1981: 138–9)

1977: 34) underlie differentials over many types of employment. Indeed, there are consistent differences in the coefficient of variation of wage distribution and in the relationship between the upper centile and lower decile of pay in these two countries (see Daubigney and Silvestre, 1972; Silvestre, 1974; Maurice, 1979), with the relative differences in pay being only part of a series of systematic disparities. Hence, the single pay structure in Germany can be contrasted with the situation in France where there are three separate pay structures (one for manual workers, one for middle management and one for upper management), a highly formal system of grades and appointments (with more ranks distinguished as well as wider pay differentials between them) and a more bureaucratic structure of authority (Phelps Brown, 1977; Maurice, 1979).

Culture also impacts on a number of variations in the *rank order* of given occupations. For instance, in the UK, in the early nineteenth century, technologists and applied scientists had been highly esteemed but their status gradually declined following a counter-revolution in the wider culture after the watershed of the Great Exhibition in 1851, when as Wiener (1981: 158) has observed, *industrial values* were systematically undermined:

> The standards of value of this new elite of civil servants, professionals, financiers, and landed proprietors, inculcated by a common education in public schools and ancient universities and reflected in the literary culture it patronized, permeated by their prestige much of British society beyond the elite itself. These standards did little to support, and much to discourage, economic dynamism. They threw earlier enthusiasms for technology into disrepute, emphasized the social evils brought by the industrial revolution, directed attention to issues of the 'quality of life' in preference to the quantitative concerns of production and expansion, and disparaged the restlessness and acquisitiveness of industrial capitalism. Hand in hand with this disparagement went the growth of an alternative set of social values, embodied in a new vision of the nation.

And the current consequence is that, except for surveyors, engineers in the UK now receive lower rates of pay than all other established professional groups (Routh, 1980: 64). Moreover, their uniquely unfavourable position compared with their counterparts in North America and the European continent extends to the small proportion of engineers on the top board of leading companies, the separation of practical and theoretical skills and the prestige of pure rather than applied sciences in the educational system (Fores and Glover, 1978; Lawrence, 1980; Sorge and Warner, 1980).

Ideology

The meanings enshrined in ideologies also enable some contrasts in pay structure to be interpreted, and particularly the relative position of routine non-manual groups. The socialist 'preference for blue-collar workers' fits in well with 'the official propaganda that the working class is the governing class under socialism' (Adam, 1972), while the Marxian view of work of a non-material kind as unproductive (coupled with the political need of the regime to retain the support of manual workers) also explains the low relative pay of non-manual groups in such countries as the Soviet Union (Phelps Brown, 1977: 46).

Table 8.2 thus compares the pay structures of Leningrad Engineering workers and British workers in mechanical engineering and reveals the relatively poor standing of white-collar employees in the pay structure of the USSR. Yet the more general effects of ideology as against, say, market forces, on pay structure are contentious. Taking Israel as an example, egalitarianism is maintained in the Kibbutzim in all aspects of the formal structure. This includes an equal voice in the organization's affairs, 'the rotation of "black-work" assignments, equality in housing, in eating, in financial arrangements, and in all other domains' (Rabkin and Spiro, 1970; Phelps Brown, 1977). But the wider ramifications of this movement are limited, despite its reinforcement by Zionism (which emphasizes equal pay for equal work, only a limited differential between the lowest- and highest-paid worker and the use of welfare and tax systems to redistribute incomes). Indeed, in general, economic pressures encouraging differentiation have been appreciably more significant, being reflected in the widespread use of job evaluation and income supplementation in Israeli enterprises (Dubin and Aharoni, 1981: 18–19).

Economic conditions

But although culture and ideology remain the overriding meanings informing disparate strategic choices on pay distribution, a series of structural conditions (notably economic) constrain outcomes, with the consequence that, while 'workers may not be paid their marginal product', the tendency towards it is the *most* 'reliable guide to what will happen to wages in the long run' (Brown, 1979: 128). And, above all, labour market theory highlights the origins of inequity in material distribution:

TABLE 8.2 *Comparison of pay structures in engineering in Leningrad and in Great Britain*
Monthly earnings in Leningrad, reported in 1967; weekly earnings in Great Britain in April 1970; expressed as relatives to the unweighted mean of eight occupational grades = 100.

Leningrad engineering workers			British workers in mechanical engineering
Management (factory directors, shop superintendents)	146	130	Managers; supervisors and foremen
Non-manual workers in highly qualified technical-scientific jobs (designers)	107	117	Engineers, scientists, technologists
Qualified non-manual workers (technologists, bookkeepers)	93	103	Technicians
Highly qualified workers in jobs with mental and manual functions (tool setters)	109	100	Machine tool setter, setter-operator
Qualified workers of superior manual work (fitters, welders)	101	103	Fitter (production); fitter, maintenance; welder, skilled
Qualified manual workers (machine-tool operators, press operators)	91	89	Machine operator (metal) semi-skilled
Non-manual workers of medium qualifications (inspection and office workers)	71	83	Clerk (intermediate), storekeeper, storeman, semi-skilled
Unqualified manual workers	82	76	Unskilled building or engineering worker

Source: Lane (1971: 64–5)

notably the 'dealings at arm's length, and the consequent predominance of the pursuit and calculation of self-interest over a concern for those, most of them personally unknown to one, with whom one is related only through the market' (Phelps Brown, 1977: 66).

To be sure, supply and demand for labour explain comparability as well as disparity in pay structures (see Phelps Brown, 1977; Kerr, 1983), the common ranking of occupations by remuneration having already been mentioned. However, there are substantial variations in the *rank order* of *particular occupations* amongst countries at least within manual grades. Indeed, as will be seen in Table 8.3, the place in rank order of the wages of a variety of workers, such as electric fitters, plumbers, carpenters, painters and machine operators is far from uniform and, as Phelps Brown (1977: 62) has pointed out, there is no occupation whose position does not vary over at least eleven places. Moreover, the *supply* of labour in each category, attributable to diverse socio-demographic structures (including the ethnic composition of the labour force, education and training level, and so on) in given countries is largely responsible for this situation. But the implications of supply and demand for labour are most pronounced in the long-term trends and movements which characterize pay structure, explaining the curvilinear or 'U'-shaped pattern in which, following a period of accentuation of inequalities accompanying the early phase of industrialism, there is a *tendency* for income and pay structure to become progressively more egalitarian.

The structure of the developing industrial part of the economy, reflected in the supply and demand for labour, thus largely accounts for the rise of inequalities in the early period. As development proceeds, the gap between the 'leading' and 'lagging' sectors widens and this exacerbates differentials until the advanced enterprises have absorbed roughly half the total labour force (Kuznets, 1955, 1963; Ahlwalia, 1976; Robinson, 1976). In the expanding 'leading' sector, skilled workers and managerial and technical personnel are in demand and hence are able to attract premium wage and salary rates. By contrast, not least because of population growth, in the 'lagging' sector, the supply of unskilled labour remains plentiful, depressing levels of remuneration. However, the situation of increasing disparities in pay is gradually remedied, partly by an increase in the supply of skilled, managerial and technical personnel through advances in education and training, but also because employment in the 'lagging' sector is most unattractive. And the up-shot is that income distribution and pay structure are more inegalitarian in developing than in developed countries (see Iwuji, 1980; Abdin et al., 1983; Bigsten, 1983), some of the differentials in Africa

TABLE 8.3 *Rank order of wages of manual workers in different countries*

Twenty occupations in twenty-two countries. October 1968: median, highest, and lowest of places in the rank order country by country, and median of the rates of pay expressed as relatives to the unweighted average of pay in occupations 1, 2, 4, 10, 12, 15 in each country.

	Place in rank order			Median relative pay
	Median	Highest	Lowest	
(1) Electric fitters (inside wiremen)	4	1	12	103
(2) Plumbers	4	1	12	102
(3) Carpenters	4	1	12	101
(4) Painters	4.5	1	15	102
(5) Machine compositors	5	1	10	118
(6) Bricklayers	5	1	12	100
(7) Tram and bus drivers	5	1	14	99
(8) Coal hewers, underground	6	1	16	103
(9) Iron and steel melters	6	1	16	97
(10) Garage mechanics (general duties)	6.5	1	14	98
(11) Pattern makers	7	2	13	101
(12) Fitters (assemblers)	7	1	15	98
(13) Cement finishers	8	1	16	97
(14) Bakers (ovenmen)	9	1	15	97
(15) Cabinet makers	9	1	18	92
(16) Tram and bus conductors	10	2	18	86
(17) Labourers (unskilled), municipal parks and gardens	13.5	3	17	75
(18) Construction labourers, unskilled	14	1	18	81
(19) Railway goods porters	14	3	20	75
(20) Spinners (male)	14	4	19	74

Algeria, Senegal, Tunisia, Argentina, Mexico, Peru, Hong Kong, Israel, Japan, Parkistan, Singapore, Austria, Belgium, West Germany, Italy, Netherlands, Spain, Sweden, Switzerland, UK, Australia, New Zealand.

The number of countries for which quotations were available for any one occupation was between fifteen and twenty except for occupations 5 and 8 (both only seven countries).

Source: Phelps Brown (1977: 61)

being appreciable. Table 8.4 shows that, in Kenya, the ratios of skilled to unskilled manual pay rates are 6.7:1 and for administrative to clerical workers 4:1.

TABLE 8.4 *Occupational wage differentials amongst six African countries – ratio of pay rates*

Country	Clerical to manual (unskilled)	Clerical to trades- and craftsmen (skilled)	Skilled (trades- and craftsmen) to unskilled manual	Administrative to clerical
Ethiopa	2	1.7	1.2	4.6
Kenya	4.9	1.4	6.7	4.0
Tanzania	2.1	1.7	1.9	2.8
Zambia	1.3	0.8	1.7	1.0
Ghana	1.3	1.1	1.2	2.9
Nigeria	1.3	1.0	1.3	3.6

Source: Iwuji (1980: 154)

But, above all, the case of the Soviet Union illuminates the universal applicability of the curvilinear relationship between level of development and inequality of pay structure. Although, after 1917, the destruction of the social hierarchy heralded a reduction in differentials, in the Stalin era these widened substantially during rapid industrialization (see Kirsch, 1972; Lane, 1982). Since the 1950s, however, there has been a clear narrowing of differentials achieved by several increases in the minimum wage, small rises for intermediary groups and a virtual freeze on upper-level salaries (Chapman, 1979). The two most fundamental changes in the Soviet wage structure have involved raising the minimum wage (between 1956 and 1960 in industry and other branches of material production and then, from 1978, across the board) and a simplification of the wage system. To be sure, the pay of a worker in the Soviet Union is still made up of: (1) a basic rate for a skill or grade; (2) a possible supplement for conditions of work; (3) a possible regional supplement; (4) a length of service supplement in areas such as the far north; (5) overtime earnings; and (6) incentive earnings. But, as Chapman (1979: 152) has noted, as a result of the reforms:

The wide variety of existing wage scales was reduced; the wage scales were simplified and made uniform; and the spread of basic wage rates was generally narrowed. At the same time, wage differentials resulting from harsh working conditions or undesirable geographic locations were made more specific and uniform. Incentive provisions were also made more uniform, and their contribution to workers' earnings were lessened. There was some reduction in piecework; progressive piecework was virtually abolished. Greater emphasis was placed on bonuses, but ceilings were established on the size of the bonus that could be earned.

These changes have dramatically narrowed differentials in the Soviet Union, not least between the average earnings of managerial-technical personnel and those of the manual workforce. The far-reaching nature of this transition is shown in Table 8.5 where the relationship between earnings of workers and earnings of managerial-technical personnel and of office workers in Soviet industry (1945–76) are set out. It will be seen that, between 1960 and 1976, although the relative average earnings of office workers hardly fluctuated at all (just over 80 per cent of workers' earnings), there was a further decline in managerial-technical personnel salaries from the very high post-war peak (on average, in 1976, these were just 122 per cent of workers' earnings).

TABLE 8.5 *Relationship between earnings of workers and earnings of managerial-technical personnel and of office workers in the Soviet Union 1945–76 (average earnings of workers = 100)*

	Average earnings of managerial-technical personnel	Average earnings of office workers
1945	230	101
1950	176	93
1955	166	89
1960	148	82
1965	142	83
1970	136	85
1971	134	84
1972	130	83
1973	127	81
1974	126	82
1975	124	82
1976	122	83

Source: Chapman (1979: 173)

Political conditions

But while level of economic development remains the best single predictor of dispersal of incomes, their distribution within the population is mediated by the nature of political systems. Certainly, this relationship is suggested by a comparison of per capita income in selected eastern and western countries (see Table 8.6), for if the ratio of the shares of the top 5 per cent to the bottom 5 per cent of the population is examined, there are pronounced disparities between private enterprise and state socialist societies. Nevertheless, there is overlap (the UK and Sweden are thus *more* egalitarian than the USSR) and, on different units of analysis (the ratio of the top 10 per cent to the bottom 10 per cent and the ratio of the top 25 per cent to bottom 25 per cent), the similarities are striking.

TABLE 8.6 *Per capita income from all sources, after income taxes, in selected industrial nations, various years, 1963–71*

	Ratio top 5% to bottom 5%	Ratio top 10% to bottom 10%	Ratio top 25% to bottom 25%
Bulgaria	3.8	2.7	1.7
Hungary	4.0	3.0	1.8
Czechoslovakia	4.3	3.1	1.8
United Kingdom	5.0	3.4	1.9
Sweden	5.5	3.5	1.9
USSR	5.7	3.5	2.0
Italy	11.2	5.9	2.5
Canada	12.0	6.0	2.4
United States	12.7	6.7	2.6

Source: Wiles (1974: 48)

Notwithstanding serious pitfalls in measurement (notably the weak data base and the obstacles which arise when rather different questions are posed for relating the experiences of given countries; see Wilensky, 1975: 88), the eradication of private ownership of the means of production under socialist political systems largely explains disparities in very high incomes. On the other hand, it should be stressed that, accompanying economic growth, the share of income from property in the national product has in any event fallen relative to that of income from employment in all advanced countries (see Kuznets, 1966; Lydall, 1968; Blinder, 1974; Phelps Brown, 1977; Wilensky, 1978). In a well-known comparative survey (that included Canada, France, Switzerland, the UK, the USA and West Germany) Kuznets (1966: 218) thus observed that:

> the proportion of property income in national income (excluding the equity of individual entrepreneurs), which ranged between 20 and 40 per cent in the mid-nineteenth century, has, after a long period of stability or slight rise, declined – in some countries beginning with the post-World War I period, in others beginning with World War II – and is now at or below 20 per cent. Even more clearly discernible is the decline in the share of income from capital, including that on equity of individual entrepreneurs, from almost half to about 20 per cent – although the allocation of entrepreneurs between service and property components has many elements of arbitrariness.

More specifically, too, inheritances account for surprisingly little of overall inequality, partly because of their small average size as compared with earned income, but also because the receipt of a large inheritance can be an effective work disincentive (Blinder, 1974).

Yet the role of *political structure* is most evident in the variations in welfare-state effort, the essence of which 'is government-protected minimum standards of income, nutrition, health, housing, and education, assured to every citizen as a political right, not as charity' (Wilensky, 1975: 1). But while level of *economic growth* largely determines social security spending (Wilensky, 1975, 1978, 1983), and as Table 8.7 reveals, expressed as a percentage of gross production, public welfare expenditures bear little relationship to ideology or political system, aspects of political structure (and notably centralization of decision making within the polity) remain vital. Hence, in a detailed analysis, Wilensky (1975) covered sixty-four countries, which he classified by type of political system; liberal democratic (UK, Sweden), authoritarian populist (Mexico, Japan), authoritarian oligarchic (Venezuela, Brazil) and totalitarian (East Germany, USSR). His results showed that social security arrangements hardly reflected these differences at all, but depended rather on per capita GNP, population age and the age of the social security system. Moreover, at least amongst rich countries, disparities in *welfare state practice and ideology* could be largely attributed to political structure, for the high welfare spenders were found to be the *corporatist democracies* (e.g. the Netherlands, Belgium, Sweden, Germany and Austria) in which social policy is an expression of economic policy and in which there is 'the interplay of strongly organized, usually centralized interest groups, especially labour, employer, and professional associations with a centralized or moderately centralized government obliged by law or informal arrangement to consider their advice' (Wilensky, 1983: 53). By contrast, countries which have either corporatist tendencies without the full participation of labour (e.g. Japan) or fragmented and decentralized political economies (e.g. Australia, Canada, the USA and the UK) are both more inegalitarian and more prone to the erosion of welfare state expenditure by the so-called 'tax-welfare backlash' (Wilensky, 1983: 56). In explaining welfare expenditure, ideology was found to be primarily a dependent variable with only weak independent or reciprocal effects, for while a people with a pro-welfare state ideology will more readily accept a further expansion of services and 'income-equalizing' benefits, it is essentially countries in which *the authority of central over regional or local government is strong* that tend to have *higher* welfare-state spending and a greater emphasis on equality.

Organizational variables: the role of the multinational corporations

But there are also strong grounds for supposing that management policies on pay structures bear upon a number of distributional outcomes (for instance, the tendency for Japanese employers to reward seniority in order to inculcate company loyalty is of direct consequence for the income levels of particular groups in the population). Moreover, although there are some doubts about the analytical placement of the role of multinational corporations (these could be examined under economic conditions), there are substantial (if still only improperly understood) repercussions here on differentials.

First and foremost, then, the presence of multinational corporations appreciably modifies the curvilinear pattern of income inequality associated with level of development. In particular, divergencies in pay structure amongst developing countries partly reflect disparate levels of penetration by multinational corporations because of the core-periphery relations

TABLE 8.7 *Public welfare expenditures as per cent of gross production, 1974 and 1976* [average of the two years]

Country	Expenditures as % of gross production
Sweden	27.8
West Germany	25.7
Austria	25.7
France	24.8
Italy	20.9
Ireland	20.7
United States	14.2
United Kingdom	13.9
Greece	10.7
Japan	5.8
Czechoslovakia	20.1
Hungary	16.9
East Germany	16.8
Yugoslavia	14.5
Bulgaria	13.4
USSR	11.9
Poland	10.4
Romania	6.9

Source: Kerr (1983: 143)

associated with the *organizational dominance* of the multinationals and the global division of labour. As Bornschier (1983: 12) has pointed out:

> The new form of the spatial-economic hierarchy which is coexisting with the classical one is the core-periphery division of labour within industrial activities. The core is specializing in control over capital, technology, innovation processes and the production of the most advanced and technologically sophisticated products – embodying much human capital – at the beginning of the product cycle, whereas the periphery is engaged in more standardized and routinized industrial production either for the domestic or the world market.

And the upshot is a further superimposed pattern of stratification or 'dualism', with inequalities being greatest in nations with a peripheral industrial and a dominant agrarian system, while higher levels of equality occur in countries with industrial systems focused on core activities (see Figure 8.2). In short, income inequality in general does not inexorably vary 'directly with development, but with surplus, power and the structural position within the world economy' (Bornschier, 1983).

To sustain this proposition Bornschier (1983) examined the effects of multinational corporations on income distribution in the seventy-two countries in the world with adequate inequality data. Penetration by MNCs was discovered to have an observable positive effect on income inequality and distinctly modified the consequences of GNP per capita (level of development) on dispersal of income. Moreover, the presence of MNCs was related both to *more* income inequality in less developed countries and 'the opposite effect in wealthy headquarter countries', while the LDCs 'would not have reached the same maximum level of income inequality without MNC penetration', and would have accomplished 'a lower maximum level of inequality at an earlier level of development' (Bornschier, 1983: 16–17).

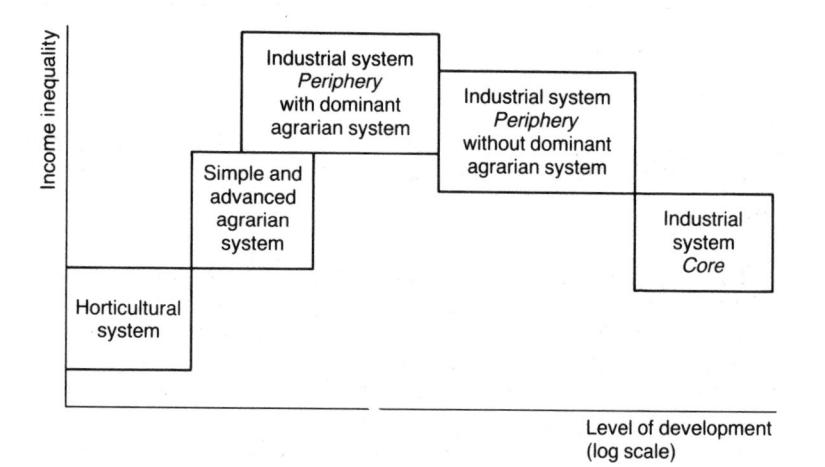

FIGURE 8.2 *Core-periphery relations, economic development and income inequality*

Source: Bornschier (1983: 18)

The distribution of power

Trade Unions

Even though a society's surplus is the product of organization and technology, power substantially influences its distribution (Lenski, 1966). The dominance of elite groups in the 'larger' society is vital here, but so are power disparities in the industrial relations system, the strength of trade unions in individual countries substantially impacting on the pay of specific groups, differentials, the degree of egalitarianism of overall income distribution, labour's share of national income and welfare-state expenditures.

Varying levels of unionization shape the rank order of occupations in terms of pay in given nations, recent investigations in the USA summarized by Parsley (1980) giving the estimate of a 10–15 per cent advantage for unionized workers. Moreover, the dual nature of the industrial relations system (national and plant-level bargaining) *accentuates* these advantages for British trade unionists, the results of studies by Pencavel (1974, 1977), Mulvey (1976), Mulvey and Foster (1976), Stewart (1976) and Nickell (1977) indicating that, if a separate local agreement has been reached, the union/non-union differential is as high as 40 to 50 per cent in the UK. Dispersal of incomes also correlates with levels of trade union density (Brown, 1979), partly because of the mediating effects of egalitarian ideologies. But, above all, the distribution of power *within* labour organizations is vital here, for, when trade union memberships are comprised of a large percentage of the working population (rather than being confined to skilled occupational groups), unskilled workers can either use the ballot box or factional policies to compress differentials.

Trade union density also underlies differences in the extent of egalitarianism of income distributions, countries such as Sweden, Australia and the UK having a high percentage of the workforce in unions and relatively equal income shares, with the obverse applying for France and the USA (Sawyer, 1976: Brown, 1979). Labour's share of national income follows a similar pattern, the proportion of total income accruing to labour being 63 per cent in the UK, compared with West Germany (59 per cent), France (56 per cent) and Japan (56 per cent), all of which have lower levels of union density. However, the evidence here is not entirely consistent, for a fairly high share for labour (60 per cent) is evident in the USA, which of all leading western countries has the lowest level of union density (Kerr, 1983). Finally, although political centralization is basic to variations in welfare-state spending amongst rich countries roughly matched for economic level, the strength of working-class-based organizations is also pertinent (see Wilensky (1975)).

The state: incomes policies

The state's presence in the industrial relations system highlighted in Chapter 5 is also reflected in the structure of pay and above all, in incomes policies, which typically alter the dispersal of wages by narrowing differentials (Dodge, 1979; Silvestre, 1979). Nevertheless, there are variable outcomes which depend on the type and success of specific incomes policies, the resistance by employers, organized labour and the rank-and-file, and the constraints of market forces. Clearly, however, incomes policies are adopted by governments to contain inflationary pressures without high unemployment and, as Flanagan, Soskice and Ulman (1983: 38) have noted, the recent phase in the 1970s produced three principal variations amongst west European nations: (1) Austria, the Netherlands and Norway (in these countries, the 1970s began with relatively formal approaches to incomes policies, but by the end of the decade there were dissonant experiences); (2) West Germany, Sweden and the UK (all began the decade with tacit restraint and then had diverse experiences); and (3) Denmark, Italy and France (which began the 1970s with 'wage and price determination unrestrained by either formal or tacit incomes policies', and were characterized by 'weak institutional structures that were dominated by employers').

But the repercussions of incomes policies on pay structure are best demonstrated through a more specific comparison of Austria and Britain. Even with the incomes policy of the 1970s, the Austrian wage structure remained highly sensitive to market forces. The general approach by both the Parity Commission (which oversees the pay of different groups) and the principal labour-market organizations has been to favour *stable functional shares*, diminishing the effects of incomes policies on differentials. Indeed, following an influx of foreign workers after 1973, there was actually a *growth* in industrial wage dispersion. That this situation did not occasion widespread unrest can be explained not just by the background consensus but also by the channeling of distributional conflict through welfare-state activities. Indeed, as Flanagan, Soskice and Ulman (1983: 81) have stressed:

> although Austria has a major commitment to redistribution, distributional conflict has been channeled into the legislative process, thereby reducing the pressure on the collective bargaining and incomes policy institutions. Unions and employers largely agree that wages should be distributed according to the worker's contribution to production, while income distribution according to the criterion of need occurs through legislation. There appears to be general agreement, moreover, that the existing wage structure and the existing functional distribution of income are appropriate by the first criterion.

By contrast with Austria, differentials in Britain did narrow in the 1970s after government intervention. In particular, the 1972–4 incomes policy of the Heath administration occurred in a period which witnessed 'a compression of differentials without precedent in peacetime' in the UK this century (Brown, 1976: 44). For example, average hourly earnings for skilled timeworkers as a percentage of timeworking labourers fell from 140.9 in June 1972 to 131.8 in June 1975 (see Brown, 1976: 40). To be sure, this may have ensued largely from the wider impact of price inflation and of other types of government legislation (e.g. on equal pay) (see Brown, 1976), but incomes policies had an appreciable effect in the period of office of the Labour administration (1974–9). The compression of skilled differentials was most apparent between 1975 and 1976, when the rate of hourly earnings of skilled workers over labourers in engineering fell from 132 to 128 (Flanagan, Soskice and Ulman, 1983: 428). And, certainly, the government favoured egalitarian 'flat-rate' rather than percentage increases, a preference which not only led to employer resistance but also engendered hostility and rank-and-file revolt amongst skilled unions and their members, contributing in no small measure to the Trade Union Congress resolution in 1977 to return to 'free collective bargaining'.

Summary

This analysis of income differentials (and redistribution through the welfare state) thus brings to a close the examination of key themes in industrial relations. Above all, we have seen that strategic choices reflected in divergencies in pattern (e.g. in differentials in pay and in the relative position of particular occupations in given countries) require detailed interpretations in terms of aspects of culture and ideology, economic forces (notably conditions of supply and demand), political structure, organizational variables and the power of the 'actors' in the industrial relations system. Moreover, a number of structural elements are responsible for disparate income redistribution and underscore those conditions which are likely, in the long run, to produce both social and economic justice and the successful accommodation of interests in the distribution sphere without undue sacrifice of economic efficiency or material prosperity.

Part 4

Conclusions

Chapter 9 Conclusions

By the mid-1980s, it had become evident that a further substantial advance in the discipline of industrial relations would be feasible if theoretical and research endeavour had a more pronounced comparative emphasis. Yet it was also fully appreciated that much of earlier abstract discourse and empirical method was ill-adapted to such a purpose. Given, too, that rigorous comparative investigations (in which a country-by-country treatment of themes is discarded in favour of their examination across different societies) were in their infancy, the obstacles to fundamental progress inevitably appeared daunting. In consequence, while interest in comparative issues intensified, there had been few milestones marking an unmistakable pattern of onward and upward ascent.

This was the background for the current attempt to establish a conceptual basis for analysis and explanation in comparative industrial relations. No claims of course can be made to have resolved the bulk of theoretical problems, but it is hoped that an insightful analysis has been conducted through the application of 'action' categories and the notion of strategic choice, the detailing of comprehensive explanatory frameworks, the formulation of specific propositions in given substantive areas and the marshalling of data from a wide range of disparate sources. It now remains to restate those arguments to which a special significance is attached and to re-emphasize and to extend central points at issue.

The comparative approach to industrial relations is, as we have seen, essentially a method of analysis in which environmental, intervening and proximal conditions are isolated and their impact upon various substantive industrial relations phenomena established. To delimit the subject of industrial relations for comparative purposes involves: (1) the recognition that employers and managers, labour and trade unions and the state and various of its agencies have common *and* divergent interests long-term and short-term (and that there are attempts to resolve these differences in all industrial relations systems); and (2) to acknowledge that these universal traits of industrial relations are manifest in both production and distribution spheres. Moreover, an adequate comparative approach should include coverage of broad societal structures and processes, a multidisciplinary and explanatory core and an historical as well as cross-sectional treatment of consequential themes.

Fundamental to the arguments advanced in this study is that, at the current stage in our knowledge, attempts to establish a general inclusive comparative industrial relations theory are likely to prove fruitless. Indeed, it is in any event implausible that the same elemental conditions will explain phenomena as diverse as, say, trade unionism in socialist societies and variations in strike activity in the west. In addition to the development and refinement of analytical frameworks, then, the optimum path for further progress would now appear to be the more precise formulation of specific theories in a series of substantive areas. Moreover, although the very broad associations identified here must be regarded as tentative, they do point to a limited number of elemental conditions which help to shape the strategies of the actors and which merit more detailed assessment in future theoretical and empirical scholarship. Examined in turn, these encompass cultural values, ideologies, politico-economic structures, the institutional framework of industrial relations, the power of the 'actors' and various temporal movements.

Cultural values

To begin with, then, the cultures of given societies are the primary sources of the *values* which supply varied meanings and reference points for the 'actors' in the industrial relations system. Certainly, as we have seen, culture is imprinted on managerial industrial relations 'styles' (e.g. Japanese paternalism, African arbitrary paternalism), on trade union strategy, structure and government under collective bargaining and where value-rational purposes are pre-eminent (the role of ethics, religious values and ideals of democracy being vital here), on the formation of independent trade unions under socialism (this applies especially, of course, to the case of 'Solidarity' where Roman Catholicism and Polish cultural nationalism have been decisive) on preferences for different types of state strategy (e.g. pluralism or corporatism), on the institutions of industrial democracy (the stress on local autonomy by groups with a common cultural identity being central to some experiments) and on the distribution of economic rewards (such differentials as the relative pay of engineers are thus linked with culture). To be sure, its contribution to variations in other areas (e.g. the incidence and 'shape' of strikes in the west) is weak and in given cases (e.g. trade union structure) it is of lesser consequence than other explanatory forces. But, in general, culture is intimately associated with diversity in the industrial relations experiences of nations and its effects will surely become progressively pronounced as more countries are industrially developed and as new sets of 'actors' seek to generate workable solutions to problems arising in both production and distribution spheres.

Moreover, it should be stressed that even the advanced cross-national methodologies currently being deployed almost invariably understate cultural influences, by being based on a 'factorial' design, and hence measuring differences of degree rather than of trait, relationship or type. But cultural disparities are mainly *configurational* and are expressed 'in location, social distance and types of social relationship between institutions or elements within a distinctive social structure', Teulings (1984: 255) arguing that:

> The weakness of the factorial design in comparative research is the intrinsic tendency to remove singular or unique configurations and produce above all major *similarities* between the units of comparison (in this case: nations). This tendency is reinforced by a preference for a specific type of variable construction. Most of the variables define variations of kind, not *in* kinds. They do not quantify qualitative differences but differences 'in degree'.

In our study, the force of this case was demonstrated in the area of industrial conflict, where the analysis of qualitative variations in disputes amongst nations has been generally submerged by the concentration on quantitative differences based on specific strike measures.

Ideologies

Nevertheless, dissimilarities in the industrial relations experiences of nations also stem from non-uniformity in ideologies. Indeed, as Kerr (1983: 84) has pointed out, when the contrasting goals of political systems encompassed in distinctive ideologies become ingrained 'within a people', they represent 'a very powerful force for continuity'. However, they limit the solutions available to problems and this 'subjects them to erosion' in the long term (Kerr, 1983: 82).

But for comparative purposes, the relationship between power, strategies for control and general ideas are validly interpretable through *ideologies*. These shape managerial strategies and 'styles' (e.g. constitutionalism and authoritarianism in Britain and France respectively), labour strategies (particularly 'radical' types), trade union density, structure and government under collective bargaining and in labour movements with predominantly 'political objectives' (etched, above all, on differences in structure), the role of the state (e.g. in the pressures for corporatism), the 'shape' of strikes (notably patterns with high member or worker involvement), the institutions of industrial democracy (e.g. co-determination and self-management) and, to a lesser extent, the distribution of economic rewards (e.g. the pay of white-collar workers under socialism). Ideologies are also vital for understanding the *objectives* of the 'actors'' strategies, they are intertwined with economic, public and legal policies and are of course integral to the programmes of political parties. In short, they are indispensable for comparative analysis and, notwithstanding possible erosion, are likely to remain a potent source of diversity in industrial relations in the years ahead.

Politico-economic structure

Yet to affirm the centrality of cultural values and ideologies is not to propose a one-sidedly 'subjectivist' interpretation of diversity in the employment relationship. Indeed, in the broadest comparisons, there is no gainsaying the significance of politico-economic structure. This is evident in managerial strategies (for instance, under state socialism the autonomy of management is so circumscribed that it is debatable whether it is reasonable to use the term managerial strategy at all), employers' associations (absent entirely from socialist countries), labour strategies (substantially limited again in 'command'-type economies), the role of the state (dominant under corporatism and centralized forms of socialism), and patterns of industrial conflict (for example, in the diverse modes of protest under the different systems).

It could of course be objected that while, for analytical purposes, politico-economic structure is indispensable for global comparisons, it is largely irrelevant for understanding variations amongst countries, say, in western Europe, where institutional explanations are more basic (see e.g. Lipset, 1961; Bain and Price, 1980). But while there is force in this argument, certain internal differences amongst broad groupings of nations are still attributable to political economy rather than to institutions. This is most obvious when the 'corporatist democracies' (e.g. the Scandinavian countries and Austria) are contrasted with countries with a more enduring commitment to pluralism (e.g. the UK). The former thus have a pronounced role for the state in industrial relations, strong employers' associations, a functional separation of industrial and political issues in the labour movement, low strike activity, extensive experimentation with industrial democracy and high welfare expenditures. Hence, freed from dogmatic restrictions, a political economy of industrial relations contributes a series of valuable (if partial) insights of profound relevance for understanding diversity amongst nations and to comparative industrial relations theorizing as a whole.

The institutional framework of industrial relations

Nevertheless, it is a general rule that the more focused the analysis (in terms of countries studied and theme), the more necessary it is for the investigator to use institutional modes of explanation to interpret the remaining differences. Not surprisingly, too, at many points in the preceding account, variations in industrial relations institutions have been found to be closely linked with divergent national patterns. This applies specifically to the role of employers' associations (constrained by decentralized collective bargaining), labour strategies (institutionalization and accommodation reduces radicalism), trade union density (the scope and depth of collective bargaining is basic here), structure (preferred methods of union regulation being consequential) and government (level of bargaining affects the development of factions), the role of the state (level of bargaining is related to its influence), strikes (their frequency is increased by domestic-level bargaining and their 'shape' is affected by types of agreement), and industrial democracy (workplace-level union organization reduces the likelihood of legally based works councils and co-determination machinery).

Nevertheless, there is much dissension which should be resolved at this point on the precise status of institutional explanations. For Clegg (1976: 11), collective bargaining is not only 'an influence on other aspects of union behaviour' but the 'main', 'major', 'foremost', or 'principal influence' and 'where collective bargaining is the predominant method of regulation, its dimensions account for union behaviour more adequately than any other set of explanatory variables can do.' By contrast, scholars who advocate the centrality of political conditions and the wider class-based strategies of labour, assert no less forcefully that collective bargaining arrangements are '*reflections* of the distribution of power and the outcomes of conflicts between the labour movements (unions and parties), employers and the state at the time when these arrangements came into being' and that, in so far as they 'subsequently acquire a measure of "functional autonomy" ', they should be understood as intervening variables with 'the task of causal explanation being reserved . . . for factors in the social, political and economic environment' (Shalev, 1980: 29). *Pari passu*, the same arguments can be extended in principle to cover institutional structures of industrial relations where collective bargaining is not the predominant means of regulating the employment relationship.

But while environmental and institutional variables are at different analytical levels (the latter are intervening and not independent in explanatory sequence), both sets of conditions are potentially 'causative' and neither should be dismissed on purely *a priori* grounds. This is illuminated in Figure 9.1, where the 'functional' separation of institutional from environmental variables is depicted. At the point when institutions become established (or a major development departs from existing arrangements), the pattern is the outcome of distinctive strategies of the 'actors', in specific cultural, ideological and politico-economic conditions and with a given distribution of power. *But once institutional structures take root they can continue without major change for prolonged periods, despite marked alterations in, say, political and economic conditions.* This is partly because of efforts of those in dominant roles in the institutions concerned who have a clear interest in 'organizational survival' (see Flanders, 1970), but also because of processes of socialization (at induction and in committee proceedings and so on) which ensure that new

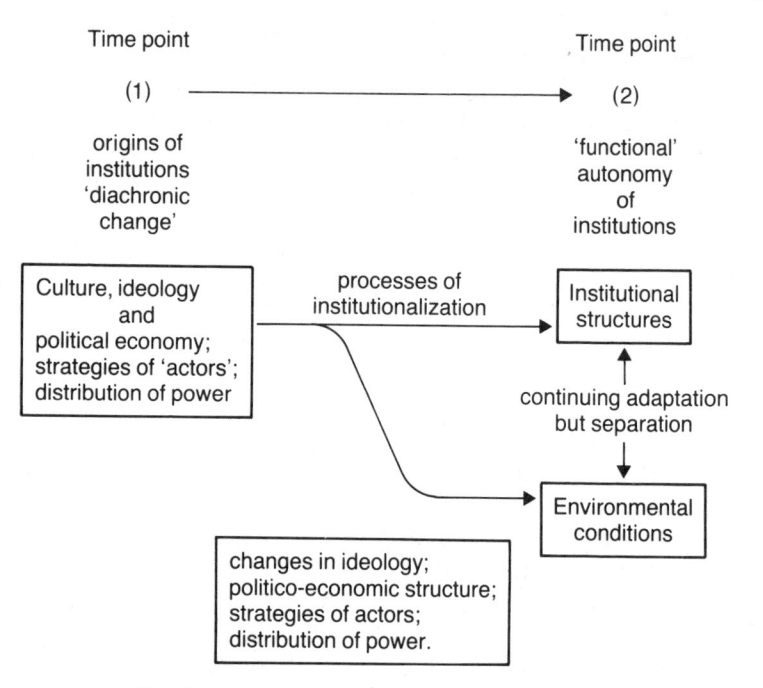

FIGURE 9.1 *The 'functional' separation of institutions from environmental conditions*

recruits continue to sustain the established machinery. To be sure, institutions do change (partly through adaptation to new environmental circumstances, partly through a gradual decline as new arrangements supersede them and partly through radical transformation in 'crisis' periods). But, over time, they can develop a degree of autonomy from the environmental conditions in which they are situated and, as such, comprise a valuable (albeit *analytically* subordinate) explanation of national differences.

Moreover, to stress again the vital role of an historical dimension, there is no doubt that an examination of past periods of major institutional construction leads to a fuller understanding of the characteristics of contemporary institutional forms, a series of *catalytical* circumstances being paramount. First and foremost, then, periods of wartime and its aftermath have been fundamental to institutional change (the industrial relations systems of eastern and western Europe thus substantially reflect the ideas and the alterations in the distribution of power 'occasioned' by the two World Wars). Economic depressions and attempts to resolve them are other cases in point (e.g. the 'political exchanges' which brought about a low level of strike activity in Scandinavia). Upsurges in disputes are also frequently associated with institutional reform (the 'wave' of stoppages in western Europe in the late 1960s and the 1970s thus helped to trigger attempts to re-institutionalize industrial conflict through the encouragement of collective bargaining at shop-floor level and the establishment or extension of machinery for industrial democracy). And finally, in developing countries, 'national liberation' struggles have been critical for subsequent industrial relations practice (where trade unions were allied with anti-colonial movements they will probably remain integral to the new order *and* politically conscious).

In short, environmental and institutional modes of explanation are complementary and not mutually exclusive. Indeed, Clegg (1976) himself has acknowledged the vital role of employers, managers and the state and of a number of wider environmental conditions (e.g. technology, industrial organization and ideologies) for the development of collective bargaining structure. Moreover, American analysts such as Kochan (1980) have been fully aware of the wider environment of industrial relations viewing centralization of collective bargaining, for example, as a result of the scope of product and labour markets in the economic context and diverse public policies as well as organizational variables and bargaining tactics and power. Ultimately, then, the adoption of a polemical position in these debates seems to be futile, the weight to be attached to environmental and institutional variables depending on rigorous empirical analysis of specific substantive themes.

The power of the 'actors'

The relationships and distribution of power amongst the 'actors' are also central to the diverse industrial relations experiences of nations. Managerial, labour and state strategies thus emerge from a calculus involving assessments of the power of the other 'actors'. Employers' associations typically arise in response to the growing power of labour and, in turn, are checked by the increasing influence of managerial personnel accompanying the growth of large-scale corporations. Specific institutions of industrial democracy can only be established under given conditions of power. And reductions in the extent of income inequality over time reflect changes in political conditions which impact on the power of the various groups in the labour market. Strategies encapsulate cultural values and ideologies but they do not affect behaviour except through the medium of power. Structures are experienced as 'constraints' on action precisely because of their anchorage in asymmetrical distributions of power. And change does not take place through shifting structural or ideological conditions alone, but rather through the relationships of power which prevail in given sets of circumstances and through which environmental forces are transmitted. Nevertheless, although power is ubiquitous and is manifested at a number of analytical levels, it is the pattern of distribution *amongst the 'actors' in the industrial relations system* which is crucial. Indeed, a signal weakness of Dunlop's (1958) original theoretical position here was to view power in defocalized terms, as an attribute of the 'larger' society, rather than as enmeshed with the parties themselves. Yet while this is in no way to dispute the potential relevance of power in the wider environment (and this is especially so if political parties are treated as exogenous to the main relationships), it is, above all, its varied distribution amongst the actors themselves that explains a wide range of differences in industrial relations phenomena.

Temporal forces and movements

We have now seen that continuing substantial dissimilarity in the industrial relations experiences of nations stems principally from varied strategic choices of the 'actors' set within disparate cultural and ideological meanings, broad politico-economic conditions, institutional structures and the distribution of power in the industrial relations system. Moreover, looking to the future, our conclusion must be that, notwithstanding a number of convergent trends, in the long run the forces for *increasing dissimilarity* may well become progressively dominant.

In his recent seminal study, Clark Kerr (1983), as we have observed, has stipulated several areas of comparability, increasing similarity and continuing substantial dissimilarity in industrial societies, many of which are relevant to the more specific sphere of industrial relations. Moreover, while it is not the aim here to challenge such a proposition (there is clear evidence of convergence in areas such as the increasing role of the state in general in industrial relations and in the distribution of economic rewards), it is to argue that the comparative scholar fills out areas within the missing fourth logical category of increasing dissimilarity. For, as more countries become industrialized, it is to be expected that, in addition to the variability contained in the nature of strategic choice itself, diversities in culture, history, demographic structures and politico-economic institutions will all impact in complex ways and produce an increasingly broad range of outcomes. This interpretation is also reinforced by the findings of research studies documented in the previous chapters, the acknowledgment of 'waves' and 'cycles' in movements in key phenomena (such as strike activity) over time, and by a recognition of the implications of the different trajectories of development of societies for greater diversity.

In the previous chapters, then, evidence of increasing dissimilarity was found in managerial industrial relations 'styles', trade union density, strike activity, forms of industrial democracy and even aspects of the distribution of economic rewards. More specifically, then, from the predominantly authoritarian or directive approach of managers to labour problems in the nineteenth century, in recent years, highly complex patterns have unfolded that embrace: (1) the continuation and reinforcement of (and even reversion to) authoritarianism; (2) the differentiation and spread of predominantly paternal, constitutional and participative 'styles' (Kerr *et al.*, 1960); and (3) the emergence of 'hybrid' forms (e.g. consultative-paternal, consultative-constitutional and arbitrary-paternal). In the case of trade unions, too, density, in particular, shows signs of more diversity even in the west, as does the form of labour legislation. Strike activity reveals a broadly *similar* pattern of movement in the early twentieth century, which has been subsequently replaced by widespread variation and the 'withering away of strikes' in the bulk of the 'corporatist' democracies of northern Europe, a continuing high level of activity in countries such as Italy and, above all, the emergence of complex, distinctive strike 'profiles'. With respect to industrial democracy, too, although there has generally been far greater experimentation in most countries since the 1960s than earlier, this situation has not caused widespread uniformity at all but rather the outgrowth of progressively rich and polymorphous types (ranging from self-management through producer co-operatives, works councils, co-determination, the extension of collective bargaining and shop-floor participatory programmes). And even in the distribution of economic rewards, core-periphery effects associated with the rise of the large-scale corporations may well have checked (if not altered completely) the seemingly universal tendency for pay differentials first to advance and then decline as industrialism progresses.

On a long-term historical view, the comparative scholar is thus sceptical about notions of unilinear or secular trends and identifies more complex patterns of movement and, not infrequently, a series of 'waves' or 'cycles' of change. Both strike activity and industrial democracy are subject to variations of this type. The 'withering away of the strike' hypothesis thus seemed untenable once the west European strike waves of the late 1960s and early 1970s, occurred and, although the 1970s witnessed a peak in the reform of industrial democracy machinery, there had been previous epochs of heightened concern (such as the early 1920s).

Finally, further dissimilarity is attributable to different trajectories of development, with the 'new' nations not passing along similar evolutionary stages to those of the west and east. On the contrary, there appear to be appreciable 'late development' effects, a much faster speed of industrial and technological development that telescopes evolutionary processes, and a varied pace and mode of adaptation in advanced societies as well. And the upshot is that already highly complex patterns at any given moment in time are likely to be compounded in the future by multiform processes of change which are likely to produce diverse, dissimilar and divergent types of industrial relations experience.

In sum, then, intricate forces of uneven consequence for industrial relations phenomena have been discovered. Of course, there remain the common elements of the identification of the three main groups of 'actors' in the industrial relations system, the focus on conflict and the resolution of disputes, the shared and the diverse interests and the location of industrial relations activities in both production and distribution spheres. But at the heart of comparative analysis remains the basic tension between the forces of creativity and control, the varied strategies, values and convictions of the 'actors' themselves and differences in culture and ideology, in politico-economic conditions, in industrial relations institutions and in power. In combination, these produce a multitude of outcomes which, in the long term are

Bibliography

AARON, B. (ed.) (1971), *Labor Courts and Grievance Settlement in Western Europe*, Berkeley and Los Angeles, University of California Press.

AARON, B. (1984), 'Future trends in industrial relations law', *Industrial Relations*, 23, pp. 52–7.

AARON, B. and WEDDERBURN, K. W. (eds) (1972), *Industrial Conflict: A Comparative Legal Survey*, London, Longman.

AARON, H. (1967), 'Social security: international comparisons', in O. Eckstein (ed.), *Studies in the Economics of Income Maintenance*, Washington DC, Brookings Institution, pp. 13–48.

ABDIN, R., BENNELL, P., FAJANA, O., GODFREY, M. and HAMDOUCH, B. (1983), *A World of Differentials*, London, Hodder & Stoughton.

ABEGGLEN, J. C. (1958), *The Japanese Factory*, Glencoe, Illinois, Free Press.

ABELL, P. (1975), *Organizations as Bargaining and Influence Systems*, London, Heinemann.

ABELL, P. (1977), 'The many faces of power and liberty: revealed preference, autonomy, and teleological explanation', *Sociology*, 11, pp. 5–24.

ABELL, P. and MAHONEY, N. (1982), 'The performance of small-scale producer cooperatives in developing countries: capital starvation and capital management', in D. C. Jones and J. Svejnar (eds), *Participatory and Self-Managed Firms*, Lexington, Mass., Heath, pp. 287–97.

ABERCROMBIE, N. and URRY, J. (1983), *Capital, Labour and the Middle Class*, London, Allen & Unwin.

ADAM, J. (1972), 'Wage differentials in Czechoslovakia', *Industrial Relations*, 11, pp. 157–71.

ADIZES, I. (1971), *Industrial Democracy: Yugoslav Style*, New York, Free Press.

ADORNO, T. W., FRENKEL-BRUNSWIK, E., LEVINSON, D. J. and SANFORD, R. N. (1950), *The Authoritarian Personality*, New York, Harper & Row.

AHLWALIA, M. S. (1976), 'Inequality, poverty and development', *Journal of Development Economics*, 3, pp. 307–42.

AJIFERUKE, M. and BODDEWYN, J. (1970), 'Culture and other explanatory variables in comparative management studies', *Academy of Management Journal*, 13, pp. 153–63.

AKINMAYOWA, J. T. (1980), 'Relationship of personnel managers to others', *Personnel Review*, 9 (4), pp. 33–6.

AKINMAYOWA, J. T. (1981), 'The cultural impact on management in Nigeria', in R. Mansfield and M. J. F. Poole (eds), *International Perspectives on Management and Organization*, Aldershot, Gower, pp. 121–31.

AKKERMANS, T. and GROOTINGS, P. (1978), 'From corporatism to polarisation: elements of the development of Dutch industrial relations', in C. Crouch and A. Pizzorno (eds), *The Resurgence of Class Conflict in Western Europe Since 1968*, vol. 1, London, Macmillan, pp. 159–89.

ALBA, V. (1968), *Politics and the Labor Movement in Latin America*, Stanford, Stanford University Press.

ALEXANDER, R. J. (1965), *Organized Labor in Latin America*, New York, Free Press.

ALTHUSSER, L. (1969), *For Marx*, London, Allen Lane.

AMSDEN, A. H. (1971), *International Firms and Labour in Kenya*, London, Cass.

ANDERSON, J. C. (1978), 'A comparative analysis of local union democracy', *Industrial Relations*, 17, pp. 278–95.

ANDERSON, J. C. (1979), 'Local union participation: a re-examination', *Industrial Relations*, 18, pp. 18–31.

ANDERSON, J. and GUNDERSON, M. (1982), *Union-Management Relations in Canada*, Ontario, Addison-Wesley.

ARMSTRONG, E. G. A. (1984), 'Employers' associations in Great Britain', in J. P. Windmuller and A. Gladstone, *Employers' Associations and Industrial Relations*, Oxford, Clarendon Press, pp. 44–78.

ASCHERSON, N. (ed.), (1982), *The Book of Lech Walesa*, New York, Touchstone.

ASHENFELTER, O. (1971), 'The effect of unionization on wages in the public sector: the case of fire fighters', *Industrial and Labor Relations Review*, 24, pp. 191–202.

ASHENFELTER, O. (1972), 'Racial discrimination and trade unionism', *Journal of Political Economy*, 80, pp. 435–64.

ASHENFELTER, O. and PENCAVEL, J. H. (1969), 'American trade union growth: 1900–1960', *Quarterly Journal of Economics*, 83, pp. 434–48.

ATKINSON, A. B. (ed.) (1981), *Wealth, Income and Inequality*, 2nd, revised edition, Oxford, Oxford University Press.

ATKINSON, A. B. (1983), *The Economics of Inequality*, 2nd edn, Oxford, Oxford University Press.

BAILY, M. N. (ed.) (1982), *Workers, Jobs and Inflation*, Washington DC, Brookings.

BAIN, G. S. and ELSHEIKH, F. (1976), *Union Growth and the Business Cycle*, Oxford, Blackwell.

BAIN, G. S. and PRICE, R. (1980), *Profiles of Union Growth*, Oxford, Blackwell.

BAIN, G. S., COATES, D. and ELLIS, V. (1973), *Social Stratification and Trade Unionism*, London, Heinemann.

BAKKE, E. W. (1933), *The Unemployed Man*, London, Nisbet.

BALIBAR, E. (1970), 'The basic concepts of historical materialism', in L.

Althusser and E. Balibar, *Reading Capital*, London, New Left Books, pp. 199–308.

BANKS, J. A. (1970), *Marxist Sociology in Action*, London, Faber & Faber.

BARBASH, J. (1984), *The Elements of Industrial Relations*, Madison, University of Wisconsin Press.

BARNETT, G. E. (1916), 'Growth of labor organization in the United States, 1897–1914, *Quarterly Journal of Economics*, 30, pp. 780–95.

BARNOUW, V. (1973), *Culture and Personality*, Homewood, Illinois, Dorsey Press.

BARRETT, G. V. and BASS, B. M. (1970), 'Comparative surveys of managerial attitudes and behaviour', in J. Boddewyn (ed.), *Comparative Management*, New York, Graduate School of Administration.

BATSTONE, E., BORASTON, I. and FRENKEL, S. (1977), *Shop Stewards in Action*, Oxford, Blackwell.

BAUMGARTNER, T., BURNS, T. R. and DeVILLE, P. (1979), 'Work, politics and social structuring under capitalism: impact and limitations of industrial democracy reforms under capitalist relations of production and social reproduction', in T. R. Burns, L. E. Karlsson and V. Rus (eds), *Work and Power*, London, Sage, pp. 173–221.

BELL, D. (1973), *The Coming of Post-Industrial Society*, New York, Basic Books.

BENDIX, R. (1956), *Work and Authority in Industry*, New York, Wiley.

BENDIX, R. (1964), *Nation-Building and Citizenship*, New York, Wiley.

BENNELL, P. S. (1981), 'Earnings differentials between public and private sectors in Africa: the cases of Ghana, Kenya and Nigeria', *Labour and Society*, 6, pp. 223–41.

BERGER, E. L. (1974), *Labour, Race, and Colonial Rule*, Oxford, Clarendon Press.

BERGER, R. (1979), 'Economic planning in China', in N. Maxwell (ed.), *China's Road to Development*, 2nd edn, Oxford, Pergamon Press, pp. 169–203.

BERGER, S. (1981), 'Introduction', in S. Berger, A. Hirschman and C. Maier (eds), *Organizing Interests in Western Europe*, Cambridge, Cambridge University Press, pp. 1–23.

BERLINER, J. S. (1957), *Factory and Manager in the USSR*, Cambridge, Mass., Harvard University Press.

BERNARDO, R. M. (1971), *The Theory of Moral Incentives in Cuba*, Montgomery, University of Alabama Press.

BERNSTEIN, I. (1954), 'The growth of American unions', *American Economic Review*, 44, pp. 301–18.

BETTELHEIM, C. (1976), *Economic Calculation and Forms of Property*, London, Routledge & Kegan Paul.

BEYME, K. VON (1980), *Challenge to Power: Trade Unions and Industrial Relations in Capitalist Countries*, London, Sage.

BEYNON, H. (1973), *Working for Ford*, Harmondsworth, Penguin.

BIGSTEN, A. (1983), *Income Distribution and Development*, London, Heinemann.

BLACKBURN, R. M. (1967), *Union Character and Social Class*, London, Batsford.

BLAIN, A. N. J. (1972), *Pilots and Management*, London, Allen & Unwin.

BLAIN, A. N. J. and GENNARD, J. (1970), 'Industrial relations theory – a critical review', *British Journal of Industrial Relations*, 8, pp. 389–407.

BLAINPAIN, R., MILLARD, F. and AARON, B. (1982), *Comparative Labor Law and Industrial Relations*, Washington DC, Bureau of National Affairs.

BLASI, J., MEHRLING, P. and WHYTE, W. F. (1984), 'Environmental influences on the growth of worker ownership and control', in B. Wilpert and A. Sorge (eds), *International Yearbook of Organizational Democracy*, vol. 2., Chichester, Wiley, pp. 289–313.

BLAUNER, R. (1964), *Alienation and Freedom*, Chicago, University of Chicago Press.

BLINDER, A. S. (1974), *Towards an Economic Theory of Income Distribution*, Cambridge, Mass., MIT Press.

BLONDEL, J. (1969), *An Introduction to Comparative Government*, London, Weidenfeld & Nicolson.

BLUESTONE, I. (1978), 'Human dignity is what it's all about', *Viewpoint*, 8, pp. 21–4.

BLUM, A. A. (1969), *Teacher Unions and Associations: A Comparative Study*, Urbana, University of Illinois Press.

BLUM, A. A. (ed.) (1981), *International Handbook of Industrial Relations*, Westport, Connecticut, Greenwood.

BOHANNAN, P. (1969), *Social Anthropology*, London, Holt, Rinehart & Winston.

BORNSCHIER, V. (1981), 'Some recent explanations of income inequality: an evaluation and critique', *International Studies Quarterly*, 25, pp. 283–8.

BORNSCHIER, V. (1983), 'World economy, level of development and income distribution: an integration of different approaches to the explanation of income inequality', *World Development*, 11, pp. 11–20.

BOSKIN, M. (1972), 'Unions and relative wages', *American Economic Review*, 62, pp. 466–72.

BRANNEN, P. (1983), *Authority and Participation in Industry*, London, Batsford.

BRANNEN, P., BATSTONE, E., FATCHETT, D. and WHITE, P. (1976), *The Worker Directors*, London, Hutchinson.

BRAVERMAN, H. (1974), *Labor and Monopoly Capital*, New York, Monthly Review Press.

BRIGHTON LABOUR PROCESS GROUP (1977), 'The capitalist labour process', *Capital and Class*, 1, pp. 3–42.

BRODERSEN, A. (1966), *The Soviet Worker*, New York, Random House.

BRODY, D. (1960), *Steelworkers in America: The Non-Union Era*, Cambridge, Mass., Harvard University Press.

BRODY, D. (1980), *Workers in Industrial America*, New York, Oxford University Press.

BRODY, D. (1983), 'On the failure of US radical politics: a farmer-labor analysis', *Industrial Relations*, 22, pp. 141–63.

BROSSARD, M. and MAURICE, M. (1976), 'Is there a universal model of organization structure?', *International Studies of Management and Organization,* 6, pp. 11–45.

BROWN, D. V. and MYERS, C. A. (1957), 'The changing industrial relations philosophy of American management', Proceedings of the Ninth Annual Winter Meetings of the Industrial Relations Research Association, Madison, Wisconsin, IRRA, pp. 84–99.

BROWN, E. C. (1966), *Soviet Trade Unions and Labor Relations,* Cambridge, Mass., Harvard University Press.

BROWN, R. K., CURRAN, M. M. and COUSINS, J. (1983), *Changing Attitudes to Employment,* London, Department of Employment.

BROWN, W. (1976), 'Incomes policy and pay differentials', *Oxford Bulletin of Economics and Statistics,* 38, pp. 27–49.

BROWN, W. (1979), 'Social determinants of pay', in G. M. Stephenson and C. J. Brotherton (eds), *Industrial Relations: A Social Psychological Approach,* Chichester, Wiley, pp. 115–30.

BROWN, W. (ed.) (1981), *The Changing Contours of British Industrial Relations,* Oxford, Blackwell.

BROWN, W. (1983), 'The impact of high unemployment on bargaining structure', *Journal of Industrial Relations,* 25, pp. 132–9.

BROWN, W. and SISSON, K. (1984), 'Current trends and future possibilities', in M. J. F. Poole, W. Brown, J. Rubery, K. Sisson, R. Tarling and F. Wilkinson, *Industrial Relations in the Future,* London, Routledge & Kegan Paul, pp. 11–38.

BROWN, W., HAYES, J., HUGHES, B. and ROWE, L. (1980), 'Occupational pay structures under different wage fixing arrangements: a comparison of intra-occupational pay dispersion in Australia, Great Britain and the US, *British Journal of Industrial Relations,* 18, pp. 217–20.

BUCK, T. (1982), *Comparative Industrial Systems,* New York, St Martin's Press.

BULLOCK, A. (1977), *Report on the Committee of Inquiry on Industrial Democracy,* London, HMSO.

BUNN, R. F. (1984), 'Employers' associations in the Federal Republic of Germany', in J. P. Windmuller and A. Gladstone, (eds), *Employers' Associations and Industrial Relations,* Oxford, Clarendon Press, pp. 169–201.

BURAWOY, M. (1979), *Manufacturing Consent,* Chicago, University of Chicago Press.

BURNS, T. and STALKER, G. M. (1961), *The Management of Innovation,* London, Tavistock.

BUSCH, J. G. K. (1983), *The Political Role of International Trade Unions,* London, Macmillan.

CARCHEDI, G. (1975a), 'On the economic identification of the new middle class', *Economy and Society,* 4, pp. 1–86.

CARCHEDI, G. (1975b), 'Reproduction and social classes at the level of production relations', *Economy and Society,* 4, pp. 359–417.

CARCHEDI, G. (1977), *On the Economic Identification of Social Classes*, London, Routledge & Kegan Paul.

CAREW, A. (1976), *Democracy and Government in European Trade Unions*, London, Allen & Unwin.

CHALMERS, W. E. (1967), *Crucial Issues in Industrial Relations in Singapore*, Singapore, Donald Moore.

CHAPMAN, J. G. (1979), 'Recent trends in the Soviet industrial wage structure', in A. Kahan and B. A. Ruble (eds), *Industrial Labor in the USSR*, New York, Pergamon, pp. 151–83.

CHAUDHARY, R. L. (1977), *Studies in Caribbean Labour Relations Law*, Barbados, Coles.

CHILD, J. (1969), *British Management Thought*, London, Allen & Unwin.

CHILD, J. (1981), 'Culture, contingency and capitalism in the cross-national study of organizations', in B. M. Staw and L. L. Cummings (eds), *Research in Organizational Behaviour*, vol. 3, Greenwich, Conn., Jai Press, pp. 303–56.

CHILD, J. and KIESER, A. (1979), 'Organization and managerial roles in British and West-German companies: an examination of the culture-free thesis', in C. J. Lammers and D. J. Hickson (eds), *Organizations Alike and Unlike*, London, Routledge & Kegan Paul, pp. 251–71.

CHILD, J., LOVERIDGE, R. and WARNER, M. (1973), 'Towards an organizational study of trade unions', *Sociology*, 7, pp. 71–91.

CLARKE, R. O. (1980), 'Labour-management disputes – a perspective', *British Journal of Industrial Relations*, 18, pp. 14–25.

CLEGG, H. A. (1975), 'Pluralism and industrial relations', *British Journal of Industrial Relations*, 13, pp. 309–16.

CLEGG, H. A. (1976), *Trade Unionism Under Collective Bargaining*, Oxford, Blackwell.

CLEGG, H. A. (1979), *The Changing System of Industrial Relations in Great Britain*, Oxford, Blackwell.

CLEGG, H. A., FOX, A. and THOMPSON, A. F. (1964), *A History of British Trade Unions Since 1889*, vol. 1, 1889–1910, Oxford, Clarendon Press.

CLEGG, S. and DUNKERLEY, D. (1980), *Organizations, Class and Control*, London, Routledge & Kegan Paul.

COLEMAN, J. (1978), 'Employee participation in the US enterprise', *British Journal of Industrial Relations*, 16, pp. 175–94.

COMMONS, J. R. (1932), 'Labour movement', *Encyclopedia of the Social Sciences*, New York, Macmillan, p. 683, p. 695.

COOPER, C. L. and KUNIYA, N. (1978), 'Participative management practice and work humanization in Japan', *Personnel Review*, 7, pp. 25–30.

COX, R. W. (1971), 'Approaches to a futurology of industrial relations', *International Institute for Labour Studies Bulletin*, 8, pp. 139–64.

COX, R. W. (1977), 'Pour une étude prospective des relations de production', *Sociologie du Travail*, 19, pp. 113–37.

CRAIG, A. W. J. (1975), 'A framework for the analysis of industrial relations systems', in B. Barrett, E. Rhodes and J. Beishon (eds), *Industrial Relations and the Wider Society*, London, Collier-Macmillan, pp. 8–20.

CRAIG, A. W. J. (1983), *The System of Industrial Relations in Canada*, Englewood Cliffs, New Jersey, Prentice Hall.

CRAIG, C., RUBERY, J., TARLING, R. and WILKINSON, F. (1982), *Labour Market Structure, Industrial Organization and Company*, Cambridge, Cambridge University Press, pp. 8–20.

CREIGH, S. W., DONALDSON, N. M. C. and HAWTHORN, E. (1980), 'Stoppage activity in OECD countries', *Employment Gazette*, 88, pp. 1174–81.

CREIGH, S. W., DONALDSON, N. M. C. and HAWTHORN, E. (1982), 'Differences in strike activity between countries', in D. Sapsford, S. W. Creigh, N. M. C. Donaldson and E. Hawthorn, *Strikes: Theory and Activity*, Management Bibliographies and Reviews, 8, pp. 32–50.

CROMPTON, R. (1976), 'Approaches to the study of white collar unionism', *Sociology*, 10, pp. 407–26.

CROMPTON, R. and GUBBAY, J. (1977), *Economy and Class Structure*, London, Macmillan.

CROUCH, C. (1977), *Class Conflict and the Industrial Relations Crisis*, London, Heinemann.

CROUCH, C. (ed.) (1979), *State and Economy in Contemporary Capitalism*, New York, St Martin's Press.

CROUCH, C. and PIZZORNO, A. (eds), (1978a), *The Resurgence of Class Conflict in Western Europe Since 1968: Vol. 1, National Studies*, London, Macmillan.

CROUCH, C. and PIZZORNO, A. (eds) (1978b), *The Resurgence of Class Conflict in Western Europe Since 1968: Vol. 2, Comparative Analyses*, London, Macmillan.

CUTLER, A. (1978), 'The romance of labour', *Economy and Society*, 7, pp. 74–95.

CUTWRIGHT, P. (1965), 'Political structure, economic development and national social security programs', *American Journal of Sociology*, 70, pp. 537–50.

DABSCHECK, B. and NILAND, J. (1981), *Industrial Relations in Australia*, Sydney, Allen & Unwin.

DACHLER, H. P. and WILPERT, B. (1978), 'Conceptual dimensions and boundaries of participation in organizations: a critical evaluation', *Administrative Science Quarterly*, 23, pp. 1–39.

DAHEIM, H. (1973), 'The practice of co-determination on the management level of German enterprises', in W. Albeda (ed.), *Participation in Management*, Rotterdam, Rotterdam University Press, pp. 17–34.

DAHRENDORF, R. (1959), *Class and Class Conflict in Industrial Society*, London, Routledge & Kegan Paul.

DAMACHI, U. G. (1974), *The Role of Trade Unions in the Development Process*, New York, Praeger.

DAMACHI, U. G. (1978), *Theories of Management and the Executive in the Developing World*, London, Macmillan.

DAMACHI, U. G., SEIBEL, H. D. and TRACHTMAN, L. (1979), 'Introduction' in U. G. Damachi, H. D. Seibel and L. Trachtman (eds), *Industrial Relations in Africa*, London, Macmillan, pp. 1–15.

DAMACHI, U. G., SEIBEL, H. D. and TRACHTMAN, L. (eds) (1979), *Industrial Relations in Africa*, London, Macmillan.

DAUBIGNEY, J. P. and SILVESTRE, J. J. (1972), *Comparison de hierarchie des salaires entre l'Allemagne et la France*, Aix-en-Provence, Laboratorie de 'économie et de sociologie du travail, Faculté de Droit et des Sciences Economiques.

DAVIS, H. B. (1941), 'The theory of union growth', *Quarterly Journal of Economics*, 55, pp. 611–37.

DAVIS, K. and MOORE, W. E. (1945), 'Some principles of stratification', *American Sociological Review*, 10, pp. 242–9.

DECKER, D. R. (1983), *The Political, Economic and Labor Climate in Argentina*, Philadelphia, Wharton School.

DECKER, D. R. and DURAN, I. (1982), *The Political, Economic and Labor Climate in Columbia*, Philadelphia, Wharton School.

DERBER, M. (1984), 'Employers' associations in the United States', in J. P. Windmuller and A. Gladstone (eds), *Employers' Associations and Industrial Relations*, Oxford, Clarendon Press, pp. 79–114.

DERELI, T. (1968), *The Development of Turkish Trade Unionism*, Istanbul, Sermet Matbaasi.

DIEJOMAOH, V. P. (1979), 'Industrial relations in a development context: the case of Nigeria', in U. G. Damachi, H. D. Seibel and L. Trachtman (eds), *Industrial Relations in Africa*, London, Macmillan, pp. 169–200.

DODGE, D. (1979), 'Impact of some government policies on wage determination: an overview', in Organization for Economic Cooperation and Development, *Collective Bargaining and Government Policies*, Paris, OECD, pp. 163–79.

DOERINGER, P. B. (ed.) (1981), *Industrial Relations in International Perspective*, London, Macmillan.

DOERINGER, P. B. and PIORE, M. J. (1971), *Internal Labor Markets and Manpower Analysis*, Lexington, Mass., Heath.

DORE, R. P. (1973), *British Factory – Japanese Factory*, London, Allen & Unwin.

DORFMAN, H. (1957), *Labor Relations in Norway*, Oslo, Norwegian Joint Committee on International Social Policy.

DOUGLAS, P. H. (1930), *Real Wages in the United States*, Boston, Houghton Mifflin.

DUBIN R. and AHARONI, Y. (1981), 'Ideology and reality: work and pay in Israel', *Industrial Relations*, 20, pp. 18–35.

DUBOIS, P. (1978), 'New forms of industrial conflict 1960–1974', in C. Crouch and A. Pizzorno (eds), *The Resurgence of Class Conflict in Western Europe Since 1968*, vol. 2, London, Macmillan, pp. 1–34.

DUBOIS, P. (1982), 'Manning levels and wage hierarchies: the case of French and English maintenance workers in serial (batch) industries', *British Journal of Industrial Relations*, 20, pp. 76–82.

DUFTY, N. F. (1975), *Changes in Labour-Management Relations in the Enterprise*, Paris, OECD.

DUFTY, N. F. (1984), 'Employers' associations in Australia', in J. P. Windmuller and A. Gladstone (eds), *Employers' Associations and Industrial Relations*, Oxford, Clarendon Press, pp. 115–48.

DULLES, F. R. (1949), *Labor in America*, New York, Crowell.

DUNLOP, J. T. (1949), 'The development of labor organization: a theoretical framework', in R. A. Lester and J. Shister (eds), *Insights into Labor Issues*, New York, Macmillan, pp. 163–93.

DUNLOP, J. T. (1958), *Industrial Relations Systems*, New York, Holt.

DUNLOP, J. T. and GALENSON, W. (eds) (1978), *Labor in the Twentieth Century*, New York, Academic Press.

DURKHEIM, E. (1947), *The Division of Labor in Society*, Illinois, Free Press.

DURKHEIM, E. (1952), *Suicide*, London, Routledge & Kegan Paul.

DUVERGER, M. (1964), *Introduction to the Social Sciences*, London, Allen & Unwin.

ECKSTEIN, A. (ed.) (1977), *Comparison of Economic Systems*, Berkeley and Los Angeles, University of California Press.

EDELMAN, M. and FLEMING, R. W. (1965), *The Politics of Wage-Price Decisions: A Four Country Analysis*, Urbana, University of Illinois Press.

EDELSTEIN, J. D. and WARNER, M. (1975), *Comparative Union Democracy*, London, Allen & Unwin.

EDWARDS, P. K. (1979), 'Methodological issues in quantitative strike analysis – criticism and comment', *Industrial Relations*, 18, pp. 117–19.

EDWARDS, P. K. (1981), *Strikes in the United States 1881–1974*, Oxford, Blackwell.

ELDER, J. W. (1976), 'Comparative cross-national methodology', *Annual Review of Sociology*, 2, pp. 209–30.

ELDRIDGE, J. E. T. (1968), *Industrial Disputes*, London, Routledge & Kegan Paul.

ELGER, A. (1979), 'Valorization and deskilling: a critique of Braverman', *Capital and Class*, 7, pp. 58–99.

ELLUL, J. (1965), *The Technological Society*, London, Jonathan Cape.

ENGLAND, G. W. (1974), *The Manager and his Values*, Cambridge, Mass., Ballinger.

ENGLAND, G. W., DHINGRA, O. P. and AGARWAL, N. C. (1974), *The Manager and the Man: a Cross-cultural Study of Personal Values*, Kent, Ohio, Kent State University Press.

ESTEY, J. E. (1950), *Business Cycles*, New York, Prentice Hall.

FALLICK, J. L. and ELLIOTT, R. F. (1981), *Incomes Policies, Inflation and Relative Pay*, London, Allen & Unwin.

FAUCHEUX, C. and ROJOT, J. (1979), 'Social psychology and industrial relations: a cross-cultural perspective', in G. M. Stephenson and C. J. Brotherton (eds), *Industrial Relations: A Social Psychological Approach*, London, Wiley, pp. 33–49.

FEARN, R. M. (1981), *Labor Economics: The Emerging Synthesis*, Cambridge, Mass., Winthrop.

FEDERAL CIVILIAN WORKFORCE STATISTICS (1974), *Age and Federal Employment: An Overview*, Washington DC, US Civil Service Commission.

FICZERE, L. (1974), *The Socialist State Enterprise*, Budapest, Akademiai Kiado.

FISHBEIN, W. H. (1984), *Wage Restraint by Consensus*, London, Routledge & Kegan Paul.

FISHER, A. G. B. (1932), 'Education and relative wage rates', *International Labour Review*, 25, pp. 742–64.

FLANAGAN, R., SOSKICE, D. and ULMAN, L. (1983), *Unions, Economic Stabilization and Incomes Policy: The European Experience*, Washington DC, Brookings.

FLANDERS, A. (1970), *Management and Unions*, London, Faber & Faber.

FOGARTY, M. P., RAPOPORT, R. and RAPOPORT, R. N. (1971), *Sex, Career and Family*, London, Allen & Unwin.

FORD, G. W., PLOWMAN, D. P. and LANSBURY, R. D. (1980), 'Employers' associations: an introduction', in G. W. Ford, J. M. Hearn and R. D. Lansbury (eds), *Australian Labour Relations*, 3rd edition, Melbourne, Macmillan.

FORES, M. and GLOVER, I. (1978), *Manufacturing and Management*, London, HMSO.

FORM, W. H. (1979), 'Comparative industrial sociology and the convergence hypothesis', *Annual Review of Sociology*, 5, pp. 1–25.

FORM, W. H. and BLUM, A. A. (eds) (1965), *Industrial Relations and Social Change in Latin America*, Gainesville, University of Florida Press.

FOULKES, F. K. (1980a), *Effective Personnel Policies: A Study of Large Non Union Employers*, Englewood Cliffs, New Jersey, Prentice Hall.

FOULKES, F. K. (1980b), *Positive Employee Relations*, Englewood Cliffs, New Jersey, Prentice Hall.

FOX, A. (1966), *Industrial Sociology and Industrial Relations*, Royal Commission on Trade Unions and Employers' Associations, Research Paper 3, London, HMSO.

FOX, A. (1973), 'Industrial relations: a social critique of the pluralist ideology', in J. Child (ed.), *Man and Organization*, London, Allen & Unwin, pp. 185–231.

FOX, A. (1974), *Beyond Contract*, London, Faber & Faber.

FOX, A. and FLANDERS, A. (1969), 'The reform of collective bargaining: from Donovan to Durkheim', *British Journal of Industrial Relations*, 7, pp. 151–80.

FRANK, A. G. (1979), *Capitalism and Underdevelopment in Latin America*, New York, Monthly Review Press.

FREEDMAN, A. (1979), *Managing Labor Relations: Organization, Objectives and Results*, New York, Conference Board.

FRENKEL, S. J. (ed.) (1980), *Industrial Action*, London, Allen & Unwin.

FREUND, J. L. 'Market and union influences on municipal employee wages', *Industrial and Labor Relations Review*, 27, pp. 391–404.

FRIEDMAN, A. L. (1977), *Industry and Labour: Class Struggle at Work and Monopoly Capitalism*, London, Macmillan.

FRIEDMANN, G. (1962), *The Anatomy of Work*, New York, Free Press.

FRY, L. W. (1982), 'Technology-structure research: three critical issues', *Academy of Management Journal*, 25, pp. 532–52.

FÜRSTENBERG, F. (1978), *Workers' Participation in Management in the Federal Republic of Germany*, Geneva, International Institute for Labour Studies.

GALBRAITH, J. K. (1952), *American Capitalism*, Boston, Houghton Mifflin.

GALBRAITH, J. K. (1981), *A Life in Our Times*, Boston, Houghton Mifflin.

GALENSON, W. (1949), *Labor in Norway*, Cambridge, Mass., Harvard University Press.

GALENSON, W. (ed.) (1952a), *Comparative Labor Movements*, New York, Prentice Hall.

GALENSON, W. (1952b), *The Danish System of Labor Relations*, Cambridge, Mass., Harvard University Press.

GALLIE, D. (1978), *In Search of the New Working Class*, Cambridge, Cambridge University Press.

GALLIE, D. (1983), *Social Inequality and Class Radicalism in France and Britain*, Cambridge, Cambridge University Press.

GARBARINO, J. (1950), 'A theory of interindustry wage structure variation', *Quarterly Journal of Economics*, 64, pp. 282–305.

GARBARINO, J. (1984), 'Unionism without unions: the new industrial relations', *Industrial Relations*, 23, pp. 40–51.

GENERAL CONFEDERATION OF ITALIAN INDUSTRY (1957), *General Confederation of Italian Industry: Its History, Organization and Purposes*, Rome, General Confederation of Italian Industry.

GEORGE, V. and LAWSON, R. (eds) (1980), *Poverty and Inequality in Common Market Countries*, London, Routledge & Kegan Paul.

GERWIN, D. (1979), 'The comparative analysis of structure and technology: a critical appraisal', *Academy of Management Review*, 4, pp. 41–51.

GIDDENS, A. (1973), *The Class Structure of the Advanced Societies*, London, Hutchinson.

GIDDENS, A. (1979), *Central Problems in Social Theory*, London, Macmillan.

GINER, S. (1972), *Sociology*, London, Martin Robertson.

GLASER, W. (1975), 'Cross-national studies of organizations', *International Studies of Management and Organization*, 5, pp. 68–90.

GOBBO, M. (1981), *The Political, Economic and Labor Climate in Spain*, Philadelphia, Wharton School.

GODSON, R. (1976), *American Labor and European Politics*, New York, Crane, Russak & Co.

GOLDTHORPE, J. H. (1974a), 'Industrial relations in Great Britain: a critique of reformism', *Politics and Society*, 4, pp. 419–42.

GOLDTHORPE, J. H. (1974b), 'Social inequality and social integration in modern Britain', in D. Wedderburn (ed.), *Poverty, Inequality and Class Structure*, Cambridge, Cambridge University Press, pp. 217–38.

GOLDTHORPE, J. H. (1980), *Social Mobility and Class Structure in Modern Britain*, Oxford, Oxford University Press.

GOLDTHORPE, J. H. and LLEWELLYN, C. (1977), 'Class mobility: intergenerational and work life patterns', *British Journal of Sociology*, 28, pp. 269–302.

GOODMAN, J. F. B., ARMSTRONG, E. G. A., DAVIS, J. E. and WAGNER, A. (1977), *Rule-Making and Industrial Peace*, London, Croom Helm.

GORDON, D. (1972), *Theories of Poverty and Underemployment*, Lexington, Mass., Heath.

GORDON, R., EDWARDS, R. and REICH, M. (1982), *Labour Market Segmentation in American Capitalism*, Cambridge, Cambridge University Press.

GORZ, A. (1967), *Strategy for Labor*, Boston, Beacon Press.

GOSPEL, H. (1983), 'The development of management organization in industrial relations: an historical perspective', in K. E. Thurley and S. Wood (eds), *Industrial Relations and Management Strategy*, Cambridge, Cambridge University Press, pp. 91–110.

GOULDNER, A. W. (1954), *Wildcat Strike*, New York, Harper & Row.

GOUREVITCH, P., MARTIN, A., ROSS, G., ALLEN, C., BORNSTEIN, S. and MARKOVITS, A. (1984), *Unions and Economic Crisis*, London, Allen & Unwin.

GRANICK, D. (1960), *The Red Executive*, London, Macmillan.

GRANICK, D. (1972), *Managerial Comparisons in Four Developed Countries*, Cambridge, Mass., MIT Press.

GRAY, P. S. (1980), 'Collective bargaining in Ghana', *Industrial Relations*, 9, pp. 175–91.

GREEN, J. R. (1978), *Grass Roots Socialism*, Baton Rouge, Louisiana State University Press.

GREENBERG, P. D. and GLASER, E. M. (1980), *Some Issues in Joint Union-Management Quality of Worklife Improvement Efforts*, Kalamazoo, Michigan, Upjohn Institute.

GREGORY, P. R. and STUART, R. C. (1980), *Comparative Economic Systems*, Boston, Houghton Mifflin.

GREYFIÉ DE BELLECOMBE (1978), *Workers' Participation in Management in France*, Geneva, International Institute for Labour Studies.

GROSSMAN, P. (1979), 'The Soviet government's role in allocating industrial labor', in A. Kahan and B. A. Ruble (eds), *Industrial Labor in the USSR*, New York, Pergamon, pp. 42–55.

GULICK, C. A. and BERS, M. K. (1953), 'Insight and illusion in Perlman's theory of the labor movement', *Industrial and Labor Relations Review*, 6, pp. 510–31.

GULLIVER, P. H. (1979), *Disputes and Negotiations: A Cross-Cultural Perspective*, New York, Academic Press.

GURR, T. R. (1970), *Why Men Rebel*, Princeton, New Jersey, Princeton University Press.

GUTMAN, H. G. (1976), *Work, Culture and Society in Industrialized America*, New York, Knopf.

GYLLENHAMMAR, P. G. (1977), *People at Work*, London, Addison-Wesley.

HABERMAS, J. (1980), 'Psychic thermidor and the rebirth of rebellious subjectivity', *Berkeley Journal of Sociology*, 25, pp. 1–12.

HANSEN, B. (1983), 'LDC labor markets: applications of internal labor market theory', *Industrial Relations*, 22, pp. 238–60.

HARARI, E. (1973), *The Politics of Labor Legislation in Japan*, Berkeley, University of California Press.

HARE, A. E. C. (1946), *Industrial Relations in New Zealand*, Wellington, Whitcombe & Tombs.

HARMAN, S. (1979), 'A peace plan for workers and bosses', *The Washington Post*, 15 April, p. 4.

HARNETT, D. L. and CUMMINGS, L. L. (1980), *Bargaining Behaviour: An International Study*, Houston, Dame.

HARTLEY, J. (1983), 'Ideology and organizational behaviour', *International Studies of Management and Organization*, 13, pp. 7–34.

HEADEY, B. W. (1970), 'Trade unions and national wage policies', *Journal of Politics*, 32, pp. 407–39.

HELLER, F. A. and WILPERT, B. (1981), *Competence and Power in Managerial Decision-Making*, Chichester, Wiley.

HENEMAN, H. G., JR. (1969), 'Toward a general conceptual system of industrial relations: how do we get there?', in G. G. Somers (ed.), *Essays in Industrial Relations Theory*, Ames, Iowa State University Press, pp. 3–24.

HERMAN, E. E. and KUHN, A. (1981), *Collective Bargaining and Labor Relations*, Englewood Cliffs, New Jersey, Prentice Hall.

HERNES, G. and SELVIK, A. (1981), 'Local corporatism', in S. Berger, A. Hirschman and C. Maier (eds), *Organizing Interests in Western Europe*, Cambridge, Cambridge University Press, pp. 103–19.

HIBBS, D. A., JR. (1976), 'Industrial conflict in advanced industrial societies', *American Political Science Review*, 70, pp. 1033–58.

HIBBS, D. A., JR. (1978), 'On the political economy of long-run trends in strike activity', *British Journal of Political Science*, 8, pp. 153–75.

HICKSON, D. J. and MacMILLAN, C. J. (eds) (1981), *Organization and Nation*, Aston Programme 4, Aldershot, Gower.

HIGGINS, B. (1968), *Economic Development*, London, Constable.

HILL, S. (1981), *Competition and Control at Work*, London, Heinemann.

HINES, A. G. (1964), 'Trade unions and wage inflation in the United Kingdom, 1893–1961', *Review of Economic Studies*, 31, pp. 221–52.

HOBSBAWM, E. J. (1964), *Labouring Men*, London, Weidenfeld & Nicolson.

HOFFMAN, E. B. (1973), *Resolving Labor-Management Disputes: A Nine Country Comparison*, New York, Conference Board.

HOFFMAN, E. B. (1974), *The Role of Labor Law in Developing Countries*, Geneva, International Labour Office.

HOFSTEDE, G. (1981), *Culture's Consequences*, London, Sage.

HOROWITZ, I. L. (1972), *Three Worlds of Development*, New York, Oxford University Press.

HOSELITZ, B. F., SPENGLER, J. J., LETICHE, J. M., MCKINLEY, E., BUTTRICK, J. and BRUTON, H. J. (1960), *Theories of Economic Growth*, New York, Free Press.

HOWARD, M. C. (1979), *Modern Theories of Income Distribution*, New York, St Martin's Press.

HUSE, E. F. and BOWDITCH, J. L. (1977), *Behaviour in Organizations: A Systems Approach to Managing*, 2nd edition, London, Addison-Wesley.

HYMAN, R. (1975), *Industrial Relations*, London, Macmillan.

HYMAN, R. (1978), 'Pluralism, procedural consensus and collective bargaining', *British Journal of Industrial Relations*, 16, pp. 16–40.

ICHIRO, N. (1975), *Industrialization and Labor-Management Relations in Japan*, Tokyo, Japan Institute of Labour.

IMAZ, J. L. de (1972), 'Management as a bankrupt power factor', in S. M. Davis and L. W. Goodman (eds), *Workers and Managers in Latin America*, Lexington, Mass., Heath, pp. 273–9.

INDIAN INSTITUTE OF PERSONNEL MANAGEMENT (1961), *Personnel Management in India*, London, Asia Publishing House.

INDUSTRIAL DEMOCRACY IN EUROPE INTERNATIONAL RESEARCH GROUP (IDE) (1976), 'Industrial democracy in Europe: an international comparative study', *Social Science Information*, 15, pp. 177–203.

INDUSTRIAL DEMOCRACY IN EUROPE INTERNATIONAL RESEARCH GROUP (IDE) (1979), 'Participation: formal rules, influence and involvement', *Industrial Relations*, 18, pp. 273–94.

INDUSTRIAL DEMOCRACY IN EUROPE INTERNATIONAL RESEARCH GROUP (IDE) (1981a), *European Industrial Relations*, Oxford, Clarendon Press.

INDUSTRIAL DEMOCRACY IN EUROPE INTERNATIONAL RESEARCH GROUP (IDE) (1981b), *Industrial Democracy in Europe*, Oxford, Clarendon Press.

INFANTE, J. T. (1980), *The Political, Economic and Labor Climate in the Philippines*, Philadelphia, Wharton School.

INGHAM, G. K. (1974), *Strikes and Industrial Conflict*, London, Macmillan.

INKELES, A. and BAUER, R. A. (1959), *The Soviet Citizen*, Cambridge, Mass., Harvard University Press.

INTERNATIONAL LABOUR OFFICE (1958), *African Labour Survey*, Geneva, International Labour Office.

INTERNATIONAL LABOUR OFFICE (1959), *Trade Union Rights in the USSR*, Geneva, International Labour Office.

INTERNATIONAL LABOUR OFFICE (1966), 'Technological change and manpower planning in a centrally planned economy', *Labour and Automation*, Bulletin no. 3, Geneva, International Labour Office.

INTERNATIONAL LABOUR OFFICE (1973–82), *Yearbook of Labour Statistics*, Geneva, International Labour Office.

INTERNATIONAL LABOUR OFFICE (1973), *Collective Bargaining in Industrialized Market Economies*, Geneva, International Labour Office.

INTERNATIONAL LABOUR OFFICE (1976a), *Industrial Relations in Asia*, Geneva, International Labour Office.

INTERNATIONAL LABOUR OFFICE (1976b), *Women Workers and Society*, Geneva, International Labour Office.

INTERNATIONAL LABOUR OFFICE (1977), *Role of Employers' Organizations in English-Speaking Caribbean Countries*, Labour-Management Relations Series no. 53, Geneva, International Labour Office.

INTERNATIONAL LABOUR OFFICE (1979), *Wage Determination in English-Speaking Caribbean Countries*, Geneva, International Labour Office.

ISENMAN, P. (1980), 'Inter-country comparison of "real" (PPP) incomes: revised estimates and unresolved questions', *World Development*, 8, pp. 61–72.

IWUJI, E. C. (1980), 'Wage structure in developing countries: a comparative study of six English-speaking African countries', *Labour and Society*, 5, pp. 151–69.

JACKSON, M. P. (1982), *Trade Unionism*, London, Longman.

JACKSON, P. and SISSON, K. (1975), 'Management and collective bargaining – a framework for an international comparison of employer organizations', Warwick Working Paper, Industrial Relations Research Unit, University of Warwick.

JACKSON, P. and SISSON, K. (1976), 'Employers' confederations in Sweden and the UK and the significance of industrial infrastructure', *British Journal of Industrial Relations*, 14, pp. 306–23.

JACOBY, S. (1979), 'The origins of internal labor markets in Japan', *Industrial Relations*, 18, pp. 184–96.

JAHODA, M., LAZARSFELD, P. F. and ZEISEL, H. (1972), *Marienthal*, London, Tavistock.

JAMES, L. (1981), 'Sources of legitimate power in polyarchic trade union government', *Sociology*, 15, pp. 251–61.

JANVRY, A. de. (1981), *The Agrarian Question and Reformism in Latin America*, Baltimore, Johns Hopkins Press.

JAPAN FEDERATION OF EMPLOYERS' ASSOCIATION (1963), *An Outline of the Japan Federation of Employers' Associations*, Tokyo, Japan Federation of Employers' Associations.

JAPAN INSTITUTE OF LABOUR (1979), *Social Tensions and Industrial Relations*

Arising in the Industrialization Processes of Asian Countries, Tokyo, Japan Institute of Labour.

JESSOP, B. (1977), 'Remarks on some recent theories of the capitalist state', *Cambidge Journals of Economics*, 1, pp. 353–73.

JOHNSON, A. G. and WHYTE, W. F. (1977), 'The Mondragon system of worker production cooperatives', *Industrial and Labor Relations Review*, 31, pp. 18–30.

JOHNSON, N. R. and DECKER, D. R. (1978), *The Political, Economic, and Labor Climate in Peru*, Philadelphia, Wharton School.

JONES, D. C. (1979), 'US producer co-operatives: the record to date', *Industrial Relations*, 18, pp. 342–57.

JONES, D. C. (1982), 'The United States of America: a survey of producer co-operative performance', in F. H. Stephen (ed.), *The Performance of Labor-Managed Firms*, New York, St Martin's Press, pp. 53–73.

JONES, D. C. and SVEJNAR, J. (eds) (1982), *Participatory and Self-Managed Firms*, Lexington, Mass., Heath.

KAHAN, A. and RUBLE, B. A. (eds) (1979), *Industrial Labor in the USSR*, New York, Pergamon.

KASSALOW, E. M. (1969), *Trade Unions and Industrial Relations: An International Comparison*, New York, Random House.

KASSALOW, E. M. (1980), 'Industrial conflict and consensus in the US and Western Europe', in B. Martin and E. M. Kassalow (eds), *Labor Relations in Advanced Industrial Societies*, New York, Carnegie, pp. 45–60.

KATZELL, R. A. (1979), 'Changing attitudes toward work', in C. Kerr and J. M. Rosow (eds), *Work in America: The Decade Ahead*, New York, Van Nostrand Reinhold, pp. 35–57.

KENDALL, W. (1975), *The Labour Movement in Europe*, London, Allen Lane.

KENNEDY, T. (1978), *European Labour Relations*, London, Associated Business Programmes.

KERR, C. (1964), *Labor and Management in Industrial Society*, New York, Doubleday.

KERR, C. (1969), *Marshall, Marx and Modern Times: The Multi-Dimensional Society*, Cambridge, Cambridge University Press.

KERR, C. (1970), 'Labor's income share and the labor movement', in C. R. McConnell (ed.), *Perspectives on Wage Determination*, New York, McGraw-Hill, pp. 263–73.

KERR, C. (1977), *Labor Markets and Wage Determination*, Berkeley and Los Angeles, University of California Press.

KERR, C. (1983), *The Future of Industrial Societies*, Cambridge, Mass., Harvard University Press.

KERR, C., DUNLOP, J. T., HARBISON, F. and MYERS, C. A. (1960), *Industrialism and Industrial Man*, Cambridge, Mass., Harvard University Press.

KIRSCH, L. J. (1972), *Soviet Wages*, Cambridge, Mass., MIT Press.

KLUCKHOLN, F. R. and STRODTBECK, F. L. (1961), *Variations in Value Orientations*, New York, Row Peterson.

KMETZ, J. (1977/78), 'A critique of the Aston studies and results with a new measure of technology', *Organization and Administrative Sciences*, 9, pp. 123–44.

KNOELLINGER, C. E. (1960), *Labor in Finland*, Cambridge, Mass., Harvard University Press.

KNOWLES, K. G. J. C. (1952), *Strikes – A Study of Industrial Conflict*, Oxford, Blackwell.

KOCHAN, T. A. (1980), *Collective Bargaining and Industrial Relations*, Homewood, Irwin.

KOCHAN, T. A. and KATZ, H. C. (1983), 'Collective bargaining, work organization, and worker participation: a return to plant-level bargaining', *Labor Law Journal*, 34, pp. 324–9.

KOCHAM, T. A., MCKERSIE, R. B. and CAPPELLI, P. (1984), 'Strategic choice and industrial relations theory', *Industrial Relations*, 23, pp. 16–39.

KOCHAN, T. A., MITCHELL, D. J. B. and DYER, L. (eds) (1982), *Industrial Relations Research in the 1970's: Review and Appraisal*, Madison, Wisconsin, Industrial Relations Research Association.

KOONTZ, H. and O'DONNELL, C. (1955), *The Principles of Management*, New York, McGraw-Hill.

KORPI, W. (1978), *The Working Class in Welfare Capitalism*, London, Routledge & Kegan Paul.

KORPI, W. (1980), 'Industrial relations and industrial conflict: the case of Sweden', in B. M. Martin and E. M. Kassalow (eds), *Labor Relations in Advanced Industrial Societies*, New York, Carnegie, pp. 89–108.

KORPI, W. and SHALEV, M. (1979), 'Strikes, industrial relations and class conflict in capitalist societies', *British Journal of Sociology*, 30, pp. 164–87.

KRIESI, H. (1982), 'The structure of the Swiss political system', in G. Lehmbruch and P. C. Schmitter (eds), *Patterns of Corporatist Policy-Making*, Beverly Hills, Sage, pp. 133–61.

KROEBER, A. L. (1969), *Configurations of Culture Growth*, Berkeley and Los Angeles, University of California Press.

KROEBER, A. L. and KLUCKHOHN, C. (1952), *Culture: A Critical Review of Concepts and Definitions*, Cambridge, Mass., Papers of the Peabody Museum of American Archaeology and Ethnology, Harvard University.

KUZNETS, S. (1955), 'Economic growth and income inequality', *American Economic Review*, 45, pp. 1–28.

KUZNETS, S. (1963), 'Quantitative aspects of the economic growth of nations: VIII, Distribution of income by size', *Economic Development and Cultural Change*, 11, pp. 1–80.

KUZNETS, S. (1966), *Modern Economic Growth: Rate, Structure and Spread*, New Haven, Conn., Yale University Press.

LAMMERS, C. J. and HICKSON, D. J. (eds) (1979a), *Organizations Alike and Unlike*, London, Routledge & Kegan Paul.

LAMMERS, C. J. and HICKSON, D. J. (1979b), 'Towards a comparative sociology of organizations', in C. J. Lammers and D. J. Hickson (eds), *Organizations Alike and Unlike*, London, Routledge & Kegan Paul, pp. 3–20.

LANE, D. (1970), *Politics and Society in the USSR*, London, Weidenfeld & Nicolson.

LANE, D. (1971), *The End of Inequality?*, Harmondsworth, Penguin.

LANE, D. (1976), *The Socialist Industrial State*, Boulder, Colorado, Westview Press.

LANE, D. (1982), *The End of Social Inequality?*, London, Allen & Unwin.

LARDY, N. R. (1978), *Economic Growth and Distribution in China*, Cambridge, Cambridge University Press.

LASH, S. (1984), *The Militant Worker*, London, Heinemann.

LASLETT, J. H. M. (1974), 'Socialism and American trade unionism', in J. H. M. Laslett and S. M. Lipset (eds), *Failure of a Dream?*, New York, Anchor, pp. 200–32.

LASLETT, J. H. M. and LIPSET, S. M. (eds) (1974), *Failure of a Dream?*, New York, Anchor.

LAWRENCE, P. (1980), *Managers and Management in West Germany*, London, Croom Helm.

LEHMBRUCH, G. (1979), 'Liberal corporatism and party government', in P. C. Schmitter and G. Lehmbruch (eds), *Trends Toward Corporatist Intermediation*, London, Sage, pp. 147–83.

LENSKI, G. (1966), *Power and Privilege*, New York, McGraw-Hill.

LESTER, R. A. (1958), *As Unions Mature*, Princeton, New Jersey, Princeton University Press.

LEVINE, S. B. (1958), *Industrial Relations in Postwar Japan*, Urbana, University of Illinois Press.

LEVINE, S. B. and TAIRA, K. (1980), 'Interpreting industrial conflict: the case of Japan', in B. Martin and E. M. Kassalow (eds), *Labor Relations in Advanced Industrial Societies*, New York, Carnegie, pp. 61–88.

LEVINSON, H. M. (1951), *Unionism: Wage Trends and Income Distribution, 1914–1947*, Ann Arbor, Bureau of Business Research, University of Michigan.

LEWENHAK, S. (1977), *Women and Trade Unionism*, London, Benn.

LEWIN, D., and FEUILLE, P. (1983), 'Behavioral research in industrial relations', *Industrial and Labor Relations Review*, 36, pp. 341–60.

LEWIN, D., FEUILLE, P. and KOCHAN, T. A. (1977), *Public Sector Labor Relations*, New York, Horton.

LEWIS, H. G. (1959), 'Competitive and monopoly unionism', in P. D. Bradley (ed.), *The Public Stake in Union Power*, Charlottesville, University of Virginia Press, pp. 181–208.

LEWIS, H. G. (1963), *Unionism and Relative Wages in the United States*, Chicago, University of Chicago Press.

LIN, FU-SHUN (1966), *Chinese Law: Past and Present*, New York, Columbia University, East Asian Institute.

LINZ, J. J. (1981), 'A century of politics and interests in Spain', in S. Berger, A. Hirschman and C. Maier (eds), *Organizing Interests in Western Europe*, Cambridge, Cambridge University Press, pp. 367–415.

LIPSET, S. M. (1961), 'Trade unions and social structure I', *Industrial Relations*, I, pp. 75–89.

LIPSET, S. M. (1962), 'Trade unions and social structure: II', *Industrial Relations*, I, pp. 89–110.

LIPSET, S. M. (1971), *Agrarian Socialism*, revised edition, Berkeley and Los Angeles, University of California Press.

LITTERER, J. A. (ed.) (1980), *Organizations – Structure and Behavior*, New York, Wiley.

LITTLER, C. (1982), 'Deskilling and changing structures of control', in S. Wood (ed.), *The Degradation of Work*, London, Hutchinson, pp. 122–45.

LITTLER, C. and LOCKETT, M. (1983), 'The significance of trade unions in China', *Industrial Relations Journal*, 14, pp. 31–42.

LITTLER, C. and SALAMAN, G. (1982), 'Braverman and beyond: recent theories of the labour process', *Sociology*, 16, pp. 251–69.

LIVERNASH, E. R. (1962), 'The general problem of work rules', Proceedings of the Industrial Relations Association, Madison, Wisconsin, IRRA, pp. 1–10.

LOCKWOOD, D. (1958), *The Blackcoated Worker*, London, Allen & Unwin.

LOCKWOOD, D. (1966), 'Sources of variation in working class images of society', *Sociological Review*, 14, pp. 249–67.

LORWIN, V. R. (1954), *The French Labor Movement*, Cambridge, Mass., Harvard University Press.

LOVERIDGE, R. (1983), 'Sources of diversity in internal labour markets', *Sociology*, 17, pp. 44–62.

LOVERIDGE, R. and MOK, A. L. (1979), *Theories of Labour Market Segmentation*, The Hague, Martinus Nijhoff.

LYDALL, H. (1968), *The Structure of Earnings*, Oxford, Clarendon Press.

MCAULEY, M. (1969), *Labour Disputes in Soviet Russia 1957–1965*, Oxford, Clarendon Press.

MCCARTHY, C. (1973), *The Decade of Upheaval*, Dublin, Institute of Public Administration.

MCCONNEL, C. R. (ed.) (1970), *Perspectives on Wage Determination*, New York, McGraw-Hill.

MacDONALD, O. (ed.) (1981), *The Polish August*, San Francisco, Ztangi Press.

MacKENZIE, G. (1977), 'The political economy of the American working class', *British Journal of Sociology*, 28, pp. 244–52.

MCKERSIE, R. B. and HUNTER, L. (1973), *Pay, Productivity and Collective Bargaining*, London, Macmillan.

MAGENAU, J. M. and PRUITT, D. G. (1979), 'The social psychology of bargaining', in M. Stephenson and C. J. Brotherton (eds), *Industrial Relations: A Social Psychological Approach*, London, Wiley, pp. 181–210.

MAITLAND, I. (1983), *The Causes of Industrial Disorder*, London, Routledge & Kegan Paul.

MALLES, P. (1973), *The Institutions of Industrial Relations in Continental Europe*, Ottawa, Labour Canada, Research and Development.

MALLET, S. (1975), *The New Working Class*, Nottingham, Spokesman.

MALLET, S. (1978), Comments in 'Preface', C. Crouch and A. Pizzorno (eds), *The Resurgence of Class Conflict in Western Europe Since 1978*, vol. 1, London, Macmillan.

MALLOY, J. M. (ed.) (1977), *Authoritarianism and Corporatism in Latin America*, Pittsburg, University of Pittsburg Press.

MANSFIELD, R. (1980), 'The management task', in M. J. F. Poole and R. Mansfield (eds), *Managerial Roles in Industrial Relations*, Farnborough, Gower, pp. 1–11.

MANSFIELD, R. and POOLE, M. J. F. (eds) (1981), *International Perspectives on Management and Organization*, Aldershot, Gower.

MARSDEN, D. (1981), 'Vive la difference: pay differentials in Britain, West Germany, France and Italy', *Employment Gazette*, 89, pp. 309–18.

MARSHALL, A. (1920), *Principles of Economics*, London, Macmillan.

MARTIN, B. and KASSALOW, E. M. (eds) (1980), *Labor Relations in Advanced Industrial Societies: Issues and Problems*, Washington, Carnegie.

MARTIN, J. (1982), 'The fairness of earnings differentials: an experimental study of the perceptions of blue-collar workers', *Journal of Human Resources*, 17, pp. 110–23.

MARTIN, R. (1968), 'Union democracy: an explanatory framework', *Sociology*, 2, pp. 205–20.

MARTIN, R. (1978), 'The effects of recent changes in industrial conflict on the internal politics of trade unions', in C. J. Crouch and A. Pizzorno (eds), *The Resurgence of Class Conflict in Western Europe since 1978*, vol. 2, London, Macmillan, pp. 101–26.

MARTIN, R. (1981), *New Technology and Industrial Relations in Fleet Street*, Oxford, Clarendon Press.

MARX, K. (1963), *The Poverty of Philosophy*, New York, International Publications.

MARX, K. (1974), *Capital*, London, Lawrence & Wishart.

MATHUR, A. S. (1968), *Labour Policy and Industrial Relations in India*, Agra-3, Ram Prasad.

MAURICE, M. (1979), 'For a study of "the societal effect": universality and specificity in organization research', in C. J. Lammers and D. J. Hickson (eds), *Organizations Alike and Unlike*, London, Routledge & Kegan Paul, pp. 42–60.

MAURICE, M. and SELLIER, F. (1979), 'Societal analysis of industrial relations: a comparison between France and West Germany', *British Journal of Industrial Relations*, 17, pp. 322–36.

MAXWELL, N. (ed.) (1979), *China's Road to Development*, Oxford, Pergamon Press.

MAYO, E. (1949), *The Social Problems of an Industrial Civilization*, London, Routledge & Kegan Paul.

MEIER, E. L. (1976), *Ageing in America: Implications for Employment*, Washington, NCOA-Harris.

MEMBER PARTICIPATION IN INDUSTRIAL ORGANIZATIONS (MPIO) (1980), paper presented by P. A. Clark, Participation Symposium, Inter-University Centre, Dubrovnik.

MESA-LAGO, C. and BECK, C. (eds) (1975), *Comparative Socialist Systems*, Pittsburg, University of Pittsburg, Center for International Studies.

MEYER, A. D., SNOW, C. C. and MILES, R. E. (1982), 'Teaching organization theory', in R. D. Freedman, C. L. Cooper and S. A. Stumpf (eds), *Management Education*, Chichester, Wiley, pp. 175–209.

MEYERS, F. (1967), 'The study of foreign labor and industrial relations' in S. Barkin, W. Dymond, E. M. Kassalow, F. Meyers and C. A. Myers (eds), *International Labor*, New York, Harper & Row, pp. 15–30.

MICHIGAN INTERNATIONAL LABOR STUDIES (1968), *Labor Relations and the Law in the United Kingdom and United States*, Ann Arbor, University of Michigan.

MILES, R. E. and SNOW, C. C. (1978), *Organization Strategy, Structure and Process*, New York, McGraw-Hill.

MILLS, D. Q. (1982), *Labor-Management Relations*, 2nd edition, New York, McGraw-Hill.

MONTESQUIEU, CHARLES DE SECONDAT, BARON DE (1977), *The Spirit of Laws*, Berkeley and Los Angeles, University of California Press.

MONTGOMERY, D. (1979), *Workers' Control in America*, Cambridge, Cambridge University Press.

MORLEY, I. E. and STEPHENSON, G. M. (1977), *The Social Psychology of Bargaining*, London, Allen & Unwin.

MORRIS, J. O. and CORDOVA, C. (1962), *Bibliography of Industrial Relations in Latin America*, Ithaca, New York State School of Industrial and Labor Relations, Cornell University.

MUELLER, G. H. (1979), 'Rationality in the work of Max Weber', *European Journal of Sociology*, 20, pp. 149–71.

MULVEY, C. (1976), 'Collective agreements and relative earnings in UK manufacturing in 1973', *Economica*, 43, pp. 419–27.

MULVEY, C. and FOSTER, J. I. (1976), 'Occupational earnings in the UK and the effects of collective agreements', *Manchester School of Economic and Social Studies*, 44, pp. 258–75.

MUNNS, V. G. and MCCARTHY, W. E. J. (1967), *Employers' Associations*, Royal Commission on Trade Unions and Employers' Associations, Research Paper 7, London, HMSO.

MYERS, C. A. (1951), *Industrial Relations in Sweden*, Cambridge, Mass., MIT Press.

MYERS, C. A. (1958), *Labor Problems in the Industrialization of India*, Cambridge, Mass., Harvard University Press.

MYERS, C. A. and KANNAPPAN, S. (1970), *Industrial Relations in India*, New York, Asia Publishing House.

MYERS, M. S. (1976), *Managing Without Unions*, London, Addison-Wesley.

MYERS, R. M. (1980), *The Chinese Economy: Past and Present*, Belmont, California, Wadsworth.

NAVILLE, P. (1961), *L'Automation et le travail humain*, Paris, Centre National de la Recherche Scientifique.

NEGANDHI, A. R. (1974), 'Cross-cultural management studies: too many conclusions, not enough conceptualization', *Management International Review*, 14, 59–67.

NELSON, D. N. (1981), 'Worker-party conflict in Romania', *Problems of Communism*, 30, pp. 40–9.

NELSON, D. and WHITE, S. (1982), *Communist Legislatures in Comparative Perspective*, London, Macmillan.

NEUBERGER, E. and DUFFY, W. (1976), *Comparative Economic Systems*, Boston, Allyn & Bacon.

NEUFELD, M. F. (1960), 'The inevitability of political unionism in underdeveloped countries: Italy, the exemplar', *Industrial and Labor Relations Review*, 13, pp. 365–86.

NG, SEK-HONG (1984), 'One brand of workplace democracy: the workers' congress in the Chinese enterprise', *Journal of Industrial Relations*, 26, pp. 56–75.

NICHOLS, T. (1969), *Ownership, Control and Ideology*, London, Allen & Unwin.

NICHOLS, T. (1977), 'Labor and monopoly capital', *Sociological Review*, 25, pp. 192–4.

NICKELL, S. J. (1977), 'Trade unions and the position of women in the industrial wage structure', *British Journal of Industrial Relations*, 15, pp. 192–210.

NIGHTINGALE, D. (1974), 'Confict and conflict resolution', in G. Strauss, R. E. Miles and C. C. Snow (eds), *Organizational Behaviour, Research and Issues*, Madison, Wisconsin, Industrial Relations Research Association.

NOBLE, D. F. (1979), 'Social choice in machine design: the case of automatically controlled machine tools', in A. Zimbalist (ed.), *Case Studies on the Labour Process*, London, Monthly Review Press.

OAKESHOTT, R. (1978), *The Case for Workers' Co-ops*, London, Routledge & Kegan Paul.

ODAKA, K. (1975), *Towards Industrial Democracy*, Cambridge, Mass, Harvard University Press.

O'DAY, S. (1981), *The Political, Economic and Labor Climate in Brazil – 1981 Supplement*, Philadelphia, Wharton School.

OFFE, C. (1975), 'The theory of the capitalist state and the problem of policy formation', in R. Alford, C. Crouch and C. Offe (eds), *Stress and Contradiction in Modern Capitalism*, Lexington, Mass., Heath.

OKOCHI, K., KARSH, B. and LEVINE, S. B. (eds) (1974), *Workers and Employers in Japan*, Tokyo, Tokyo University Press.

ORGANIZATION FOR ECONOMIC COOPERATION AND DEVELOPMENT (1977), *The Development of Industrial Relations Systems: Some Implications of Japanese Experience*, Paris, OECD.

ORGANIZATION FOR ECONOMIC COOPERATION AND DEVELOPMENT (1979), *Collective Bargaining and Government Policies*, Paris, OECD.

ORGANIZATION FOR ECONOMIC COOPERATION AND DEVELOPMENT (1981), *Microelectronics, Productivity and Employment*, Paris, OECD.

O'TOOLE, J. (1977), *Work, Learning and the American Future*, San Francisco, Jossey-Bass.

OWEN SMITH, E. (ed.) (1981), *Trade Unions in the Developed Economies*, London, Croom Helm.

PANITCH, L. (1980), 'Recent theorizations of corporatism: reflections on a growth industry', *British Journal of Sociology*, 31, pp. 159–87.

PARKIN, F. (1971), *Class, Inequality and the Social Order*, London, MacGibbon & Kee.

PARKIN, F. (1979), *Marxism and Class Theory*, London, Tavistock.

PARSLEY, C. J. (1980), 'Labor union effects on wages gains and wages: a survey of recent literature', *Journal of Economic Literature*, 18, pp. 1–31.

PARSONS, T. (1951), *The Social System*, Glencoe, Illinois, Free Press.

PAUKERT, F. et al., (1981), *Income Distribution, Structure of the Economy and Employment*, London, Croom Helm.

PEEL, J. (1979), *The Real Power Game*, London, McGraw-Hill.

PENCAVEL, J. H. (1974), 'Relative wages and trade unions in the United Kingdom', *Economica*, 41, pp. 194–210.

PENCAVEL, J. H. (1977), 'The distributional and efficiency effects of trade unions in Great Britain', *British Journal of Industrial Relations*, 15, pp. 137–56.

PERLMAN, S. (1928), *A Theory of the Labor Movement*, New York, Kelley.

PERSKY, S. and FLAM, H. (1982), *The Solidarity Sourcebook*, Vancouver, New Star Books.

PERSONICK, M. E. (1974), 'Union and non union pay patterns in construction', *Monthly Labor Review*, 97, pp. 71–5.

PETERSON, R. B. and TRACY, L. (1977), 'Testing a behavioral theory model of labor negotiations', *Industrial Relations*, 16, pp. 35–50.

PETTENGILL, J. S. (1980), *Labour Unions and the Inequality of Earned Income*, Amsterdam, North-Holland.

PFEFFER, J. and ROSS, J. (1981), 'Unionization and income inequality', *Industrial Relations*, 20, pp. 271–85.

PHELPS, E. S. (1972), *Inflation Policy and Unemployment Theory*, London, Macmillan.

PHELPS BROWN, H. (1977), *The Inequality of Pay*, Oxford, Oxford University Press.

PIORE, M. J. (1979), *Birds of Passage*, Cambridge, Cambridge University Press.

PIZZORNO, A. (1978a), 'Political exchange and collective identity in industrial conflict', in C. J. Crouch and A. Pizzorno (eds), *The Resurgence of Class Conflict in Western Europe Since 1968*, vol. 2, London, Macmillan, pp. 277–98.

PIZZORNO, A. (1978b), 'Preface' in C. Crouch and A. Pizzorno (eds), *The Resurgence of Class Conflict in Western Europe Since 1968*, vol. 1, London, Macmillan.

PLOWMAN, D., DEERY, S. J. and FISHER, C. H. (1980), *Australian Industrial Relations*, revised edition, Sydney, McGraw-Hill.

POLLARD, S. (1965), *The Genesis of Modern Management*, London, Edward Arnold.

POOLE, K. E. (1951), *Fiscal Policies and the American Economy*, New York, Prentice-Hall.

POOLE, M. J. F. (1974), 'Towards a sociology of shop stewards', *Sociological Review*, 22, pp. 57–82.

POOLE, M. J. F. (1975), 'Ideas, institutions and economic development', *Sociological Analysis and Theory*, 5, pp. 331–57.

POOLE, M. J. F. (1976), 'A power analysis of workplace labour relations', *Industrial Relations Journal*, 5, pp. 331–57.

POOLE, M. J. F. (1978), *Workers' Participation in Industry*, revised edition, London, Routledge & Kegan Paul.

POOLE, M. J. F. (1979), 'Industrial democracy: a comparative analysis', *Industrial Relations*, 18, pp. 262–72.

POOLE, M. J. F. (1980), 'Managerial strategies and industrial relations', in M. Poole and R. Mansfield (eds), *Managerial Roles in Industrial Relations*, Farnborough, Gower, pp. 38–49.

POOLE, M. J. F. (1981), 'Industrial democracy in comparative perspective', in R. Mansfield and M. J. F. Poole (eds), *International Perspectives on Management and Organization*, Aldershot, Gower, pp. 23–38.

POOLE, M. J. F. (1982a), 'Personnel management in Third World countries', *Personnel Review*, 11 (4), pp. 37–43.

POOLE, M. J. F. (1982b), 'Theories of industrial democracy: the emerging synthesis', *Sociological Review*, 30, pp. 181–207.

POOLE, M. J. F. (1984), *Theories of Trade Unionism*, revised edition, London, Routledge & Kegan Paul.

POOLE, M. J. F. (1985), 'Participation through representation: a review of constraints and conflicting pressures', in R. Stern (ed.), *International Yearbook of Organizational Democracy*, Chichester, Wiley.

POOLE, M. J. F., BROWN, W., RUBERY, J., SISSON, K., TARLING, R. and

WILKINSON, F. (1984), *Industrial Relations in the Future*, London, Routledge & Kegan Paul.

POOLE, M. J. F., MANSFIELD, R., BLYTON, P. R. and FROST, P.E. (1981), *Managers in Focus*, Aldershot, Gower.

POOLE, M. J. F., MANSFIELD, R., BLYTON, P. R. and FROST, P. E. (1982), 'Managerial attitudes and behaviour in industrial relations: evidence from a national survey', *British Journal of Industrial Relations*. 20, pp. 285–307.

PORKET, J. L. (1978), 'Industrial relations and participation in management in the Soviet-type communist system', *British Journal of Industrial Relations*, 16, pp. 70–85.

POULANTZAS, N. (1975), *Classes in Contemporary Capitalism*, London, New Left Books.

PRANDY, K. (1965), *Professional Employees*, London, Faber & Faber.

PRAVDA, A. (1979), 'Spontaneous workers' activities in the Soviet Union', in A. Kahan and B. A. Ruble (eds), *Industrial Labor in the USSR*, New York, Pergamon, pp. 333–66.

PRICE, R. and BAIN, G. S. (1976), 'Union growth revisited: 1948–1974 in perspective', *British Journal of Industrial Relations*, 14, pp. 339–55.

PRICE, R. and BAIN, G. S. (1983), 'Union growth in Britain: retrospect and prospect', *British Journal of Industrial Relations*, 21, pp. 46–68.

PRUITT, D. G. (1981), *Negotiation Behaviour*, New York, Academic Press.

PRUITT, D. G. and KIMMEL, M. (1977), 'Twenty years of experimental gaming', *Annual Review of Psychology*, 28, pp. 363–92.

PRYOR, F. L. (1968), *Public Expenditures in Communist and Capitalist Nations*, Homewood, Illinois, Irwin.

PUGH, D. S., HICKSON, D. J., HININGS, C. R. and TURNER, C. (1968), 'Dimensions of organization structure', *Administrative Science Quarterly*, 13, pp. 65–105.

PURCELL, J. (1983), 'The management of industrial relations in the modern corporation: agenda for research', *British Journal of Industrial Relations*, 21, pp. 1–16.

PURCELL, J. and SISSON, K. (1983), 'Strategies and practice in the management of industrial relations', in G. S. Bain (ed.), *Industrial Relations in Britain*, Oxford, Blackwell, pp. 95–120.

RABKIN, L. Y. and SPIRO, M. E. (1970), 'Postscript: the kibbutz in 1970', in M. E. Spiro (ed.), *Kibbutz, Venture in Utopia*, New York, Schocken.

RAMSAY, H. (1977), 'Cycles of control', *Sociology*, 11, pp. 481–506.

RAMSAY, H. (1983), 'Evolution or cycle? Worker participation in the 1970s and 1980s', in C. Crouch and F. A. Heller (eds), *International Yearbook of Organizational Democracy*, vol. 1, Chichester, Wiley, pp. 203–25.

RAZA, M. A. (1963), *The Industrial Relations System of Pakistan*, Karachi, Bureau of Labour.

REES, A. (1970), 'The effects of unions on resources allocation', in C. R. McConnell (ed.), *Perspectives on Wage Determination*, New York, McGraw-Hill, pp. 226–33.

REYNAUD, J. D. (1980), 'Industrial relations and political systems: some reflections on the crisis in industrial relations in western Europe', *British Journal of Industrial Relations*, 18, pp. 1–13.

RICHARDS, V. and WILLIAMS, A. N. (1982), 'Institutional and economic aspects of the Jamaican sugar cooperatives', in D. C. Jones and J. Svejnar (eds), *Participatory and Self-Managed Firms*, Lexington, Mass., Heath, pp. 299–312.

RIDDELL, D. S. (1968), 'Social self government: the background of theory and practice in Yugoslav socialism', *British Journal of Sociology*, 19, pp. 47–75.

ROBERTS, B. C. (1964), *Labour in the Tropical Territories of the Commonwealth*, London, Bell.

ROBERTS, K. H. (1970), 'On looking at an elephant: an evaluation of cross-cultural research related to organizations', *Psychological Bulletin*, 74, pp. 327–50.

ROBERTS, K. H. and BOYACILLIGER, N. (1983), 'A survey of cross-national organizational researches', *Organization Studies*, 4, pp. 379–86.

ROBERTS, K. H., HULIN, C. L. and ROUSSEAU, D. M. (1978), *Developing an Interdisciplinary Science of Organizations*, San Francisco, Jossey-Bass,

ROBINSON D. (1979), 'The development of collective bargaining in relation to national economic, employment and related policies', in Organization for Economic Cooperation and Development, *Collective Bargaining and Government Policies*, Paris, OECD, pp. 111–25.

ROBINSON, S. (1976), 'A note on the U-hypothesis relating to income inequality and economic development', *American Economic Review*, 63, pp. 50–72.

ROKKAN, S. (1970), *Citizens, Elections, Parties: Approaches to the Comparative Study of the Process of Political Development*, Oslo, Universitetsforlaget.

ROSE, M. (1977), *French Industrial Studies*, Farnborough, Saxon House.

ROSE, M. (1979), *Servants of Post-Industrial Power*, New York, Sharpe.

ROSENBERG, W. G. and YOUNG, M. B. (1982), *Transforming Russia and China*, New York, Oxford University Press.

ROSNER, M., KAVCIC, B., TANNENBAUM, A. S., VIANELLO, M. and WEISER, G., (1973), 'Worker participation and influence in five countries', *Industrial Relations*, 12, pp. 200–12.

ROSS, A. M. (1966), *Labor Law and Practice in India*, Washington, United States Department of Labor.

ROSS, A. M. and GOLDNER, W. (1950), 'Forces affecting the inter-industry wage structure', *Quarterly Journal of Economics*, 64, pp. 254–81.

ROSS, A. M. and HARTMAN, P. T. (1960), *Changing Patterns of Industrial Conflict*, New York, Wiley.

ROSS, A. M. and IRWIN, D. (1951), 'Strike experience in five countries', 1927–1947: an interpretation', *Industrial and Labor Relations Review*,' 4, pp. 323–42.

ROSOW, J. M. (1979), 'Quality-of-work-issues for the 1980's', in C. Kerr and J. M. Rosow (eds), *Work in America: The Decade Ahead*, New York, Van Nostrand Reinhold, pp. 157–87.

ROTHENBERG, I. H. and SILVERMAN, S. B. (1973), *Labor Unions, How to Avert Them, Beat Them, Out-Negotiate Them, Live with Them, Unload Them*, Elkins Park, Pa., Management Relations.

ROUTH, G. (1980), *Occupation and Pay in Great Britain 1906–79*, London, Macmillan.

ROYAL COMMISSION ON THE DISTRIBUTION OF INCOME AND WEALTH (1975), *Initial Report on the Standing Reference*, Report No. 1, London, HMSO.

RUBIN, J. Z. and BROWN, B. R. (1975), *The Social Psychology of Bargaining and Negotiation*, New York, Academic Press.

RUBLE, B. A. (1979), 'Factory unions and workers' rights', in A. Kahan and B. A. Ruble (eds), *Industrial Labor in the USSR*, New York, Pergamon, pp. 59–84.

RUBLE, B. A. (1981), *Soviet Trade Unions*, Cambridge, Cambridge University Press.

RUNCIMAN, W. G. (1966), *Relative Deprivation and Social Justice*, London, Routledge & Kegan Paul.

RYBICKI, Z., BLAZEJCZYK, M., KOWALIK, A., TRZECIAK, M. and WACLAWEK, J. (1978), *Workers' Participation in Management in Poland*, Geneva, International Institute for Labour Studies.

RUS, V. (1970), 'Influence structure in Yugoslav enterprises', *Industrial Relations*, 9, pp. 148–60.

RYSCAVAGE, P. M. (1974), 'Measuring union-non union earnings differences', *Monthly Labor Review*, 97, pp. 3–9.

SAHAY, A. (1973), *Sociological Analysis*, London, Routledge & Kegan Paul.

SAUNDERS, C. and MARSDEN, D. (1979), *A Six-Country Comparison of the Distribution of Industrial Earnings in the 1970s*, London, HMSO.

SAUNDERS, C. and MARSDEN, D. (1981), *Pay Inequalities in the European Community*, London, Butterworth.

SAWYER, M. (1976), *Income Distribution in OECD Countries*, Paris, OECD.

SCHELLING, T. (1960), *The Strategy of Conflict*, Cambridge, Mass., Harvard University Press.

SCHLAGHECK, J. L. (1977), *The Political, Economic and Labor Climate in Mexico*, Philadelphia, Wharton School.

SCHMENNER, R. W. (1973), 'The determination of municipal employee wages', *Review of Economics and Statistics*, 55, pp. 83–90.

SCHMITTER, P. C. (1974), 'Still the century of corporatism?', *The Review of Politics*, 36, pp. 85–131.

SCHMITTER, P. C. and LEHMBRUCH, G. (1979), *Trends Towards Corporatist Intermediation*, London, Sage.

SCHMITTER, P. C. (1981), 'Interest intermediation and regime governability in contemporary Western Europe and North America', in S. Berger, A. Hirschman and C. Maier (eds), *Organizing Interests in Western Europe*, Cambridge, Cambridge University Press, pp. 287–327.

SCHREGLE, J. (1978), 'Co-determination in the Federal Republic of Germany', *International Labour Review*, 117, pp. 81–98.

SCHREGLE, J. (1981), 'Comparative industrial relations: pitfalls and potential', *International Labour Review*, 120, pp. 15–30.

SCHREGLE, J. (1982), *Negotiating Development: Labour Relations in Southern Asia*, Geneva, International Labour Office.

SCHUMPETER, J. (1943), *Capitalism, Socialism and Democracy*, London, Allen & Unwin.

SCITOVSKY, T. (1966), 'An international comparison of the trend of professional earnings', *American Economic Review*, 57, pp. 25–42.

SCOVILLE, J. G. (1982), 'A review of international and comparative research in the 1970s', in T. A. Kochan, D. J. B. Mitchell and L. Dyer (eds), *Industrial Relations Research in the 1970's: Review and Appraisal*, Madison, Wisconsin, Industrial Relations Research Association.

SELOWSKY, M. (1981), 'Income distribution, basic needs and trade-offs with growth: the case of semi-industrialized Latin American countries', *World Development*, 9, pp. 73–92.

SHABON, A. (1981), *The Political, Economic and Labor Climate in the Countries of the Arabian Peninsula*, Philadelphia, Wharton School.

SHALEV, M. (1978a), 'Lies, damned lies and strike statistics: the measurement of trends in industrial conflict', in C. Crouch and A. Pizzorno (eds), *The Resurgence of Class Conflict in Western Europe Since 1968*, vol. 1, London, Macmillan, pp. 1–19.

SHALEV, M. (1978b), 'Problems of strike measurement', in C. Crouch and A. Pizzorno (eds), *The Resurgence of Class Conflict in Western Europe Since 1968*, vol. 1, London, Macmillan, pp. 321–34.

SHALEV, M. (1978c), 'Strikers and the state: a comment', *British Journal of Political Science*, 8, pp. 479–92.

SHALEV, M. (1980), 'Industrial relations theory and the comparative study of industrial relations and industrial conflict', *British Journal of Industrial Relations*, 18, pp. 26–43.

SHALEV, M. (1983a), 'Class politics and the western welfare state', in S. E. Spiro and E. Yuchtman-Yaar, *Evaluating the Welfare State*, New York, Academic Press, pp. 27–49.

SHALEV, M. (1983b), 'Strikes and the crisis', *Economic and Industrial Democracy*, 4, pp. 417–60.

SHINODA, Y. (1967), *Japan's Management Associations*, Tokyo, Sophia University, Socio-Economic Institute, Industrial Relations Section.

SHIROM, A. (1984), 'Employers' associations in Israel', in J. P. Windmuller and A. Gladstone (eds), *Employers' Associations and Industrial Relations*, Oxford, Clarendon Press, pp. 294–317.

SHISTER, J. (1953), 'The logic of union growth', *Journal of Political Economy*, 61, pp. 413–33.

SHONFIELD, A. (1965), *Modern Capitalism*, New York, Oxford University Press.

SHORTER, E. and TILLY, C. (1974), *Strikes in France 1830–1968*, Cambridge, Cambridge University Press.

SILVESTRE, J. J. (1974), 'Industrial wage differentials: a two-country comparison', *International Labour Review*, 110, pp. 495–514.

SILVESTRE, J. J. (1979), 'Comment on Dodge's paper', in Organization for Economic Cooperation and Development, *Collective Bargaining and Government Policies*, Paris, OECD, pp. 181–86.

SINFIELD, R. (1981), *What Unemployment Means*, Oxford, Martin Robertson.

SINGER, D. (1982), *The Road to Gdansk*, New York, Monthly Review Press.

SINGH, R. (1976), 'System theory in the study of industrial relations: time for a reappraisal?', *Industrial Relations Journal*, 7, pp. 59–71.

SINGH, R. (1978), 'Theory and practice in industrial relations', *Industrial Relations Journal*, 9, pp. 57–64.

SINGH, V. B. and SARAN, A. K. (eds) (1960), *Industrial Labour in India*, London, Asia Publishing House.

SIRIANNI, C. (1982), *Workers' Control and Socialist Democracy*, London, New Left Books.

SISSON, K. (1985), *The Management of Collective Bargaining*, Oxford, Blackwell.

SKOGH, G. (1984), 'Employers' associations in Sweden', in J. P. Windmuller and A. Gladstone (eds), *Employers' Associations and Industrial Relations*, Oxford, Clarendon Press, pp. 149–68.

SLICHTER, S. (1941), *Union Policies and Industrial Management*, Washington DC, Brookings.

SLICHTER, S. (1952), 'Wage policies since World War II', *The Commercial and Financial Chronicle*, 4 December.

SLICHTER, S., HEALY, J. J. and LIVERNASH, E. R. (1960), *The Impact of Collective Bargaining on Management*, Washington DC, Brookings.

SMITH, J. S. (1981), 'Implications of developments in micro-electronics technology on women in the paid workforce', in Organization for Economic Cooperation and Development, *Micro-electronics, Productivity and Employment*, Paris, OECD, pp. 240–55.

SNYDER, D. (1975), 'Institutional setting and industrial conflict', *American Sociological Review*, 40, pp. 259–78.

SNYDER, D. (1977), 'Early North American strikes: a reinterpretation', *Industrial and Labor Relations Review*, 30, pp. 325–41.

SOMBART, W. (1906), *Why is There no Socialism in the United States?*, Tübingen, Mohr.

SOMERS, G. G. (ed.) (1969), *Essays in Industrial Relations Theory*, Ames, Iowa State University Press.

SORGE, A. (1976), 'The evolution of industrial democracy in the countries of the European Community', *British Journal of Industrial Relations*, 14, pp. 318–33.

SORGE, A. (1977), 'The cultural context of organization structure: administrative rationality, constraints and choice', in M. Warner (ed.), *Organizational Choice and Constraint*, Farnborough, Saxon House, pp. 57–78.

SORGE, A. and WARNER, M. (1980), 'Manpower training, manufacturing organization and workplace relations in Great Britain and West Germany', *British Journal of Industrial Relations*, 18, pp. 318–33.

SORGE, A., HARTMANN, G., WARNER, M. and NICHOLAS, I. (1983), *Microelectronics and Manpower in Manufacturing*, Aldershot, Gower.

SOSKICE, D. (1978), 'Strike waves and wage explosions, 1968–1970: an economic interpretation', in C. Crouch and A. Pizzorno (eds), *The Resurgence of Class Conflict in Western Europe Since 1968*, vol. 2, London, Macmillan, pp. 221–46.

STAFFORD, F. P. (1968), 'Concentration and labor earnings: a comment', *American Economic Review*, 58, pp. 174–81.

STAGNER, R. C. (1956), *Psychology of Industrial Conflict*, New York, Wiley.

STAGNER, R. C. (1957), *Union-Management Relations in Italy: Some Observations*, Reprint no. 49, University of Illinois Institute of Labor and Industrial Relations.

STAGNER, R. C. and ROSEN, H. (1965), *Psychology of Union-Management Relations*, Monterey, California, Brooks/Cole.

STEPAN, A. (1978), *The State and Society*, Princeton, New Jersey, Princeton University Press.

STEPHEN, F. M. (ed.) (1982), *The Performance of Labor-Managed Firms*, New York, St Martin's Press.

STEPHENS, J. (1979), *The Transition to Socialism*, London, Macmillan.

STEPHENSON, G. M. and BROTHERTON, C. J. (eds) (1979), *Industrial Relations: A Social Psychological Approach*, Chichester, Wiley.

STERN, R. N. (1978), 'Methodological issues in quantitative strike analysis', *Industrial Relations*, 17, pp. 32–42.

STEVENS, C. M. (1963), *Strategy and Collective Bargaining Negotiation*, New York, McGraw-Hill.

STEWART, F. (ed.), (1983), *Work, Income and Inequality: Payment Systems in the Third World*, London, Macmillan.

STEWART, M. (1976), *Determinants of Earnings: Estimates from the General Household Survey*, mimeo, Centre for Economics of Education, London School of Economics.

STOREY, J. (1983), *Managerial Prerogative and the Question of Control*, London, Routledge & Kegan Paul.

STOUFFER, S. A., LUMSDAINE, A. A., LUMSDAINE, M. H., WILLIAMS, R. M. J., SMITH, M. B., JANIS, I. L., STAR, S. A. and COTTRELL, L. S., JR. (1949), *The American Soldier*, Princeton, New Jersey, Princeton University Press.

STRAUSS, G. (1977), 'Union government in the US: research past and future', *Industrial Relations*, 16, pp. 215–42.

STRAUSS, G. (1979), 'Social psychology and industrial relations, perspectives and suggestions', in G. M. Stephenson and C. J. Brotherton (eds), *Industrial Relations: A Social Psychological Approach*, London, Wiley, pp. 365–97.

STRAUSS, G. (1980), *Quality of Worklife and Participation as Bargaining Issues*, Reprint no. 434, Institute of Industrial Relations, University of California, Berkeley.

STRAUSS, G. (1982), *Bridging the Gap Between Industrial Relations and Conflict Management: An Introduction*, Reprint no. 449, Institute of Industrial Relations, University of California, Berkeley.

STRAUSS, G. (1984), 'Industrial relations: time for change', *Industrial Relations*, 23, pp. 1–15.

STREECK, W. (1984), *Industrial Relations in West Germany*, London, Heinemann.

STRINATI, D. (1979), 'Capitalism, the state and industrial relations', in C. Crouch (ed.), *State and Economy in Contemporary Capitalism*, New York, St Martin's Press, pp. 191–236.

STRINATI, D. (1982), *'Capitalism, the State and Industrial Relations*, London, Croom Helm.

STURMTHAL, A. F. (1951), 'Comments on Selig Perlman', *Industrial and Labor Relations Review*, 14, pp. 483–96.

STURMTHAL, A. F. (1957), *Contemporary Collective Bargaining in Seven Countries*, Ithaca, New York, Cornell University Press.

STURMTHAL, A. F. (1972), *Comparative Labor Movements*, Belmont, California, Wadsworth.

STURMTHAL, A. F. and SCOVILLE, J. G. (eds) (1973), *The International Labor Movement in Transition*, Urbana, University of Illinois Press.

SUMIYA, M. (1977), 'Japanese industrial relations revisited: a discussion of the *Nenko* system', *Japanese Economic Studies*, 5, pp. 3–65.

SUMIYA, M. (1981), 'The Japanese system of industrial relations', in P. B. Doeringer (ed.), *Industrial Relations in International Perspective*, London, Macmillan, pp. 287–323.

SWEDISH EMPLOYERS' CONFEDERATION (1950), *Constitution of the Swedish Employers' Confederation*, Stockholm, Swedish Employers' Confederation.

SWEDISH EMPLOYERS' CONFEDERATION (1974), *Agreement on Rationalisation Between the Swedish Employers' Confederation (SAF) and the Swedish Confederation of Trade Unions (LO)*, Stockholm, Swedish Employers' Confederation.

TAJFEL, H. (1981), *Human Groups and Social Categories*, Cambridge, Cambridge University Press.

TANNENBAUM, A. (ed.) (1968), *Control in Organizations*, New York, McGraw-Hill.

TANNENBAUM, A., KAVCIC, B., ROSNER, M., VIANELLO, M. and WEISER, G. (1974), *Hierarchy in Organizations*, San Francisco, Jossey-Bass.

TEULINGS, A. W. M. (1984), 'The social cultural and political setting of industrial democracy', in B. Wilpert and A. Sorge (eds), *International Yearbook of Organizational Democracy*, vol. 2, Chichester, Wiley, pp. 233–56.

THOMAS, H. (1982), 'The performance of the Mondragon cooperatives in Spain', in D. C. Jones and J. Svejnar (eds), *Participatory and Self-Managed Firms*, Lexington, Mass., Heath, pp. 129–51.

THOMAS, H. and LOGAN, C. (1982), *Mondragon: An Economic Analysis*, London, Allen & Unwin.

THOMPSON, A. W. and HART, F. (1972), *The UCS Work-In*, London, Lawrence & Wishart.

THOMPSON, E. P. (1963), *The Making of the English Working Class*, Harmondsworth, Penguin.

THROOP, A. W. (1968), 'The union-non union wage differential and cost-push inflation', *American Economic Review*, 58, pp. 79–99.

THURLEY, K. E. and WOOD, S. J. (1983), 'Business strategy and industrial relations strategy', in K. E. Thurley and S. J. Wood (eds), *Industrial Relations and Management Strategy*, Cambridge, Cambridge University Press, pp. 197–224.

TORRINGTON, D. (ed.) (1978), *Comparative Industrial Relations in Europe*, Westport, Connecticut, Greenwood.

TOURAINE, A., DURAND, C., PECAUT, D. and WILLENER, A. (1965), *Workers' Attitudes to Technical Change*, Paris, Organization for Economic Cooperation and Development.

TREU, T. and MARTINELLI, A. (1984), 'Employers' associations in Italy', in J. P. Windmuller and A. Gladstone (eds), *Employers' Associations and Industrial Relations*, Oxford, Clarendon Press, pp. 264–93.

TRISKA, J. and GATI, C. (eds), *Blue-Collar Workers in Eastern Europe*, London, Allen & Unwin, 1981.

TUGENDHAT, C. (1971), *The Multinationals*, London, Eyre & Spottiswoode.

TURNER, H. A. (1962), *Trade Union Growth, Structure and Policy*, London, Allen & Unwin.

TURNER, H. A. (1969), *Is Britain Really Strike-Prone? A Review of the Incidence, Character and Costs of Industrial Conflict*, Occasional Paper no. 20, University of Cambridge, Department of Applied Economics.

TURNER, H. A. (1980), *The Last Colony: But Whose?* Cambridge, Cambridge University Press.

ULMAN, L. (1982), *Unions, Economists, Politicians, and Incomes Policy*, Reprint no. 444, Institute of Industrial Relations, University of California, Berkley.

ULMAN, L. (1982), *Unions, Economists, Politicians, and Incomes policy*, Reprint no. 444, Institute of Industrial Relations, University of California, Berkley,

UNDY, R. and MARTIN, R. (1984), *Ballots and Trade Union Democracy*, Oxford, Blackwell.

VALENTE, C. M. (1979), *The Political, Economic and Labor Climate in Venezuela*, Philadelphia, Wharton School.

VANEK, J. (1970), *The General Theory of Labor-Managed Market Economies*, Ithaca, New York, Cornell University Press.

VANEK, J. (1977), *The Labor-Managed Economy*, Ithaca, New York, Cornell University Press.

VENKATACHALAM, V. and SINGH, R. K. (1982), *The Political, Economic and Labor Climate in India*, Philadelphia, Wharton School.

VOORDEN, W. VAN (1984), 'Employers' associations in the Netherlands', in J. P. Windmuller and A. Gladstone (eds), *Employers' Associations and Industrial Relations*, Oxford, Clarendon Press, pp. 201–31.

WALKER, K. F. (1956), *Industrial Relations in Australia*, Cambridge, Mass., Harvard University Press.

WALKER, K. F. (1967a), 'The comparative study of industrial relations', *International Institute for Labour Studies, Bulletin no. 3*, pp. 105–32.

WALKER, K. F. (1967b), 'Strategic factors in industrial relations systems – a programme of international comparative studies', *International Institute for Labour Studies, Bulletin no. 6*, pp. 187–209.

WALKER, K. F. (1970), *Australian Industrial Relations Systems*, Cambridge, Mass., Harvard University Press.

WALKER, K. F. (1974), 'A neglected dimension in industrial relations theory – psychological factors', *International Conference on Industrial and Labor Relations*, pp. 436–49.

WALKER, K. F. (1977), 'Towards useful theorising about industrial relations', *British Journal of Industrial Relations*, 15, pp. 307–16.

WALKER, K. F. (1979), 'Psychological industrial relations: a general perspective', in G. M. Stephenson and C. J. Brotherton (eds), *Industrial Relations: A Social Psychological Approach*, Chichester, Wiley, pp. 5–32.

WALLERSTEIN, E. (1974), *The Modern World System*, New York, Academic Press.

WALTON, R. E. (1975), *Criteria for Quality of Working Life*, in L. E. Davis and A. B. Cherns (eds), *The Quality of Working Life*, vol. 1, London, Macmillan, pp. 91–104.

WALTON, R. E. and MCKERSIE, R. B. (1965), *A Behavioral Theory of Labour Negotiations*, New York, McGraw-Hill.

WARNER, M. (1981), 'British and American trade union organizational structures: convergence or divergence?', *Journal of General Management*, 6, pp. 63–77.

WEBB, S. and WEBB, B. (1897), *Industrial Democracy*, London, Longmans Green.

WEBB, S. and WEBB, B. (1902), *A History of Trade Unionism*, London, Longmans Green.

WEBER, M. (1930), *The Protestant Ethic and the Spirit of Capitalism*, London, Allen & Unwin.

WEBER, M. (1968), *Economy and Society*, New York, Bedminster Press.

WEDDERBURN, D. and CROMPTON, R. (1972), *Workers' Attitudes and Technology*, Cambridge, Cambridge University Press.

WEDDERBURN, K. W. and DAVIES, P. L. (1969), *Employment Grievances and Disputes Procedures in Britain*, Berkeley and Los Angeles, University of California Press.

WEDDERBURN, K. W., LEWIS, R. and CLARK, J. (1983), *Labour Law and Industrial Relations: Building on Kahn-Freund*, Oxford, Clarendon Press.

WEISS, L. W. (1966), 'Concentration and labor earnings', *American Economic Review*, 56, pp. 96–117.

WESCHLER, L. (1982), *Solidarity*, New York, Fireside.

WEYFORTH, W. O. (1917), *The Organizability of Labor*, Baltimore, Johns Hopkins Press.

WHEELER, C. (1975), *White-Collar Power*, Urbana, University of Illinois Press.

WHEELWRIGHT, E. L. and MCFARLANE, B. (1970), *The Chinese Road to Socialism*, New York, Monthly Review Press.

WIARDA, H. J. (1981), *Corporatism and National Development in Latin America*, Boulder, Colorado, Westview Press.

WIENER, M. J. (1981), *English Culture and the Decline of the Industrial Spirit 1850–1980*, Cambridge, Cambridge University Press.

WILCZYNSKI, J. (1983), *Comparative Industrial Relations*, London, Macmillan.

WILENSKY, H. (1975), *The Welfare State and Equality*, Berkeley and Los Angeles, University of California Press. .

WILENSKY, H. (1976), *The 'New Corporatism', Centralization and the Welfare State*, London, Sage.

WILENSKY, H. (1978), 'The political economy of income distribution', in M. Yinger and S. J. Cutler (eds), *Major Social Issues: A Multidisciplinary View*, Glencoe, Illinois, Free Press, pp. 87–108.

WILENSKY, H. (1979), *The Political Economy of Income Distribution: Issues in the Analysis of Government Approaches to the Reduction of Inequality*, Reprint no. 425, Institute of Industrial Relations, University of California, Berkeley.

WILENSKY, H. (1981), 'Family life cycle, work, and the quality of life: reflections on the roots of happiness, despair and indifference in modern society', in B. Gardell and G. Johansson (eds), *Working Life*, Chichester, Wiley, pp. 235–65.

WILENSKY, H. (1983), 'Political legitimacy and consensus: missing variables in the assessment of social policy', in S. E. Spiro and E. Yuchtman-Yaar, *Evaluating the Welfare State*, New York, Academic Press, pp. 51–74.

WILES, P. (1974), *Distribution of Income: East and West*, Amsterdam, North Holland.

WILES, P. (1977), *Economic Institutions Compared*, Oxford, Blackwell.

WILES, P. (ed.) (1982), *The New Communist Third World: An Essay in Political Economy*, London, Croom Helm.

WILKINSON, F. (ed.) (1981), *The Dynamics of Labour Market Segmentation*, London, Academic Press.

WILPERT, B. (1975), 'Research on industrial democracy: the German case', *Industrial Relations Journal*, 6, pp. 53–64.

WILSON, G. K. (1982), 'Why is there no corporatism in the United States?', in G. Lehmbruch and P. C. Schmitter (eds), *Patterns of Corporatist Policy Making*, Beverly Hills, Sage, pp. 219–36.

WINDMULLER, J. P. (1967), 'Employers and employers' associations in the

Netherlands industrial relations system', *Relations Industrielles*, 22, pp. 47–73.

WINDMULLER, J. P. (1969), *Labor Relations in the Netherlands*, Ithaca, New York, Cornell University Press.

WINDMULLER, J. P. (1984), 'Employers' associations in comparative perspective: organization, structure, administration', in J. P. Windmuller and A. Gladstone (eds), *Employers' Associations and Industrial Relations*, Oxford, Clarendon Press, pp. 1–23.

WINDMULLER, J. P. and GLADSTONE, A. (1984) (eds), *Employers' Associations and Industrial Relations*, Oxford, Clarendon Press.

WINKLER, J. T. (1977), 'The corporate economy: theory and administration, in R. SCASE (ed.), *Industrial Society: Class, Cleavage and Control*, London, Allen & Unwin, pp. 43–58.

WITTE, E. E. (1954), *The Evolution of Managerial Ideas in Industrial Relations*, Bulletin no. 27, Ithaca, New York State School of Industrial and Labor Relations, Cornell University.

WOOD, S. J. (1979), 'Ideology in industrial relations theory', *Industrial Relations Journal*, 9, pp. 42–56.

WOOD, S. J. (ed.) (1982), *The Degradation of Work?*, London, Hutchinson.

WOOD, S. J., WAGNER, A., ARMSTRONG, E. G. A., GOODMAN, J. F. B. and DAVIS, J. E. (1975), 'The "industrial relations system" concept as a basis for theory in industrial relations', *British Journal of Industrial Relations*, 13, pp. 291–308.

WOODWARD, J. (1965), *Industrial Organization: Theory and Practice*, London, Oxford University Press.

YANKEBVITCH, D. (1979), 'Work, values and the new breed', in C. Kerr and J. M. Rosow (eds), *Work in America: The Decade Ahead*, New York, Van Nostrand Reinhold, pp. 3–26.

YODER, D. and STAUDOHAR, P. D. (1982), *Personnel Management and Industrial Relations*, 7th edition, Englewood Cliffs, New Jersey, Prentice-Hall.

YUNKER, J. A. (1979), 'The microeconomic efficiency argument for socialism revisited', *Journal of Economic Issues*, 13, pp. 77–112.

ZAPATA, F. (1981), 'Mexico', in A. A. Blum (ed.), *International Handbook of Industrial Relations*, Westport, Connecticut, Greenwood, pp. 351–92.

ZEFFANE, R. (1981), 'Participative management in Algeria', in R. Mansfield and M. Poole (eds), *International Perspectives on Management and Organization*, Aldershot, Gower, pp. 67–74.

ZIEGER, R. H. (1983), 'Industrial relations and labor history in the eighties', *Industrial Relations*, 22, pp. 58–70.

ZIMBALIST, A. (ed.) (1979), *Case Studies in the Labor Process*, New York, Monthly Review Press.

ZISKIND, D. (1976), 'The labor laws of the Third World', *Comparative Labor Law*, Summer, pp. 59–70.

ZUKIN, S. (1981), 'The representation of working-class interests in socialist society: Yugoslav labour unions', *Politics and Society*, 10, pp. 281–316.

Author index

Subject index